Advancing Education:

School Leadership in Action

Dedicated to the memory of William Walker, Founder President of the Commonwealth Council for Educational Administration, whose pivotal contribution to this Twentieth Anniversary volume was completed before his untimely death

To mark the Twentieth Anniversary in 1990 of
THE COMMONWEALTH COUNCIL FOR EDUCATIONAL
ADMINISTRATION (CCEA)

Advancing Education: School Leadership in Action

Edited by

William Walker, Robin Farquhar and
Meredydd Hughes

CCEA Presidents 1970–82, 1982–86 and
1986–90 respectively

The Falmer Press
(A member of the Taylor & Francis Group)
London · New York · Philadelphia

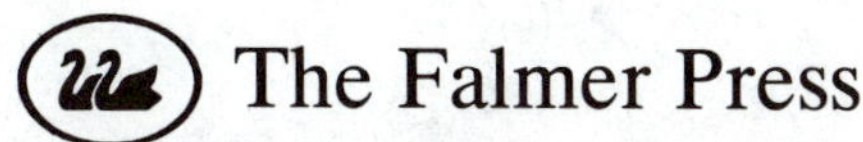

UK The Falmer Press, 4 John St., London, WC1N 2ET
USA The Falmer Press, Taylor & Francis Inc., 1900 Frost Road, Suite 101, Bristol, PA 19007

First published 1991

British Library Cataloguing in Publication Data
Advancing education: School leadership in action.
I. Walker, William II. Farquar, Robin
III. Hughes, Meredydd
371.200609171

ISBN 1-85000-924-4
ISBN 1-85000-925-2 pbk

Library of Congress Cataloging-in-Publication Data available on request

Set in 10/12pt Times by
Graphicraft Typesetters Ltd., Hong Kong

Printed in Great Britain by Burgess Science Press, Basingstoke on paper which has a specified pH value on final paper manufacture of not less than 7.5 and is therefore 'acid free'.

Contents

Foreword

If there were ever a time when education needed to be 'advanced', it is now. How appropriate then that the Commonwealth Council for Educational Administration (CCEA), an organization which has fostered many significant advances in education throughout the world, chose to mark its twentieth anniversary with a publication entitled *Advancing Education: School Leadership in Action.*

How equally appropriate that the respective Presidents of the CCEA over that twenty years, and three of the Commonwealth's leading figures in the educational administration field, Bill Walker from Australia, Robin Farquhar from Canada, and Meredydd Hughes from the UK, agreed to edit the publication. It is clear that the editors have taken great care to recruit authors who are not only university officers and scholars, directors of major institutions for administrative training and education, heads of schools and school systems and senior government and association officials, but also people who are known to be highly knowledgeable, and have impressive records of success in the study and practice of educational administration and represent a broad cross section of Commonwealth countries. The volume is published with the assistance of the Harry Harris Memorial Fund, and it is fitting to note here the contribution to CCEA's development over twenty years of successive Executive Directors: John Ewing, Harry Harris, Basil Kings and John Weeks.

This is a timely, impressive and historic publication and one that clearly achieves its objectives.

Bill Mulford
(President, Commonwealth Council for Educational Administration)
October 1990

Preface

The Commonwealth Council for Educational Administration (CCEA) was founded in 1970, its prime objective being to further the quality of educational administration through the development of a network of practitioners and scholars in the field. As the chapters in this book by Walker and Weeks clearly show, the growth of the CCEA has been remarkable, educators in all parts of the Commonwealth now being linked through conferences, regional meetings, directories, case studies, journals, travel grants and a host of other activities. Many, though by no means all, of these activities emanate from the CCEA Secretariat in Armidale, Australia.

During 1988 the Board of the Council determined that an appropriate means of marking the CCEA's twentieth anniversary in 1990 would be the publication of a book which would appeal to all with an interest in the administration of schools and school systems, but in particular to practitioners in the field. The Board invited the Council's first three Presidents — Bill Walker of Australia, Robin Farquhar of Canada and Meredydd Hughes of the UK — to edit such a volume, which was to include contributions from across the length and breadth of the Commonwealth. The editors responded by meeting in Winnipeg during early 1989, planning a book with wide-ranging appeal to educational leaders and extending invitations to contribute chapters to distinguished administrators and scholars in every region.

Their remit was far from simple. The book's main objectives were stated as:

- (i) to illuminate significant issues in educational administration and promising responses to them;
- (ii) to sensitize readers to the rapidity and inevitability of change in the field;
- (iii) to guide well-informed administrative action;
- (iv) to provide a succinct but comprehensive overview of emergent developments in the study and practice of educational administration;
- (v) to generate improved understanding of countries in the Commonwealth and appreciation of the Commonwealth itself;

(vi) to demonstrate the leadership of the CCEA, as a Commonwealth Professional Association, in regard to the above.

It says a great deal for the spirit of 'Commonwealth' that the authors invited to contribute, did so most ably and promptly. This book is the result.

Section 1 briefly describes the changes which have taken place in the Commonwealth, highlights the roles of the Commonwealth Secretariat and the Commonwealth Foundation and describes the development of the CCEA as an international leader in educational change.

Section 2 analyzes some key issues which have persistently challenged — and no doubt will continue to challenge — policy makers from London to Lagos, from Sydney to Singapore. These are the issues of centralization and decentralization, autonomy and accountability, effective schooling, the professionalization of teachers, and equity and diversity in multicultural societies.

The roles played by two key educational administrators — the principal/headteacher and the superintendent/education officer — are described and analyzed in section 3, which provides some excellent guidelines for the future through contrasting and comparing the work of such administrators in a range of countries at different stages of development.

The fourth and final section identifies some significant resources which can illuminate, support and expand the administrative process. Attention is focused first on the preparation and training of educational administrators, an area in which some Commonwealth countries already provide world leadership. The next chapter explores the relevance of new theoretical perspectives for better understanding, and hence for improved practice. The concluding chapter completes a feedback loop to the first chapter of the book, providing a broad view of the CCEA and its role in future development.

While the authors and the contexts of what they write are based in the Commonwealth, we consider the contributions to this volume to be of worldwide interest and significance. One need not be a member of the Commonwealth to find much of value in the book. And yet, without the existence of the Commonwealth, and the operation of the CCEA, it could not have been produced.

Emeritus Professor W.G. Walker, Mt Eliza, Australia
Professor R.H. Farquhar, Ottawa, Canada
Emeritus Professor M.G. Hughes, Birmingham, UK

Section 1

Introduction

1 The Changing Commonwealth

William Walker

What is 'the Commonwealth'? The first Commonwealth Secretary-General, Arnold Smith of Canada, complained in 1967, just two years after his appointment, that the concept of Commonwealth was widely misunderstood. There were four images of the Commonwealth, he asserted, and three of them were false. As Chan (1988) summarizes Smith's argument, 'it was false ... to view the Commonwealth as a form of British "kith and kin"; false to see it as a ghost of empire; and false to see in it a surrogate or placebo for that empire' (p. 3).

Arnold Smith saw the Commonwealth as an association of equals, in which Britain's voice was but one. If the Commonwealth had a charter like that of the United Nations, no doubt this relationship would have been spelled out. But it has no charter – merely a set of common ideals agreed upon by Commonwealth leaders in 1971 – and, some would say, no legal existence! Yet it *does* exist and its head is the Queen. Few students of politics have not read of Prime Minister Nehru of India's 1949 speech in which he welcomed republican India's membership in the Commonwealth and referred to the latter as a 'touch of healing' in a sick world. Perhaps surprisingly, it remains thus forty years on.

The origins of the contemporary Commonwealth clearly lie in Britain's imperial past, a past which, however, ended *de facto* with the formal acknowledgement of the sovereign equality of the 'dominions'. As Groom and Taylor (1984) put it, 'if there was to be unity, it would be unity in diversity, and by consent, not by command' (p. 3).

The post-war period of decolonization was not without its strains, especially in Africa, but the Indian-inspired precedent of republican membership provided a model for a relatively peaceful transition from empire to loose association. There were tensions associated with the Suez campaign in 1956, with South Africa's continuing membership of the Commonwealth until its withdrawal in 1961, with Amin's excesses in Uganda, and with Rhodesian independence, to name but a few events of note. On a different level, there was concern within the Commonwealth about Britain's attitude towards immigration from the 'new' Commonwealth countries and, in recent years, her increasing participation in the European Economic Community.

In 1956 the Commonwealth had eight members (the Third World countries being India, Pakistan and Ceylon); in 1960 eleven, and by 1965, the year in which the Commonwealth Secretariat was established, twenty-one. By 1990 there were fifty, the latest to be admitted being Namibia. A full list is included in figure 1, which has kindly been made available by the Commonwealth Secretariat.

In spite of the inevitable tensions associated with decolonization, the Commonwealth continued to grow — and its roots in Britain remain obvious in spite of that nation's deliberate efforts not to act in an Anglocentric mode. That this British heritage remains is reflected not only in the Queen's position as head of the Commonwealth, but in the existence of the Commonwealth Secretariat, situated close to Buckingham Palace and just around the corner from the Foreign and Commonwealth Office in Lancaster House.

The establishment of the Commonwealth Secretariat was a significant direct step, both symbolically and operationally, in the growth of Commonwealth governmental relationships (Doxey, 1989, p. 146) and, less directly, in the development of non-governmental bodies, of which the Commonwealth Council for Educational Administration (CCEA), to be discussed in this chapter, is one. The Secretariat resulted from the 1964 Commonwealth Prime Ministers' meeting where a clear division between the older 'white' members and the new membership emerged. The new members felt that Britain was trying to manipulate them in her own interests, especially over the Rhodesian question. Nkrumah of Ghana proposed the establishment of a Commonwealth Secretariat and was widely supported, notably by Williams of Trinidad, Obote of Uganda and Kenyatta of Kenya. Of the 'white' Commonwealth only Canada was supportive, so it was perhaps appropriate that the first Secretary-General of the Commonwealth, Arnold Smith, should be a Canadian.

The Commonwealth Secretariat quickly established itself as an instrument of functional cooperation, its modest budget being supported by contributions ranging from about 30 per cent from Britain to 0.75 per cent from Western Samoa. Secretariat programme came to include the Commonwealth Science Council, the Commonwealth Youth Programme and the extremely important Commonwealth Fund for Technical Cooperation, designed to assist development in poorer countries. The Secretariat set out to assist and lead the Commonwealth in a host of ways ranging from organizing Commonwealth Heads of Government Meetings (CHOGM) to running specialized conferences in fields as diverse as agriculture, medicine and, of course, education.

Looking back over a quarter of a century of its history, it is obvious that the Secretariat has become a significant force in the political, economic and educational affairs of the official Commonwealth. As those in the arena of education, especially in small countries, will readily attest, the Secretariat has proved to be a reliable and efficient source of information and ideas, as well as aid and support generally. Groom and Taylor (1984) put this relationship well:

> The Commonwealth is used by all its members; but it is held dearest by those who have few other avenues into the world. In particular it enables small countries to act on a worldwide stage in a familiar and supportive setting without the encumbering and overwhelming framework of the United Nations and its agencies. (p. 10)

Since the vast majority of the members of the Commonwealth are small, even tiny countries, the importance of this channel is obvious. Those who have attended Commonwealth Education Conferences, whether international or regional, can hardly have avoided noting this relationship; certainly it was crystal clear as early as 1971 to the present author when a participant in the Commonwealth Educational Conference held in Canberra during that year.

It is another Commonwealth-wide agency, however, which is of crucial importance for understanding the development of the Commonwealth Council for Educational Administration. The Commonwealth Foundation was largely a British initiative, inspired in part by the meetings of two Commonwealth statesmen, Lord Casey of Australia and Patrick Gordon Walker. Both had emphasized the roles of the professions in strengthening the Commonwealth and had sought the creation of a body to encourage cooperation among them.

This special foundation designed to foster professional links throughout the Commonwealth was set up by the Heads of Government Conference in 1965. The first Chairman was the distinguished Australian Nobel Prizeman Sir Macfarlane Burnet and the founding Director was Mr John Chadwick (Chadwick, 1982), a far-seeing and enthusiastic ex-diplomat whose contribution to the establishment of the CCEA just a few years later on cannot be overestimated.

The aims of the Foundation indicate clearly its firm roots in the concept of 'Commonwealth' and suggest the reasons why it so enthusiastically supported the establishment and development of the CCEA. The aims were set out as follows:

> To:
>
> encourage and support fuller representation at conferences of professional bodies within the Commonwealth;
>
> assist professional bodies within the Commonwealth to hold more conferences between themselves;
>
> facilitate the exchange of visits among professional people, especially the younger element;
>
> stimulate and increase the flow of professional information exchanged between the organizations concerned;

Figure 1.1

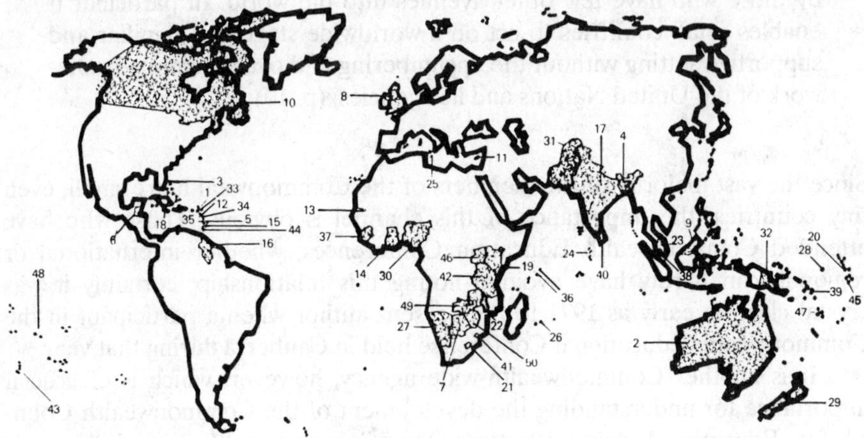

The Commonwealth

At the threshold of a new century, the Commonwealth, an offshoot of nineteenth century colonialism, has grown to fifty member states and become a leading instrument of North-South cooperation. The membership adds up to a quarter of the world's nations and people. It spans the continents and is a bridge between races and religions and between rich and poor. It enables them to discuss common problems frankly and to work together for solutions.

The Commonwealth bears little resemblance to the Empire from which it has grown. It began to take its modern form at India's independence in 1947. Two years later, India became a republic and the Commonwealth adapted itself to having within it countries owing no allegiance to the British crown. The newest member is Namibia which became independent in March 1990.

Commonwealth countries regard Queen Elizabeth II as a symbol of the association and as such the Head of the Commonwealth.

The Commonwealth has grown as former colonies in Asia, Africa, the Caribbean, the Mediterranean and the Pacific won their independence but chose to be its members. It has become firmly multiracial and more representative of the world community.

All members are equal but each is free to follow its own policies: all subscribe to a set of common ideals agreed by Commonwealth leaders in 1971. Their Declaration of Commonwealth Principles expresses commitment to international peace and order, equal rights for all citizens and the liberty of the individual; opposition to colonial domination and racial oppression; and their resolve to achieve a fairer global society.

Promoting Development

In the last four decades, the Commonwealth has played a key role in decolonization and in promoting social and economic development. It has launched many programmes of cooperation, and works with other organizations and groupings in seeking to correct the imbalances between rich and poor countries. It is in the vanguard of international action to help dismantle apartheid and bring about political freedom for South Africa.

Source: Commonwealth Secretariat, July 1990.

	Country	Capital	Population	
1	Antigua and Barbuda	St Johns	84,000	M
2	Australia	Canberra	16,506,000	M
3	Bahamas	Nassau	247,000	M
4	Bangladesh	Dhaka	108,851,000	R
5	Barbados	Bridgetown	255,000	M
6	Belize	Belmopan	182,000	M
7	Botswana	Gaborone	1,164,000	R
8	Britain	London	57,019,000	M
9	Brunei Darussalam	Bandar Seri Begawan	243,000	M*
10	Canada	Ottawa	26,104,000	M
11	Cyprus	Nicosia	686,000	R
12	Dominica	Roseau	81,000	R
13	The Gambia	Banjul	822,000	R
14	Ghana	Accra	14,040,000	R
15	Grenada	St George's	102,000	M
16	Guyana	Georgetown	799,000	R
17	India	New Delhi	813,990,000	R
18	Jamaica	Kingston	2,429,000	M
19	Kenya	Nairobi	23,021,000	R
20	Kiribati	Tarawa	67,000	R
21	Lesotho	Maseru	1,673,000	M*
22	Malawi	Lilongwe	8,155,000	R
23	Malaysia	Kuala Lumpur	16,921,000	M*
24	Maldives	Male	203,000	R
25	Malta	Valletta	345,000	R
26	Mauritius	Port Louis	1,048,000	M
27	Namibia	Windhoek	1,262,000	R
28	Nauru	Nauru	8,000	R
29	New Zealand	Wellington	3,339,000	M
30	Nigeria	Abuja	110,131,000	R
31	Pakistan	Islamabad	105,677,000	R
32	Papua New Guinea	Port Moresby	3,804,000	M
33	St Kitts and Nevis	Basseterre	43,000	M
34	St Lucia	Castries	145,000	M
35	St Vincent	Kingstown	122,000	M
36	Seychelles	Victoria	68,000	R
37	Sierra Leone	Freetown	3,938,000	R
38	Singapore	Singapore	2,639,000	R
39	Solomon Islands	Honiara	304,000	M
40	Sri Lanka	Colombo	16,565,000	R
41	Swaziland	Mbabane	737,000	M*
42	Tanzania	Dar es Salaam	24,739,000	R
43	Tonga	Nuku'alofa	101,000	M*
44	Trinidad and Tobago	Port of Spain	1,241,000	R
45	Tuvalu	Funafuti	9,000	M
46	Uganda	Kampala	16,195,000	R
47	Vanuatu	Port Vila	151,000	R
48	Western Samoa	Apia	168,000	R
49	Zambia	Lusaka	7,486,000	R
50	Zimbabwe	Harare	9,257,000	R

M Monarchy under Queen Elizabeth II
M Country with its own monarchy R Republic*
Population: mid-1988 figures, World Bank and Commonwealth Secretariat

> request to assist with the setting up of national institutions or associations in countries where these do not at present exist;
>
> promote the growth of Commonwealth-wide associations or regional Commonwealth associations in order to reduce the present centralization in Britain. (Commonwealth Heads of Government, 1965)

With such a wide-ranging remit it was not surprising that the Foundation was able to support not only conferences and meetings, but also Secretariat services in the early days of the CCEA. It is of interest that the Foundation has always welcomed complementary activities within the CCEA funded by other agencies. Good examples of this were the CCEA case studies in school and university administration and the Directory of Commonwealth Courses in Educational Administration, which were funded by the Commonwealth Secretariat, and travel grants provided by the Commonwealth Fund for Technical Cooperation and other agencies.

It is appropriate at this stage to turn to the Commonwealth Council for Educational Administration itself, for in its establishment and growth the aims, purposes, governance and achievements of 'Commonwealth' are in large measure exemplified. The origins of the CCEA date from the mid-sixties, as I have described elsewhere (Walker 1972, 1986a and 1986b). An important source of inspiration was the International Intervisitation Programme (IIP) held in the USA and Canada in 1966 under the auspices of the University Council for Educational Administration (UCEA), and attended by participants from Australia, New Zealand and Great Britain, as well as from the United States and Canada. During the IIP I discussed with colleagues the possibility of establishing a Commonwealth-wide body along the lines of the UCEA, though we always saw the body as being essentially a practitioner-based, rather than an academe-based, enterprise.

Within a year or so of the IIP we learned of the existence of the Commonwealth Foundation. Since the Foundation's remit was, as we have seen, to encourage the development of non-governmental organizations, and especially those representing the professions, it seemed appropriate to seek its support. George Baron and Bill Taylor of the University of London Institute of Education and Bill Russell, an Australian who was attached to the Victorian Agent-General's office in London, began the process of introducing the notion of the CCEA to the Foundation.

The encouragement and support of the CCEA by the Commonwealth Foundation presents an excellent case study of the Commonwealth at work. During 1969 the Vice-Chancellor of the University of New England, Alec Lazenby, agreed in principle to contribute towards the support of a secretariat for a proposed Commonwealth Council within his University's Faculty of Education. Armed with this generous offer it was possible informally to approach the Commonwealth Foundation for funding.

Meanwhile, the key step of establishing the Commonwealth Council took place during the second International Intervisitation Programme, held in Australia during 1970. This peripatetic four-week programme began in Sydney, involved two weeks of small group visits to Australian universities, colleges and school systems and ended at the University of New England at Armidale. In the course of the Armidale phase the Commonwealth members present, drawn not only from the 'old', but from several members of the 'new' Commonwealth, unanimously supported the establishment of the Commonwealth Council for Educational Administration. Moreover, it was resolved to seek the establishment of the Council's Secretariat at Armidale (Walker, 1970).

Following this, an interim Board was set up and a formal approach for funding made to the Foundation. The proposal was a unique one not only because it suggested the establishment of a secretariat in a small Australian town rather than in London or another major city, but also because unlike all other professional organizations it proposed an organization which would *begin* as a Commonwealth-wide body and would gradually break down into national, state, provincial and regional groups.

Before approval was given, John Chadwick visited Armidale and expressed satisfaction with what he saw. With an allocation of funds an Executive Director of the Council was appointed, the successful applicant being John Ewing, previously Director of Primary Education in New Zealand, and a participant in IIP 70.

Steps were then quickly taken to establish the Australian Council for Educational Administration and regional councils in various parts of Australia (Walker, 1974). The British Educational Administration Society (later the British Educational Management and Administration Society) followed, as did Councils in several other parts of the Commonwealth. In true 'Commonwealth' fashion regional conferences were soon held in Malaysia and Fiji. By 1974, when the Commonwealth Education Conference was to be held in Kingston, Jamaica, the present author, as Foundation President of the CCEA, was invited to join the Australian delegation. John Ewing, too, travelled to Jamaica where he arranged a number of receptions for national delegations. It is of interest to note that since that time the Executive Director of the CCEA has attended all Commonwealth Education Conferences not as a representative of Australia, but as an official observer at the invitation of the Commonwealth Secretariat.

The developments which followed under a succession of Executive Directors – John Ewing was followed by Harry Harris of Australia, Basil Kings of New Zealand and John Weeks of Great Britain – were textbook 'Commonwealth' developments. Some of these are vividly described by John Weeks in chapter 18 of this volume. There is no point in anticipating John Weeks' narrative here. What is worth noting, however, is just how pungently the development of the Commonwealth Council highlights those key characteristics of 'Commonwealth' referred to earlier in this chapter.

Firstly, CCEA was never Anglocentric, the existence of a Secretariat

12,000 miles from London no doubt being a contributing factor. Like the rings produced by pebbles in a mill pond the concept of the CCEA spread outwards from Australia to South-East Asia and the Pacific, then from Canada to the Caribbean and from Britain to Africa and the Mediterranean and beyond. Interestingly, the small Republic of Singapore has produced one of the largest and most active groups in the world.

Secondly, there was little order or rationality in the Council's growth. Development often depended upon a local man or woman having the appropriate 'fire in the belly' to lead colleagues forward. Vast inequalities in teachers' incomes across national borders mitigated against an orderly system of membership subscriptions. In many countries a single element subscription is paid, while in others, like Australia, the subscription can consist of three elements — state, national and international.

Thirdly, financial support was always a problem, in spite of the fact that CCEA Executive Directors have to a man made considerable personal sacrifices to keep the costs of administration and travel to a minimum. It was assumed when the first Commonwealth Foundation grants were made that the Council would be self-funding within a decade. After two decades, in spite of the generosity of the Foundation, the support of the University of New England and the ingenuity of its executive directors, it is still by no means self-supporting.

Moreover, the financial arrangements, as is so often the case in the Commonwealth, continue to rely heavily on contributions from the 'old' Commonwealth, Australian and British members in particular contributing rather more than their fair share to the maintenance of international activities. In recent years it has become more and more difficult to ensure that this generosity continues. In Britain, for example, the Commonwealth has become more distant as Europe (with its CCEA-inspired European Forum on Educational Administration) has drawn closer.

Further, the CCEA includes many small nations within its membership. If ever there was needed a clear demonstration of the importance of the Commonwealth for the small countries referred to above, it is seen in the work of the Council.

It is not always realized that some of the independent nations of the Commonwealth, for example, Tuvalu, have a smaller population than an English county town and others, for example, Fiji, a smaller population than a medium-sized Australian or Canadian city. Yet at Commonwealth-wide or regional gatherings there is a feeling of fraternity, an ease and familiarity which common traditions of language, law and education obviously engender. The difference between the Commonwealth and, for example, UNESCO meetings is very obvious in this regard.

Fifthly, the CCEA has sought leadership from right across the Commonwealth. Its Presidents have hailed from Australia (W.G. Walker and W. Mulford), Canada (R.H. Farquhar) and Britain (M.G. Hughes), and Board Members from nearly every corner of the globe.

It has organized conferences and provided advice and consultancy services across the world. It has published directories, newsletters, case studies and articles covering almost every part of the Commonwealth. It has joined with bodies as diverse as the Australian College of Education, the Inter-American Council for Educational Administration, UNESCO, and the South-East Asian and Pacific Regional Educational Administrators Meetings, in order to work for the furtherance of educational administrators, teachers and children in Commonwealth schools and school systems.

In short, I suspect that no non-government organization better typifies Arnold Smith's assertion with which we began this chapter. It can confidently be said of the Council, which I was privileged to lead and nurture through its infant years, that it was and is indeed no form of British 'kith and kin', no ghost of empire, no surrogate or placebo of empire, but very much an association of equals. Unlike the Commonwealth itself, however, it *does* have a constitution and it daily demonstrates across the schools and school systems of the Commonwealth the truth and beauty not only of Arnold Smith's 'unity in diversity' but above all of Nehru's 'touch of healing'.

References

CHADWICK, J. (1982) *The Unofficial Commonwealth: The Story of the Commonwealth Foundation 1965–80*, London, Allen and Unwin.

CHAN, S. (1988) *The Commonwealth in World Politics: A Study in International Action. 1965–1985*, London, Lester Crook.

COMMONWEALTH HEADS OF GOVERNMENT (1965) *Agreed Memorandum on the Commonwealth Foundation*, London, The Commonwealth Secretariat.

DOXEY, M. (1989) *The Commonwealth Secretariat and the Contemporary Commonwealth*, London, Macmillan.

GROOM, A.J.R. and TAYLOR, P. (1984) 'The continuing Commonwealth: Its origins and characteristics' in GROOM, A.J.R. and TAYLOR, P. (Eds) *The Commonwealth in the 1980s: Challenges and Opportunities*, London, Macmillan.

WALKER, A. (1978) *The Commonwealth: A New Look*, Oxford, Pergamon, p. 83.

WALKER, W.G. (1970) 'The International Intervisitation Programme, Australia, 1970', *The Journal of Educational Administration*, **IX**, 1, pp. 3–9.

WALKER, W.G. (1972) 'UCEA's bright sun at morning: The Commonwealth Council for Educational Administration', *Educational Administration Quarterly*, **8**, 2, pp. 16–25.

WALKER, W.G. (1974) 'The genesis of the Australian Council for Educational Administration', *ACEA Bulletin*, **1**, 1, pp. 8–11.

WALKER, W.G. (1986a) 'IIP 66: Source of an operating manual for educational administration on spaceship earth?' in HOYLE, E. and MCMAHON, A. (Eds) *World Yearbook of Education 1986: The Management of Schools*, London, Kogan Page, pp. 310–18.

WALKER, W.G. (1986b) 'Spaceship earth twenty years on: The six international intervisitation programs' in EDWARDS, W.L. (Ed.) *Record of Proceedings of Sixth International Intervisitation Program in Educational Administration, Equity and Diversity: Challenges for Educational Administrators*, Palmerston North, Massey University, pp. 155–66.

Section 2

Some Issues of Practice

Introduction

William G. Walker

Seventy years ago that great British educator Sir Percy Nunn described teachers in his '*Education: Its Data and First Principles*' as 'ambassadors of society to the kingdom of the child'. How right he was — and how complex are the social, political, economic and curricular implications of what he had to say.

What is 'society'? What is the cultural heritage which is to be transmitted by the ambassador? In reality, since time at school is finite, what *parts* of the cultural heritage are to be taught? What priorities are to be given to mathematics, literature, science, art, music and history, for example? And what balance do we seek among, in Bloom's terms, the cognitive, the affective and the psychomotor? These are political questions, i.e. questions of power, and they reflect the fact that in all societies schools are in some measure 'political animals'.

The distinguished American scholar Igor Ansoff has described contemporary Western society as being characterized by three key words: ambiguity, paradox and risk. Many teachers employed in the schools of the 'old' Commonwealth countries — and I suspect in the great majority of the schools of the 'new' Commonwealth, too — will have little difficulty in recognizing the relevance of Ansoff's key words to their own educational systems and institutions.

Teachers virtually everywhere have watched the increasing intervention of government in schools, whether in matters of funding, control, management or curriculum. In many cases the traditional education department bureaucracies with their Westminster-style 'permanent' heads have found themselves with 'contract' heads, and in more than one case with their Minister of Education virtually playing the role of senior civil servant.

When the Commonwealth came into being the overwhelming problem facing education was one of quantity. Today more and more questions are being asked about quality. Moreover, as educational systems throw off their colonial trappings they are looking around the global village and comparing their performance, or lack of it, with that of their neighbours. Words like 'equality of opportunity', 'gender' and 'equity' for example are being heard much more widely than was the case two or three decades ago.

Since the end of the Second World War teachers have grown considerably in numbers and qualifications in most parts of the Commonwealth. In addition there has been much more attention given to the question of what 'professionalism' means and to the rather fuzzy operational concept of 'professionalization'. While education departments and governments have adopted one set of criteria, burgeoning teachers' unions have often adopted other criteria.

At the same time there has been an immense growth of interest in the processes of educational administration, with an explosion of long and short courses in universities, colleges and education departments around the world.

This combination of political developments, economic imperatives, rapid social change and teacher professionalization, among other factors, has led to a host of developments which have assisted teachers to understand more clearly what John Dewey meant when he wrote, in the early days of this century, 'upright and firm I stand on a star unstable'.

There has developed a public demand for 'excellence' in education, but few have been able to say just what they mean by 'excellence' — and there has also developed an extraordinary interest in 'effective schooling' with rather rigid and inflexible definitions of 'effectiveness', often limited to test scores, being the order of the day.

In many countries reports have been commissioned in order to seek this 'excellence' and 'effectiveness' and major reorganization of schools systems, often referred to as 'restructuring' has followed. This restructuring has invariably resulted in organizational tensions: on the one hand schools have usually been given more autonomy, but both schools and teachers have found that this apparent freedom carried with it a much greater degree of accountability than they had previously experienced.

A term which came into common use during recent years was 'loose coupling', which describes the movement of power away from the centre to the periphery — from, for example, the education department to the individual school. A great deal of such loose coupling has occurred in the form of decentralization of both policy making and administration, but at the same time much greater central power has been introduced in other areas, notably in the area of curriculum.

Much of the terminology of educational reform has been adapted from business corporations. Increasingly there has been a tendency to follow contemporary business theory which usually emphasizes a powerful corporate culture, but a devolution of authority within that culture. Yet at the same time in other countries — and sometimes in the *same* country — traditional bureaucratic procedures have been re-emphasized.

Ambiguity, paradox, risk indeed!

2 Centralization and Decentralization in Curriculum and Evaluation: Looking Both Ways at Once

Hedley Beare and Andrew Sturman

The one common characteristic of school systems around the world in the 1980s was structural reform, although it has taken different courses in different countries. The reforms did not always focus on the curriculum of schools, although test scores were often used as evidence of the need to put in place the restructuring being proposed. The reforms targeted such aspects as governance patterns, or the relationship between the economic providers, or the efficiency of the systems themselves, or the way schools used their resources, but not primarily what schools teach.

Many examples could be cited. In the United States the release of *A Nation at Risk* (National Commission on Excellence in Education, 1983) and a spate of similar reports in the early part of the decade gave impetus to widespread pressure to change schools. Test scores were used to demonstrate that US education was in crisis. The Japanese government set up a National Council on Educational Reform in 1984 because of concerns about school discipline and the appropriateness of the curriculum in Japanese schools. Four reports were received by 1988 but they did not appear to have a great impact either on schools or on their programmes.

In Great Britain, the Thatcher government replaced the Schools Council with bodies more closely tied to government, passed the Education Reform Act (1988), pressured local authorities and contained their spending by devices like rate-capping, reconstituted the certification and assessment schemes in secondary education, and put in place a number of post-school training schemes.

In New Zealand, the Picot Report (Taskforce to Review Educational Administration, 1988) led to the scrapping of Regional Boards of Education, sponsored a huge devolution of both money and powers to schools, and introduced a form of privatization in which each school was required to spell out its curricular objectives in a charter. Earlier in the decade an Integration Act had permitted independent schools to become incorporated in the national system.

In Australia every one of the eight state and territory school systems underwent waves of restructuring which impacted on how schools were provided with curricular advice and supervision. The federal Schools Commission and Tertiary Education Commission which had played dominant roles through the 1970s were collapsed into a National Board more closely tied to the national Minister; and the national meeting of the Ministers of Education (the Australian Education Council) became more powerful, developing a set of national goals for schools and setting up a jointly funded Curriculum Corporation. The federal government also substantially reworked the country's post-school provisions. The binary system was replaced in favour of a 'unified national system of higher education'.

The reforms in Canada addressed the questions of minority language and religious rights, and multiculturalism. Although the Royal Commission on the Economic Union and Development Prospects for Canada (the Macdonald Commission) paid scant attention in its three-volume report (1985) to elementary or secondary education, it provided a salutary picture of where Canada stood in the world economy. It was also convinced of the need for a 'national body to develop achievement-testing procedures' for Canada, a predictable economists' reaction.

Are there common threads about the curriculum running through this galaxy of reforms? Yes, there are some, but by the beginning of the century's last decade, the trendlines were not easy to distinguish with any confidence. Indeed, attempting to outline them throws into relief the apparent uncertainty over whether the school systems in Western countries are decentralizing or recentralizing, and particularly in matters relating to the curriculum. They appear to be doing both, and simultaneously. We have selected for discussion here three factors which seem to have a recurring influence on curricula of the 1980s, namely the school effectiveness movement, the economics of schooling, and the intervention of national governments.

The School Effectiveness Movement

The so-called 'school effectiveness movement' of the 1980s, which will be considered in detail in chapter 4, was in many respects a conservative reaction to the experimentation and innovation in education which had accompanied the social reforms of the 1970s, especially the emphasis on school-based curriculum development (Beare, Caldwell and Millikan, 1989, pp. 2–22). The Coleman Report (1966) had shown that the outcomes of schooling depended only to a small extent on what the school itself did, and that the single most powerful determinant of success at school was the child's socioeconomic background. Government programmes of the 1970s had largely been driven by a desire to give to all children equality of access to schooling and supplements which would balance out their deprivations. The consequence, in a policy sense, was increasing intervention by both national and state or provincial governments in the schooling process, through specially targeted funding. The policy initiatives were centralist in tendency, allowing local decision-making to be overridden by state or national policies.

But the school effectiveness movement also produced significant decentralization. Its main thrust was to reassert that individual schools *do* make a difference. It reaffirmed the primacy of the conventional school, together with many of its traditional curricular activities — including measuring school performance through standardized tests; a tight management structure under a principal as the instructional leader; a consistent curriculum policy for the school backed by a formal, school-wide assessment programme; and an emphasis on student learning as the prime focus of the school.

In summary, then, the widespread, indeed international, emphases during the 1980s on school effectiveness had the effect of pulling schools back to the conventional curriculum, and of making schools more accountable in the way they provided for their students. It was a climate to produce conformities in what schools taught.

The Economics of Schooling

The world economy and the newly-forming trading patterns of the 1980s had a pervasive impact on what schools taught, on the reforms being put into place, and on the standards being asked for in the students who graduated from high schools.

The interlocking, international, economic order which developed in the 1980s removed from national governments around the globe a significant amount of the power to control their own finances. The nations with a well entrenched industrial base to their economies found themselves competing with aggressive, newly industrialized countries (NICs) which had an edge by reason of their ability to incorporate from the outset new technologies capable of outpacing the dated 'smoke stack industries'. A different set of 'rich' and 'poor' nations emerged. Eastern and Western trading blocs were also breaking down, particularly after 1989 and the emergence of the new European Economic Community. The superpowers of Russia, USA, Japan, China and India combined with vigorous new Asian economies like those of Taiwan, Hong Kong, South Korea, Singapore and Thailand to make the North Pacific a new focus for wealth creation. 'High tech', financial, service and information industries — all heavily dependent for their success on education — became the determinants of a nation's market superiority. Oil production also dominated world politics and currencies, especially with the Gulf War crisis.

Because countries not supported by a highly educated workforce were thereby in trouble, nation after nation poured effort into increasing its school retention rates (especially in the senior secondary years) and in reforming higher education firstly so that it could take in more students and secondly so that the teaching and research at this level were geared to goals of national development. Economic stringency forced countries to get better return for money outlays, in schools no less than in industry. Increasing productivity and efficiency became important.

Of particular interest is the extent to which in many countries the examination and certification provisions for the final year of secondary school went through a similar reconstruction (Beare and Lemke, 1986). In Great Britain, the long-established GCE at 'O' and 'A' level was revised, the General Certificate of Secondary Education (GCSE) appeared, and several post-school training programmes were amalgamated as part of a policy for youth. Ireland revised its curriculum and assessment bodies and built a youth guarantee scheme. Most states and territories in Australia tried to consolidate their Higher School Certificate (year 12) provisions to accommodate the wider spectrum of students feeding through to the final year of schooling. In the Caribbean steps were taken to set up a centralized regional examination council. Clearly the demands of the national economy, the changing employment patterns, and the intense competition for world markets had forced attention on senior school curricula and the credentials which went with them.

It thus became popular to describe education in terms of a business enterprise with instrumental goals, and reformed along the lines of the private sector competing in a market economy. As has characteristically happened at other times of rapid social and economic change, the restructuring which took place in education in the 1980s simply copied the models of organization found in business administration.

Each school was in consequence expected to identify its clients and to sell its services to them in a way which satisfied the customers. Metaphors about the market economy abound in the educational literature and in the reports of the 1980s. Not surprisingly, then, the decade saw a widespread tendency to devolve to schools as many decision-making powers as possible. School boards or governing councils became common in Australia, New Zealand, and the United States, for example. Several countries moved towards a single-line budget for each school. Increased control over the selection of their own staff was given to schools and tight accountability systems were imposed on them; in the one process, schools became more autonomous but also more tightly controlled in terms of their performances and over documentation of their learning outcomes.

The movement thus produced the three Es of education — effectiveness (setting objectives and achieving them), efficiency (achieving those objectives with the best use of the available resources), and excellence (achieving the objectives with a performance of such quality that it sets one above one's competitors). These terms were part of the international education vernacular throughout the 1980s, and they kept cropping up in the titles of the restructuring reports and in materials about the curriculum. The word appears in the title of the documents from the Singapore Minister, for example, and the New Zealand Picot Report (1988) is called *Administering for Excellence*.

The result was further confusion in the patterns of centralization and decentralization over the curriculum. On the one hand, schools were set up as though they were individual enterprises competing for their niches in the market; they had their own governing councils and their own budgets, they made their own staffing appointments (as far as the teacher unions would allow), they were encouraged to survey and then meet the demands of their own constituencies, and they were subject to mandatory audit and accountability processes.

In the United Kingdom, for example, schools were encouraged to dissociate themselves from local authorities and to go it alone with national monies. The Education Reform Act remade the powers and the membership of school governing bodies. In the United States there were several attempts to 'deregulate' schools so that they could adapt to market forces with greater speed and creativity. There was an historic reconstruction of the huge Chicago school system. In New Zealand, each school was required to use its block financial grants in ways best tailored to fulfil its charter; the centre simply imposed an accountability check by setting up an Education Review Office, which itself then regionalized, as described in chapter 14. And in Australia the huge New South Wales system introduced a sweeping decentralization of powers following the Scott Report (1990) appropriately titled *School-Centred Education*.

On the other hand, the frameworks or guidelines imposed by the centre became more insistent, imposing conformities in the curriculum where freedom and diversity had existed in the 1970s. In the United States, for example, the downturn in support from locally levied taxes had the effect of shifting the locus of control towards the state legislatures, which seemed more concerned about standards. Meanwhile, the federal government, under Presidents Reagan and Bush, was prepared to offer advice but not much money, to divest itself of responsibilities for education while at the same time it told those who *were* responsible what they ought to be doing. It led the federal authorities to use what Jung and Kirst (1989) have called 'the bully pulpit'.

In all, finance — or the lack of it, especially from traditional sources — dominated both curriculum and evaluation in the 1980s.

National Priorities and National Intervention

The 1980s saw national governments playing a consistently strong role in setting education priorities, even when there was little constitutional power for them to do so. In the federal systems of Canada, Australia, and the United States, education was a residual power of the states and provinces, but from the end of the 1939–45 war governments had learned how to circumvent this legal inhibition. In the 1980s, it was very clear that competitiveness, if not national economic survival, hung on whether the whole workforce could become better educated, multi-skilled, and adaptable, qualities needed as the prerequisites for a post-industrial economy.

The effect was to emphasize the instrumental and utilitarian in education rather than to revere the value of a 'liberal education' or education for personal fulfilment, as the reforms of the 1960s and the 1970s were depicted. The effects were particularly strong in the last two years of secondary education, in post-school programmes (which tended to emphasize training rather than education) and in higher education where the policies called for changes geared to the needs of the economy. The Education Reform Act in the United Kingdom (1988) was in fact explicit on this point. So also was the US Report of the National Commission on Excellence in Education (1981–83) which had been set up by the President himself. By the end of the 1980s, then, national governments everywhere had become one of the powerful players in education at all levels.

Centralization and Decentralization of Curriculum and Evaluation

Because the trends concerning the decentralization or recentralization of curriculum and evaluation are so confused, it is informative to trace elements of the issue by considering a particular case. We consider here briefly that of Australia.

The main responsibility for the provision of education in Australia's federal system of government lies constitutionally with the six states. There are also two territories which were under federal administration until the 1970s but have now received some state-type powers. Even so, since the 1930s visiting educators have commented upon the uniformity in educational policies and structures which have existed in Australia (Andersen, 1966), including a centralized provision of curriculum materials, a conformity in teaching styles, reliance upon the inspectorate, and the use of external examinations to assess student performance as well as to regulate for curricular uniformity.

From the 1950s onwards, however, the states began to decentralize by setting up regional offices and by progressively encouraging the participation of parents, the community, school administrators and teachers. Of the Queensland regional structure, one of the first to be established, Borchardt (1966) commented in the 1960s:

> The setting up of education regions in Queensland has not decentralized education, for true decentralization must include a large measure of local responsibility for finance, policy, courses and techniques. Perhaps the regional system in Queensland could be best described as a partial devolution of certain administrative functions from head office to regions. (p. 6)

To what extent did these changes affect decision-making in the areas of student and school evaluation and the curriculum, in course programmes and teaching strategies, and what type of curriculum and evaluation structures emerged?

Until the 1970s, the administration of education in Australia was still highly centralized at the state level. Central offices had the prime responsibility for policy making and for the structure of the curriculum, the inspectorate assessed teacher and school performance, and external public examinations existed in all states to assess student achievement. While some devolution of authority to schools and regions had occurred, the traditions guiding education enhanced a centralized approach. The model of governance which existed then has been described as 'administrative' (Sturman, 1989). Kandel (1938) characterized Australian schooling as education for 'efficiency' and Connell (1970) referred to the 'prudential' and 'administering' traditions of Australian education.

By the 1970s, however, the 'administrative' model of governance was being replaced with what might be called a 'professional' model, where teachers and administrators within schools were given a more important role in curriculum decision-making, in school evaluation and in student assessment. The changes included the abolition of several examinations; the inspectorate became advisory rather than directive; schools were encouraged to conduct their own evaluations of school performance; and school-based curriculum decision-making became common.

By the 1980s the 'administrative' model of governance and, to some extent, the 'professional' model were themselves being challenged by what might be called a 'participatory' model, where educational administration was seen as a joint enterprise involving central and regional administration, schools, parents and the community. This model in some ways supersedes the Westminster system of representative democracy with a type of participatory democracy aimed at involving 'lay' people. Whereas a parliamentary system retains the ultimate authority at the centre, with participatory democracy that authority is increasingly farmed out to other bodies set up to allow participation at school and regional levels.

The move towards the participatory model was reflected in the formation of, or increase in powers to, school councils. In one state, Victoria, in addition to the creation of school councils with curriculum responsibilities, regional boards of education were set in place in the early 1980s (only to be abolished at the end of the eighties!). In other states or territories, parents and the community were placed on school councils or, where councils did not exist, on state-level bodies set up to provide advice on education.

The pressures which brought about a move to these two models were emerging also at both national and state levels although, not surprisingly in a federal system, some states were reforming their educational administration to a greater extent than others. There was widespread acknowledgement, in the wake of student activism in a range of social issues and following the increasing militancy of teacher unions, that the patterns of relationships in education would have to change. 'It was not just that administrators and politicians had to cope with vocal political pressure but also that teachers, who were at that time on average younger and better trained than in the past, were presenting well-reasoned arguments for reform' (Sturman, 1989, p. 98).

The establishment by the federal government in the 1970s of the Schools Commission and the Curriculum Development Centre provided a significant national boost to this reform. In the early years, for example, these bodies strongly encouraged school-based curriculum decision-making, regionalization, parent and community participation in education, aid to disadvantaged schools, attention to the transition from school to work, teacher in-service development, and higher rates of student retention in senior secondary years.

These influences were being mirrored in the changes occurring at the state level. For example, Queensland did away with its external examinations and replaced them with a system of school assessment, while in other states the number of public examinations was reduced and elements of school assessment were incorporated into the examination system. The concept of school-initiated evaluation was being advanced nationally and in states like Victoria, South Australia and Queensland. For the less able students, school-based curriculum packages were being designed, such as the Tertiary Entrance Certificate, or STC, in Victoria. More generally, schools were encouraged to develop their own subjects, such as the 'school subjects' which emerged in Queensland alongside Board-registered subjects. At the same time as these changes were taking place, South Australia, Victoria and the Australian Capital Territory were encouraging wider parent and community participation in curriculum decision-making through reforming the structure and functions of school councils.

By the late 1970s the period of expansionary funding for education came to an end. High rates of youth unemployment and more generally a down-turn in the economy led people to question whether the education system was preparing school leavers for their working lives, and whether the devolution of decision-making particularly over the curriculum had gone too far. For example, at the national level the Quality of Education Review Committee (1985) noted:

> Tensions have been created by these attempts to achieve more diversity among schools. Some parents fear that their children will be disadvantaged by divergence from standard curriculum provisions and that, in deciding what is appropriate for the students of a particular school, teachers may provide offerings which limit their students' subsequent options. (p. 80)

The Committee called for 'rigorous', 'consistent' and 'coordinated' curriculum planning, advocated more 'open' evaluation of activities and proposed national and state monitoring of student achievement. Similarly, the Schools Commission, which had been in the forefront of the decentralization movement, commented that this should not 'detract from the importance of action taken beyond the confines of school or locality, or fail to acknowledge political accountability which exists in public systems' (Schools Commission, 1978, p. 6). The reservations focused on professional autonomy, not community participation; an educational partnership between schools and communities was increasingly being seen as a way to achieve educational accountability at a time when public support for state education was at a low level.

The national trends were quickly reflected at the state level. For example, the need for central guidelines for the curriculum was a key facet of the reforms which appeared in the 1980s in those Australian states where decentralization had been an important policy in the 1970s. The changes taking place in these states can be understood through the comments made by the Director-General of Education in South Australia in 1981:

> If we wanted to make a marker point, we would have to take a memorandum issued by the then Director-General, in 1968 or 1969, in which he said to schools — 'For some ninety years or so the Education Department in Flinders Street has told you meticulously what you should do and when you should do it. You should recognize now that schools are required to meet the needs of communities. Those needs vary from place to place. Therefore the schools should have much more autonomy than they had in the past. We expect schools to react to local things as expressed by local people in terms of general guidelines administered by the Department'. Those movements are watersheds which affected profoundly what happened in the 1970s. My predecessor took that line very hard and gave schools a great deal of autonomy. One of the things which I think went too far was that schools were told that their curriculum was pretty much a matter for them. I believe the facts are that teachers are not able to prepare their own curriculum. It is a waste of time for them to do so. It is stupid in my view for all schools to invent a maths curriculum. The change in that area has been completed and in the last four or five years there has been a slight swing back to the centre. (Quoted in South Australia, House of Assembly Public Accounts Committee, 1981, p. 20)

This view was reiterated in the reports of the Committee of Enquiry into Education in South Australia published in 1981 and 1982.

Does Restructuring Bring Curriculum Renewal?

Although the rationale for change is multifaceted, one of the constant expectations is that both the curriculum provisions and student achievements will improve. Have these policy initiatives, however, produced any changes to the curriculum that schools offer? Just what is the connection between decentralization/recentralization and both teaching styles and learning outcomes? Does restructuring improve learning?

The relationship between curriculum provision and decentralization in Australia has been examined by Sturman (1989). His study compared the curriculum of schools in three states which were considered to differ in the extent of the decentralization which had occurred since the 1960s. It was argued that educational administration in the most decentralized state closely resembled the 'participatory' model of governance, that administration in the most centralized state more closely resembled the 'administrative' model and that in a third state, which in terms of decentralization lay between the other two, educational administration would resemble the 'professional' model.

The study revealed differences in the curriculum among the three states, although one of the most notable facets of the results was the similarity in the responses of teachers to school curriculum organization and teaching styles. While teachers in the most centralized system attached somewhat greater importance to sources of authority for the curriculum from outside the school (such as the Education Department and the examining bodies), in all states sources *within* the school were accorded the most importance. Compared with the more decentralized states, teachers in the centralized state attached greater importance to the curricular advice from people in positions of authority (such as principals and subject heads). These findings suggest that the configuration of the system does influence the way schools organize themselves, particularly as it affects curriculum and teaching.

The analyses revealed also that the curriculum in the state which operated more closely within the professional model was the least traditionally organized. There was a greater use of a semester system, a more flexible approach to student grouping, greater time devoted to elective offerings, more elective subjects offered in total and more school-developed courses. Furthermore, there was a tendency for teachers in this state to favour an 'open' teaching style. They placed relatively greater emphasis on student negotiation of the curriculum, an enquiry approach to learning, the use of a wide range of materials, and group work. Conversely they made less use of traditional practices such as whole-class instruction, testing and grading, 'practical work', textbooks, and giving students advanced knowledge of the curriculum to be covered. Teachers in this state placed the greatest emphasis on values, personal and social skills, and skills of originality, decision-making and inquiry. They placed least emphasis on factual knowledge related to the disciplines.

At the other end of the continuum were the responses of the teachers who operated more closely within the administrative model. Curriculum organization, emphases and teaching styles were all more traditional than was revealed in the state operating within the professional model. The responses of teachers who were viewed as working within a participatory system fell between those of the other two states. In some areas, such as curriculum structures, stress on factual knowledge about subjects, stress on social skills, social and humanitarian values, and the use of a textbook, they more closely resembled the teachers in the 'administrative' system whereas in others, such as sources of authority for the curriculum, broad emphases within it and stress on cognitive skills, they more closely resembled teachers operating within the professional model.

The study revealed that the relationship between decentralization and curriculum renewal was not a straightforward one. While differences did exist across systems, it was also the case that, no matter what type of administrative system or model teachers worked within, the curriculum was affected by school organization and style and by teachers' individual views of the way knowledge should be organized. In fact, these relationships with the curriculum were as strong as, if not stronger than, those which were revealed at a system level.

Nevertheless, outwardly there does appear to be a consistency in the differences that did emerge. The state reflecting the 'administrative' model had the most traditional curriculum, the state reflecting the 'professional' model the most open style of curriculum, and the state reflecting the 'participatory' model had a mixed pattern.

The results of the study suggested that decentralization does alter the relationship that develops between the centre and schools. If schools are to make changes, away from well-known, traditional and established practices, they require appropriate support from the central and regional offices to do so. Even so, the study showed that decentralization or centralization only partially, and possibly only minimally, affects the nature of the curriculum and the way teachers teach. If there was a strong relationship, then we would expect that the effects of changing the locus of control, especially for decisions about the curriculum, would have been well researched, but such is not the case.

Conclusion

The changes which have occurred since the 1960s reflect a range of influences. In part there has been a genuine desire on the part of education systems operating in democratic countries to allow a wider range of participants to influence decision-making, but the relinquishing of control by the centre at a time when the educational system was increasingly being criticized could also be seen as a device to displace the criticism, away from the centre and onto schools and their communities. It is also obvious that wider issues — economic, political, national — have driven much of the change.

So it is time that the centralization/decentralization debate is again focused on the curriculum. This probably requires tackling the crucial issue, which systems have tended to avoid, of researching what effects, if any, administrative organization does have on student achievement and on learning outcomes. Is restructuring primarily educational or economic/political in its intentions? To put it bluntly, does it *improve* education?

References

ANDERSEN, W.E. (1966) '"To see ourselves ..." — Australian education as viewed by overseas visitors', *Australian Journal of Education*, **9–10**, pp. 229–42.

BEARE, H. (1987) 'Changing structures in education', in SIMPKINS, W.S., THOMAS, A.R. and THOMAS, E.B. (Eds) *Principal and Change: The Australian Experience*, Armidale, NSW, University of New England Teaching Monographs.

BEARE, H. (1990) *Educational Administration in the 1990s* (ACEA Monograph Series No. 6), Melbourne, Australian Council of Educational Administration.

BEARE, H., CALDWELL, B.J. and MILLIKAN, R.H. (1989) *Creating an Excellent School*, London, Routledge.

BEARE, H. and LEMKE, H. (1986) *Education and the Economy: How Educational Practices Assist in Structural Change to the Economy*, Report on the OECD Project 'Education and the Economy', Paris, OECD.

BORCHARDT, F.T. (1966) *The Regional System of Education Administration in the Wide Bay Region in Queensland* (Information Bulletin No. 1), Melbourne, Australian Council for Educational Research.

BUTTS, R.F. (1955) *Assumptions Underlying Australian Education*, Melbourne, Australian Council for Educational Research.

COLEMAN, J.S. (1966) *Equality of Educational Opportunity*, Washington, DC, US Department of Health, Education and Welfare.

CONNELL, W.F. (1970) 'Myths and traditions in Australian education', *The Australian Journal of Education*, **14**, 3, pp. 253–64.

JUNG, R. and KIRST, M. (1989) 'Beyond mutual adaptation, into the bully pulpit; Recent research on the federal role in education' in BURDIN, J.L. (Ed.) *School Leadership: A Contemporary Reader*, London, Sage Publications.

KANDEL, J.L. (1938) *Types of Administration*, Melbourne, Australian Council for Educational Research.

LAWTON, S.B. (1989) 'The octopus and the elephant and the five dragons: Commentary on the impact of national and international trends on Canadian schools in the waning years of the 20th century', paper presented at the annual meeting of the American Educational Research Association, San Francisco, March.

NATIONAL COMMISSION ON EXCELLENCE IN EDUCATION (1983) *A Nation at Risk: The Imperative for Educational Reform*, Washington, DC, US Department of Education.

QUALITY OF EDUCATION REVIEW COMMITTEE (1985) *Quality of Education in Australia* (The Karmel Report), Canberra, AGPS.

ROYAL COMMISSION ON THE ECONOMIC UNION AND DEVELOPMENT PROSPECTS FOR CANADA (Macdonald Commission) (1985) *Report: Royal Commission on the Economic Union and Development Prospects for Canada*, vols 1, 2 and 3, Ottawa, Minister of Supplies and Services.

SALLIS, J. (1988) *Schools, Parents and Governors: A New Approach to Accountability*, London, Routledge.

SCHOOLS COMMISSION (1978) *Report of the Triennium 1976–78*, Canberra, AGPS.

SCOTT, B.W. (1990) *School-Centred Education: Building a More Responsive School System*, Report of the Management Review, New South Wales Education Portfolio, Milsons Point, NSW.

SOUTH AUSTRALIA, HOUSE OF ASSEMBLY, PUBLIC ACCOUNTS COMMITTEE (1981) *Eighteenth*

Report from the Public Accounts Committee: Accountability in the Education Department and Schools, Adelaide, South Australia Government Printer.

STURMAN, A. (1989) *Decentralization and the Curriculum: The Effects of the Devolution of Curriculum of Decision Making in Australia* (ACER Research Monograph No. 35), Hawthorn, Victoria, Australian Council for Educational Research.

TASKFORCE TO REVIEW EDUCATIONAL ADMINISTRATION (1988) *Administering for Excellence: Effective Administration in Education* (The Picot Report), Wellington, New Zealand Government Printer.

3 Accountability and Autonomy: Dual Strands for the Administrator

Wayne L. Edwards

Introduction

In today's fast changing world, the emphasis in many organizations is placed on gaining optimal performance in return for the resources needed to achieve the goals which are pursued by the organization and its members. This emphasis is frequently embodied in catchcries such as, 'We must have value for money!' Oh the other hand, strategies might be used in endeavours to identify and ensure links between 'inputs' and 'outputs'. Both the providers and the managers of resources want to be sure that resources are used wisely and applied for the purposes for which they were provided — tasks which require close monitoring and clear reporting of performance. The thrust of this emphasis, therefore, is on the concept of 'accountability'. It is difficult neither to perceive value in the concept nor to understand the reasons which give an attraction to its application.

Educational places, however, do not take easily to some features of accountability. Educators, for example, are quick to note that the goals of education are not easy to define or measure. People involved in teaching and learning activities like to exercise a considerable amount of control over their work while preferring to be treated as responsible professionals who can work with minimal supervision, who can be trusted to use resources wisely and who can be regarded as possessing knowledge appropriate to the tasks of teaching and learning. These desires for some degree of freedom to work with minimal interference and hierarchical oversight are embodied in the concept of 'autonomy'. Again, the value and reasoning which underlie the concept are easily understood.

Accountability and autonomy, therefore, are dual strands which create a dilemma for the administrator. Although it is easy and convenient to discuss the concepts separately, they function in a linked fashion in educational organizations. Rather than being discrete entities for the administrator, accountability and autonomy are closely entwined. They are, too, the concern of such diverse groups as policy makers and planners at the national level, school governing bodies, people in administrative and leadership positions and practitioners working directly in teaching and learning situations. The issue lies in the degree to which accountability and autonomy are applied in relation to each other in order to ensure that people work simultaneously within guidelines and with a degree of independence. Herein lies the dilemma for the administrator: to what extent should either concept be accorded precedence? Put simply, the question is, 'To what extent should the members of an organization be able to be called to account for their work, on the one hand, while being given freedom to function, on the other hand?'

In simple terms, the most extreme outcomes of the question are easily described. Rigid, unbending emphasis on accountability is likely to lead to an autocratic organization whereas unbridled autonomy holds the potential for anarchy! Rather than being concerned with such extremes, however, the facts of life in contemporary educational places involve the striking of a balance between accountability and autonomy.

The Central Issue of Control

The dilemma of accountability and autonomy is inextricably bound to the central issue of 'control'. 'Good' management is sometimes perceived as being synonymous with the presence of structures to control what people are doing and how they are doing it — structures and procedures to which people must adhere or comply. This emphasis on such features as lines of authority and reporting, systems for checking and supervising and channels for communicating has an in-built danger: the structures and procedures can easily become the focus of any activity with the resulting potential for lessened commitment and morale. The emphasis, then, focuses on the meeting of deadlines, the pursuit of targets, communication only through official channels and a concern with structures. The consequent danger becomes manifest in forms such as increased emphasis on developing further systems of control and the increase of staff members' feelings of anxiety and dissatisfaction and time spent either in circumventing systems or complying with continuous organizational demands. Control of this kind, with these outcomes, represents a narrow view of accountability and the part it should play in organizational life.

Conversely, when control is perceived as letting people enjoy maximal freedom to 'do their own thing', the danger lies in individual parts of the organization becoming mini-institutions without any agreed standards of performance or any coordinated use of resources or any shared goals towards which all members are striving. The trick for the administrator or the governing body lies in bringing balance to enabling staff members to meet the requirements of the organization while, at the same time, having the freedom to work in ways which are meaningful and rewarding for the individual.

Reforming a System of Education Administration: The New Zealand Case

Since the late 1980s, the delivery of New Zealand's system of education administration has undergone radical reform. The nature and scope of these changes are useful in illustrating the concepts of accountability and autonomy as they have emerged in practice in the New Zealand context. Other aspects of the changes, relevant to their impact on the role of the education officer, will be considered in chapter 14.

In 1986, the Parliamentary Science and Education Select Committee in its report, *The Quality of Teaching*, (1986) noted the outmoded administrative practices underlying the system of education administration and suggested procedures for developing accountability. Little practical action, however, resulted from the report although the pace of events quickened markedly after the national elections in late 1987. The Prime Minister assumed control of the education portfolio and a successful businessman, Brian Picot, was appointed to head a small group charged with examining the system of education administration with a view to developing decentralized functions where possible, increasing the delegated powers and responsibilities of bodies governing local institutions and recommending ways of repositioning the system in order to increase its flexibility, responsiveness and efficiency. Finding an overcentralized, overly complex administrative structure, the Picot Taskforce proposed a new structure in which individual learning institutions would become the basic units of education administration and in which professionals and communities would become partners in the enterprise of identifying clear objectives to reflect local and national needs and for which each institution would be held accountable. In its report, *Administering for Excellence*, (1988) the Taskforce commented:

> Those who use public funds must be accountable for what is achieved with those funds. To be accountable, individuals and organizations must know what they are to achieve and must have control over the resources needed to do this — otherwise, accountability cannot exist. As well, those who are accountable must know who they are accountable to: the lines of accountability must be clear.

Accountability was one of eight central features upon which the proposed new system was based. Other features included openness and responsiveness, coordinated and appropriately placed decision-making and simplicity. In addition, two further features indicated a concern for accountability and autonomy. The Taskforce proposed a clarifying of responsibilities and goals: it should be clear who would be responsible for particular activities while conflicts of interest should be avoided. Further, the Taskforce proposed, 'to enable them to exercise responsibility and meet objectives, individuals must have control over the resources they require'. Some devolution of authority, therefore, was intended but a major emphasis was placed on the notion of people and institutions being accountable. The Taskforce explained:

> Those who exercise power and responsibility on behalf of others must expect to have their performance monitored and to be held accountable for what they have achieved ... Genuine accountability involves three major elements:
> * clear and specific aims and objectives, expressed as outcomes;
> * control over the resources available to achieve those outcomes;
> * monitoring by an outside agency of how well those objectives are met.

In a subsequent publication, *Tomorrow's Schools* (1988), the government began the implementation of many of the proposals made by the Picot Taskforce. There were three structural elements of relevance to the theme of this chapter. First, a new Ministry of Education emerged from the former multi-function Department of Education. The lean Ministry would provide policy advice to its Minister with other functions including the responsibility for setting national guidelines for education and curriculum objectives, the approval of the charter by which each learning institution would contract with the state to apply resources to obtaining student outcomes, the funding of institutions and the ownership of educational property.

Second, each institution began the process of electing its Board of Trustees which would accept responsibility for overall policy direction of its institution whereas the day-to-day management would be under the control of the principal. Boards would collaborate with principals, staff members and communities to prepare the charters on which funding would be based. Boards, too, would become the employers of staff and would be accountable for the degree of achievement of the institution's chartered objectives. Funding would be received by boards which would approve institution budgets and be responsible for the preparation of audited accounts.

Third, an Education Review Office was established as an independent state agency which would ensure that institutions were accountable for their use of public funds and for meeting the objectives stated in the charter and agreed between Ministry and institution. Officers of this agency would visit institutions every three years and report on the degree of attainment of objectives and the quality of administrative action. Reports would become a matter of public record.

During the same period, other taskforces investigated the early childhood and tertiary education sectors and subsequent reports have resulted in reforms of education administration in these areas, too (*Before Five* (1988) and *Learning for Life* (1988)).

The implementation of the reforms was an arduous process; as was noted in their report to the Minister of Education by the team which was established in late 1989 to review the implementation process (*Today's Schools*, 1990). Chairperson Noel Lough, a retired senior Treasury officer, wrote of a 'tough transitional period' characterized by the hard work and dedication of the people who were involved and widespread support for Picot's concepts. In addition, he commented:

> However, there is a perception that what has emerged in practice is increased central bureaucratic control, increased burdensome administrative tasks, inadequate resourcing and support for the institutions, and inadequate attention to educational outcomes.

Lough's review team recommended some thirty actions to focus the reform implementation. In the school sector, these proposals included providing administrative models for developing objectives and managing educational, personnel, property and financial programmes as well as monitoring and appraising internal activities. In addition, clearer definitions of roles was sought for principals, boards and administrative officers (where institutions were sufficiently large to warrant the employment of such people). Finally, a task force of successful principals was proposed in order to provide resources and support for schools in the implementation process while a detailed reporting process was proposed 'to ensure that schools lift their performance'.

The review team also proposed that the Ministry of Education be downsized and become focused to a major extent on its policy development role. The report noted,

> As its part in achieving improved educational outcomes for students, the primary objective within the Ministry of Education is to develop a strategy for providing high-quality educational policy assessment, advice, development and implementation on behalf of the Minister. Specifically programmes will include elements of:
> * policy development and implementation;
> * operations;
> * finance and support.
>
> Of these elements, policy development and implementation is the most important role for the ministry.

The team sought a 'methodology' on which the Ministry's policy activities would be managed and administered so that, for each policy project, procedures, analysis, consultation, evaluation and the determination of critical paths would be pursued in the interests of consistent analysis, intellectual rigour and administrative efficiency.

From the early days of the reforms, a review and audit agency had been proposed as a central feature for ensuring the examination of accountability. *Tomorrow's Schools* (1988) stated,

> An independent body — the Review and Audit Agency — will be established to ensure that institutions are accountable for the government funds they spend and for meeting the objectives set out in their charter.

Now operational as the Education Review Office, this body also received the Lough team's attention which recommended, 'that redirecting a significant portion of the present funding for the Education Review Office to schools will be the most cost-effective way of improving educational outcomes for students' (*Today's Schools*, 1990). The slimmed down Education Review Office would examine each school at least once every three years for the purpose of making a tightly focused review of outputs and outcomes in four key areas (education, personnel, property and finance) and of equity issues and community consultation. The Review Office was charged with developing a clear and well reasoned methodology for school reviews.

How New Zealand's Reformed System of Education Administration Provides For Accountability: a Summary

* The individual learning institution becomes the 'building block' of the system and should reflect a partnership with its community.
* The Ministry of Education provides funding and national education policy.
* School Boards of Trustees employ staff, manage funds, negotiate an institutional charter with the Ministry of Education and are accountable for the achievement of chartered objectives.
* Charters reflect national and local educational needs and take the form of a negotiated agreement.
* The Education Review Office visits schools at least once every three years in order to examine progress in terms of the charter. Four key functions are reviewed in relation to chartered objectives: education, personnel, property and finance.

Accountability and Autonomy: Some Dilemmas

In seeking a suitably balanced relationship between accountability and autonomy, educational policy makers and practitioners face a number of dilemmas.

A Technology to Control or to Release?

A significant dilemma concerning accountability and autonomy relates to the purpose which underlies any system which seeks to determine the level and quality of performance of an individual or group of people. A major criticism of strategies designed to examine performance focuses on the use of accountability as a technology of control. Such systems seek narrow measures of performance in order to produce data between which relationships are easily identified and which can be used to highlight aspects of performance — not only the positive but also such negative features as overspending, departure from objectives or failure to meet targets. In these cases the data are used to seek easy answers or either as a basis of reward or punishment or as a means of extending future targets. The emphasis is placed squarely on the careful monitoring and control of work performance. Such an approach might work successfully in a factory which uses specific inputs to produce a certain number of finite products and in which workers have only few decisions to make. However, the extension of the approach to the educational context becomes a technology of control when the ultimate end is that of maintaining close direction over classroom performance by decreeing precisely how resources will be used and how their use will be monitored and measured. Codd (1989) explained further:

> As society has become more and more technological, that is, more accustomed to regarding technical solutions as the only acceptable solutions to various human problems, it has become less tolerant of uncertainty and more obsessed with gaining control over every situation and state of affairs.

The converse of this approach lies in perceiving accountability and autonomy as bases for the reasoned release of human potential in which data are used to make judgments intended to help performance and to facilitate creative ways of solving problems. In such an approach, staff who implement policy will be meaningfully involved — at the very least — in making decisions about how and why work will be undertaken, what will be measured and how this will be done. The approach, of course, calls for knowledge and skill on the part of the implementer as much as the policy maker. It is hardly likely that learning places will be characterized by openness, creativity and receptivity to change when control is tight and negative. The outcome is likely to be an emphasis on conservatism and the domestication of teachers and administrators which, in turn, will hinder independent thinking and the creative resolution of problems.

The Difficulty of Measuring Educational Outcomes

The 'accountability as control' approach assumes that educational outcomes are easily quantified. There are two dilemmas inherent in this position. First, as many students of human nature readily know, frequent testing or measuring tends to result in an overemphasis on readily tested or measured activities at the expense of less easily quantified activities. Secondly — and of much greater complexity, attempts tightly to link the efficient use of resources in educational places with measurable outcomes draws us into a complex domain which centres on the key question, 'What is the output of an educational place?' Hanson (1979) notes a range of responses to the question — cognitive learning gain, attitudinal change, vocational preparation, good citizenship, custodial control, peer socialization and the like. Not only is it difficult to gain agreement on the relative value of such outcomes or ways of measuring them but also the outcomes of an educational programme might not be easy to determine in the short term. Accountability cannot be concerned only with the efficient use of resources but it must take account of the wide range of possible student learning outcomes and the multifaceted performance of staff in learning places.

In New Zealand, Snook (1990) has noted the difficulties of measuring and comparing educational outcomes and their causes and of establishing relationships between the variables which might characterize successful schools. He has argued strongly against holding educators accountable for student learning. Teachers, Snook posits, provide situations in which learning can occur rather than causing learning themselves: 'To hold teachers responsible for learning failure is like holding doctors responsible for ill health or social workers responsible for delinquency'.

Moral Accountability or Contractual Accountability?

There is an important aspect of accountability about which it is impossible to legislate. This is the inherent — almost 'natural' — accountability which many educators feel for their work. Renwick (1983) termed this a sense of moral obligation. He explained:

> ... the idea of accountability points to each of us as individuals, requiring us to consider our obligations in relation to the educational roles we perform, the relationships those roles bring us into, and the power or influence associated with them.

Barton *et al.* (1980) further distinguished between answerability to one's clients (*moral* accountability) and the responsibility which one feels to oneself and to one's colleagues (*professional* accountability). Codd (1989) explained accountability as being neither a political nor a social demand but the recognition by the individual that the professional powers invested in that person also carry a responsibility to account for the exercise of those powers.

These perceptions of accountability, quite obviously, are much wider than the 'outputs and outcomes' view of accountability which is so strongly promoted in reforms such as those occurring in New Zealand. Barton *et al.* (1980) explain this perception as accountability to one's employers or political masters (*contractual* accountability). The danger with an overreliance on this perspective is that the imposition of such systems may cause educators to move from their moral commitment if a new ideology and reward system involves too many competing demands or if it devalues the traditional strength of moral and professional accountability. At the end of the day, in fact, this traditional perspective may even be the most powerful and effective kind of accountability in the educational arena!

The Professional Person in the Public Organization

The issue of accountability and autonomy poses a dilemma for people charged with the running of educational organizations in which staff members see themselves as being competent professional practitioners. The dilemma involves the degree to which staff members should be called to account for their work, on the one hand, while being given freedom to function, on the other hand. In his study of a group of American schools, Hanson (1979) found that teachers felt they were the ultimate authorities on the teaching-learning process because of their expertise in specialized fields. They felt they had the right to organize the learning process in the fashion they chose and that their position as teachers gave them a right to differ from stated policy positions and instructions. Hanson considered, too, that the position of teachers was strengthened by an instructional process which was relatively unencumbered by a network of rules defining how teaching and learning events should be shaped.

In educational places, the activities which teachers and learners undertake occur largely independently of administrative systems. In fact, changing systems will not necessarily change the ways in which teachers and learners will interact. Much of their activity occurs within classroom walls without direct oversight by principals or departmental heads and often without rigorous or planned integration with other programmes and without regular, careful, continuous evaluation. In practice, these features are often difficult — if not impossible — to achieve. It is difficult, therefore, for people charged with the oversight of other people (whether at department, institution or system level) to be able to oversee or judge the finer details of events and behaviours which occur in the 'frontline' or at the 'chalkface'.

A way of conceptualizing this dilemma is provided by Weick (1976) who considers that the contributing elements of an organization are usually linked in a loose fashion rather than through tight, clearly defined linkages. In this loose coupling, which is characteristic of educational places, people tend to work independently and events tend to occur without strong links between them. Tighter agreement is probably more desirable over such features as a school's agreed mission and goals rather than over agreement on ways of achieving those features in the teaching-learning process. The search for a balance between accountability and autonomy for the professional person, therefore, should seek to ensure that the strengths of a loosely coupled system are not lost in the quest for tightening the links through close scrutiny and measurement.

In their work on successful companies in USA, Peters and Waterman (1982) similarly found that a considerable degree of autonomy and innovation signalled success in companies which enabled autonomy for staff and, in return, gained creativity. The same writers concluded, 'The intense, informal communication system acts as a remarkably tight control system'. However, once again, the dilemma with determining any degree of autonomy is one of striking the right balance. Quite obviously, when an organization is using the tax payer's money, total autonomy is just not possible; the question becomes, 'What is a reasonable balance?'

Locus of Policy

A further dilemma concerning accountability and autonomy bears on the issue of the locations in which policy making and policy implementation occur. In the reformed system of education administration in New Zealand, two major levels of policy development are apparent. At the national level, the new Ministry of Education is responsible for providing its Minister with policy advice from which the state will set national guidelines (or, establish policy) — the implementation of which will be overseen by the Ministry. At the local level, each institution's Board of Trustees is responsible for the development of broad policy objectives within the overall national guidelines and for the efficient and effective running of the school. Is this a process of centralization or decentralization? In reality, it is a blend of both features. As distinct from the pre-reform centralized decision-making, the new structure comprises centralized decision-making on national policy positions and the structure facilitates decentralized decision-making in which boards and their schools implement national policy in response to local needs. Goff (1989) explained the position:

> The basic premise of the reforms is that decisions should be made as close as possible to where they are carried out. The reforms are intended to promote more responsiveness, flexibility and accountability ... The government is, however, not withdrawing from its responsibilities. It funds the system.

The Education Review Office is the mechanism by which the government will ensure that institutions are accountable for the funds they spend and for meeting the objectives they identify in relation to local needs and national guidelines.

Policy, therefore, can be established and implemented at different levels.

A related concept is useful in further explaining the New Zealand situation. Child's (1977) explanation of 'delegation' provides an accurate summary.

> Delegation is an approach where decision making is passed downwards and outwards within the formal structure, but where there are strict limits imposed on the scope and type of decisions that can be made without referral upwards.

In these terms, the Education Review Office clearly has a major role to play in ensuring the accountability of institutions in the New Zealand system and, consequently, influencing the degree of autonomy or freedom to manoeuvre which is delegated to administrators and practitioners in those places.

A Note on Autonomy

Almost inevitably, this chapter is concerned more with accountability than autonomy as the former concept has become a major feature on the contemporary scene in a number of Western countries which are involved in education administration reform. Autonomy, however, requires confidence and capability in one's professional knowledge and skills in order that responsibility can be taken for one's own performance. Torrington and Weightman (1989) warn, 'Where particular staff have not been trusted to behave in this way they may be uncertain and unsure how to react'. This warning implies that the giving of autonomy carries with it not only the responsibility for ensuring that people can work with a degree of independence and responsibility but also that they are provided with the knowledge, skills and resources successfully to exercise that autonomy. The advice of the same writers concludes,

> A balance between a tight central mission of a school coupled with a loose, decentralized autonomy of how to put that into practice seems to make for effectiveness.

The New Zealand Reforms In Education Administration: A Changed Central Value

The reforms heralded the arrival of a new set of structures and values to underpin New Zealand's education administration system. Individual learning institutions became the basic 'building blocks' of education administration — largely able to determine their use of resources within the overall objectives of the state education system and local needs. This change represented a major shift from a centralized system and promoted the notion of a partnership between professional educators and the community at the local level. This devolution of decision-making to Boards of Trustees, in reality, brought with it a major emphasis on the value of accountability. In their first paragraphs of the proposed reforms, the Picot Taskforce commented, 'Those who have responsibility for decision making should be accountable for the decisions they make' (*Administering for Excellence*, 1988). Any examination of the central documents soon reveals this emphasis on an endeavour to ensure outputs and to determine level of performance. Not only was a large degree of decision-making passed to local levels but also the expectation was highlighted that decisions on resource use should be made with maximum efficiency.

Resolving the Dilemmas

How might the dilemmas be resolved? The scope of a single chapter allows an exploration of only two possible courses of action: the practical technique of constructing batteries of performance indicators and the more philosophical approach of expanding the 'pool' of control.

The Use of Performance Indicators

The key problem in assessing accountability is to identify areas in which performance should be monitored and to construct ways of assessing that performance. The use of 'performance indicators' provides a useful means of undertaking this task. Performance indicators provide some standard or criteria against which progress or accomplishment can be measured (*Draft Performance Indicators*, 1989). 'Criteria' are the topics on which judgments will be made while 'standards' are the baselines which will be used as a basis for assessment. It is relatively easy to develop performance indicators on direct inputs and outputs such as the total cost of teachers' salaries in relation to examination results. It is much more difficult to be so accurate in measuring the benefits or outcomes of, for example, a pastoral care programme in relation to the resources which are required to run the programme.

But careful thought can result in a battery of indicators which will provide a useful means of doing this task. In Britain, the document, *Performance Indicators in Schools* (1988), suggests a series of indicators which are helpful in determining effectiveness and efficiency in the most important contexts within which those concerned with the management and appraisal of schools might need to make judgments:

* management of staff;
* management of the curriculum and programmes of study;
* pastoral management;
* financial management;
* liaison with other agencies and the community; and
* management of information.

The batteries of indicators include both *quantitative* (or countable) items and *qualitative* (or less easily measured but more easily commented upon) items. *Performance Indicators in Schools* (1988) provides a range of useful sample indicators in each of the six areas. In the area of financial management, there is little difficulty in identifying quantitative or readily measurable indicators of an institution's performance. Examples of the sample indicators include:

* teaching staff cost per pupil;
* books and equipment costs per pupil;
* fuel and light costs per pupil;
* library and computer resources expenditure;
* evidence of spending all monies or justified carry-over and a clear spending pattern which does not exhaust resources before the end of the financial year;
* any shortfall in provision over identified needs; and
* the level of funding available from sources other than capitation.

Such areas as pastoral management, however, are less easily measured or counted. Further easily quantified sample indicators include:

* attendance patterns;
* incidence of vandalism;
* incidence of graffiti; and
* rates of suspensions and exclusions.

However, the effectiveness of a pastoral management programme cannot be determined on such quantifiable measures alone. The full picture will only be disclosed when observations, comments and opinions are gathered on a wide range of additional *necessary* indicators – examples of which might include:

* involvement of senior staff;
* systems of rewards and sanctions;
* relationships between teachers and pupils;
* opportunities for responsibility;
* provision of vocational guidance;
* accommodation for pastoral staff;
* provision of social areas for pupils; and
* opportunities for staff training. (*Performance Indicators in Schools*, 1988)

Five essential principles should be borne in mind when indicators are being constructed. Indicators should be:

* as few as are needed to achieve their purpose;
* related to the organization's aims and objectives;
* as acceptable as possible to those who use them;
* as reliable as possible and able to be standardized; and
* capable of conveying messages and throwing up warning signs. (*Performance Indicators in Schools*, 1988)

Braithwaite and Low (1988) consider that performance indicators should assist practitioners to improve their performance as well as providing guidance and management information. Indicators, too, should be useful in guiding policy formulation and in providing consumers and the public with indicators of institutional effectiveness.

The same writers note that indicators can be categorised into three areas. *Input* indicators include those items which are provided to enable the system to operate — such as the resource inputs of money, space, time and people. *Process* indicators determine what is done during the processes of managing, teaching and learning — such as the choices available to students, the quality of specific programmes and the nature of the organization's climate; it is in this area that emphasis is placed on the less easily measured qualitative features. *Output* indicators include the results of activities and these items might be more readily counted or measured — such as achievement rates, skills gained or resources used. Performance indicator batteries with the greatest possibility of fulfilling the demands of accountability will cater for the three types of indicator without solely relying on a single area of inquiry or on either quantitative or qualitative measures.

Expanding Control

Whereas the use of performance indicators is more of a practical strategy, it is useful also to consider the more philosophical issue of the amount of control which is exercised within an organization. A common perception of control is to consider it as a fixed commodity. In this view, a manager could claim to exercise a certain amount of control or to share a certain amount with staff members. The 'worst case scenario' occurs when we feel that our control over events is being lessened or lost. But control is a means by which the behaviour of people is influenced by the decisions of those holding control. Therefore, the concept of control raises issues such as the rights of the individual, the place of democratic principles and the morality of means of ensuring or enforcing control.

The work of Tannenbaum (1968) refutes the 'fixed amount' perspective of control and encourages policy makers and administrators to take a different view. Tannenbaum's work has been used in New Zealand to describe an alternative view in which control is not a finite resource and, in fact, is able to be increased by the 'baking of bigger pies':

> The easiest way to demonstrate this is the example of the weak, permissive manager. He exercises little control himself in terms of any attempt to influence the behaviour of members toward desired ends. It is likely that the other members of the organization exercise a similarly small amount of control over each other's behaviour. In such an organization, behaviour tends to become increasingly idiosyncratic, coordinated working relationships break down, and people do their own thing. In short, the total amount of control in the organization is relatively small. If that manager is replaced by a more energetic, task-oriented person then the total amount of control being exercised in the organization will almost certainly increase quite quickly as she starts to bring influence to bear on the behaviour of other members. If that same manager then encourages members to share in important management decisions, set team goals, and supervise each other's work, the total amount of control being exercised will probably rise yet again. At each step, organizational behaviour becomes more ordered and coordinated, and more members of the organization come to acquire influence in shaping the work of their colleagues and themselves. In short, the total amount of control increases, but the crucial point is that the manager need not lose any of his or her own control by encouraging other members to exercise control themselves. (Stewart and Prebble, 1985)

In his research, Tannenbaum (1968) sought to measure the total amount and distribution of control in an organization. Three important points stem from the evidence which he examined in a variety of organizations:

* organizations with influential rank and file members are likely to be more effective than organizations whose members do not have influence;
* organizations with powerful leaders are likely to be more effective than organizations whose leaders are less powerful; and
* organizations with influential members *and* influential leaders are likely to be more effective than organizations with less influential membership and leadership.

These findings suggest that control is not a fixed commodity and that it can be exercised effectively by people at different levels of an organization. Control is not lost or diluted when a powerful or strong leader encourages participation by other colleagues. Tannenbaum's work suggests, too, that the amount of control which is generated and shared in an organization is a useful predictor of staff involvement in the organization's activities and of the effectiveness of the organization. This view, of course, will appeal to people who value participant involvement but it does not signify the beginnings of an uncontrolled, anarchic organization. On the contrary, Tannenbaum's perspective indicates that maximum and meaningful involvement of participants in important aspects of the life of an organization will foster commitment and the pursuit of shared goals and, in the process, will increase the amount of control which is exercised. The view is aptly explained by the earlier culinary metaphor of baking bigger pies:

> The success of participative approaches, Tannenbaum suggests, hinges not on reducing control, but on achieving a system of control that is more effective than that of other systems. Likert has coined the term 'influence pie' to refer to the total amount of control being exercised within the organization. The pie may be cut and shared in many different ways, but the best way to ensure that everyone gets a bigger slice is to bake a bigger pie! (Stewart and Prebble, 1985)

Therefore, when degrees of accountability and autonomy are considered, an important question becomes, 'How can a bigger pie be baked?' An answer based on Tannenbaum's findings suggests that any system which seeks accountability should ensure that participants in that system are clearly knowledgeable about the nature of the tasks, the degree of discretion and authority which they may exercise and the way in which results will be determined. But, as much as possible, too, participants should be involved in determining and planning those measures. Tannenbaum's work suggests that the more control that is generated in an organization amongst its members, the greater is the likelihood of the organization being effective. Put another way, if people can be empowered to control their work with a good deal of autonomy, then they are likely to accept considerable responsibility for the outcomes of their own work and the use of resources required to do it.

Principals Supporting Principals in New Zealand

The Principals' Implementation Task Force was established in New Zealand in mid–1990 as an outcome of *Today's Schools* (1990). A group of successful school principals was brought together to develop a variety of administrative models and systems for guidance, support and better performance in the areas of property, finance, personnel, the delivery of education (learning and teaching) and government — policy in relation to management and operations. The preparation of support material ('packages') in the five areas denotes the importance of improving school management performance so:

* that the resources of buildings, land and facilities, dollars and people are used wisely and to best effect;
* that teachers and learners are able to do as well as they possibly can; and
* that schools function on the basis of sound policies which are able to be implemented by staff members.

In preparing its support packages, the Task Force drew on the expertise of many principals and other educators from throughout New Zealand while a large network of schools participated in trials of the materials.

The Task Force exercise was an example of a large pool of professional expertise being used to identify specific target areas for improvement in the management of skills and to draw on the practical knowledge of successful school administrators as a basis for the preparation and validation of materials.

Towards Effective Systems of Accountability

Any system which is designed to exercise control over an activity or to ensure that the performers of an activity can be brought to account for their involvement in that activity should be characterized by a number of important features. Management writers (for example, Mitchell, 1982; Van Fleet, 1988) commonly offer batteries of advice on such features from which a number of points can be applied to the education administration situation.

Integration

Effective systems to determine accountability for performance need to be integrated into the overall procedures and values which are fundamental to the organization. This implies that people at all levels clearly understand the purposes of accountability and the ways in which it is determined. Similarly, those procedures should become almost habitually included in planning and preparation activities. For instance, when a staff group plans a new programme, its members should realize almost instinctively that tools should be selected for determining and demonstrating the effectiveness of the programme so that they and the providers of the resources will be well placed to make decisions on the programme's future. Systems to determine accountability are unlikely to be effective when they are not perceived as an integral part of the way in which things are done in the organization.

Accuracy and Reliability

Good systems are based on good information. The effective system for making judgments of accountability will provide the tools for gathering information which is reliable, able to be interpreted with accuracy and provides a useful base for making decisions. Of course, there is value in being able to gather objective data about such areas as programmes and expenditures — quantitative data which are usually gathered and processed with relative ease. Of use, too, in the educational setting are the more subjective comments, reactions and judgments which might be made by educators whose activities are being assessed. Counting and measuring of this kind of qualitative data will be less important than will be care to ask meaningful questions and to seek to gather useful perceptions.

Understanding

When the people who are being held accountable possess an understanding of the nature and purpose of accountability and the processes being applied to their own performance, they are less likely to be offended, anxious or disruptive when their work is examined. This is likely to be particularly so when these people have had the opportunity to participate in the planning of the system of accountability which is being used.

Utility

Simply because something *can* be measured or counted it does not follow that it *should* be measured or counted. Systems for determining accountability should produce useful information on which judgments and decisions can be made. The essential question is, 'Is that which is being measured worth being measured?' The question implies that neither questions nor data are trivial but, rather, that they assist in the seeking of worthwhile answers and truth about the elements for which they are designed. Similarly, they will provide a useful means of determining links between goals, activities, resources and outcomes.

Timeliness

Any process of accountability should be planned in order that data not only are gathered at appropriate times but also are used, processed and disseminated in time for the meeting of targets for future planning and budgeting or dispute. Timeliness does not solely mean speed but it does mean ensuring that information is placed in the hands of those who require it and at the time for which it is needed.

Fairness

Fairness and justice must be important facets of accountability. Natural justice suggests that people subject to accountability should know the limits of their responsibility, the nature of the information being gathered about their performance and the uses to which that data will be put. Fairness implies that similar requirements will be made of people with similar responsibilities so that individuals or groups will not be disadvantaged or treated unfairly. Dialogue, disclosure and participation in the planning of accountability procedures are useful means of ensuring fair and just systems.

Flexibility

Flexibility involves the capacity to accommodate adjustments and change. While predictability and adherence to timeliness and systems might be desirable and useful, an effective system of accountability will be able to cope with changed circumstances. There may be sound reasons for increasing expenditure to take advantage of a 'once only' offer or to understand the reasons for not meeting a scheduled deadline or for accommodating a shift in direction in order to use new knowledge. An inflexible system might cause the organization to lose valuable opportunities. The real problem occurs when flexibility assumes greater importance than accountability!

When conditions such as these are met, accountability, as Barton *et al.* (1980) concluded, becomes 'not so much a programme, more a way of life'.

Key Elements of School Management and Leadership in New Zealand's Education Administration Reforms

Today's Schools (1990) clarified the relationship between the professional and lay administrators of schools:

> The key role of boards of trustees is to develop policy guidelines and to ensure that satisfactory educational outputs are achieved. In pursuing this goal the fundamental decision for boards of trustees to make is the recruitment of their principal; and then to conduct an annual appraisal of this person's performance on a basis that is consistent with the agreed job definition/contract. Management of the school then becomes the principal's role, not that of the board of trustees.
>
> The key components of the various roles include:
>
> * **Boards of Trustees**
> — To oversee and direct the process of selecting new principals.
> — To provide continuing support to the principal in the execution of his/her duties.
> — To make policy — this does not involve direct participation in operation management.
> — To ensure the school communicates effectively with its community.
>
> * **The Principal**
> — To manage the day to day educational, personnel and administrative affairs of the school.
> — To delegate enough of the daily operational administrative tasks so that the principal can perform effectively as the educational leader of the school.
> — To provide educational leadership by establishing an educational plan for the school and by communicating it to all staff and students.
> — To implement policies and programmes for achieving the school's education plan.
> — To ensure decisions on major personnel questions follow the agreed policies of the school.
> — To support teachers in carrying out their professional role.
> — To ensure through a collaborative process that heads of departments and individual teachers have both clear roles and clear sets of objectives; and also the ability to monitor their performance in achieving these objectives.

Debate during the first two years of the reforms has highlighted the amount of non-educational work required of principals and whether or not instructional leadership by principals is a realistic expectation. One perception of professional educational leadership which seems appropriate for the 1990s contains four skill areas essential to the principal's role:

* management of 'business' activities — planning, budgeting, reporting, etc;
* leadership of people — motivating, assessing, supporting, etc;
* development of curriculum — guiding, advising, evaluating, planning, etc;
* facilitating change — promoting a vision, thinking strategically, managing change, etc. (Edwards, 1989)

Conclusion

This chapter has distinguished between the entwined concepts of accountability and autonomy. The central concept of control was introduced and a series of dilemmas for administrators was highlighted. In an era in which we are concerned to do as best we can with available resources, policy makers, administrators and 'chalkface' practitioners face the task of balancing both the central phenomena examined in the chapter.

In addition to features characterizing effective systems of accountability, two current approaches were proposed for attacking the accountability-autonomy dilemma: the practicalities of applying performance indicators and the more philosophical approach of generating a greater pool of control. The reforms of education administration in New Zealand in recent years provided a case example throughout the chapter. An essential part of these reforms continues to involve the central issues explored in this chapter.

Endeavouring to achieve an appropriate balance between accountability and autonomy remains one of the most challenging and exciting policy and management tasks facing today's and tomorrow's educational leaders in their pursuit of the dual results of the best use of resources and enhanced teaching and learning.

References

Barton, J. *et al.* (1980) 'Accountability and education' in Bush, T. *et al.* (Eds) *Approaches to School Management*, London, Harper and Row, pp. 98–120.

Before Five (1988) White Paper on Early Childhood Care and Education in New Zealand, Wellington, Government Printer.

Braithwaite, J. and Low, B. (1988) 'Determining school effectiveness through performance indicators: Have we got it right?', paper presented to Directors-General of Education Conference, Australia.

Child, J. (1977) *Organization: A Guide to Problems and Practice*, London, Harper and Row.

Codd, J. (1989) 'Evaluating tomorrow's schools: Accountability or control?', *Delta 41*, May, pp. 3–11.

Draft Performance Indicators (1989) Wellington, Implementation Unit, Department of Education.

Edwards, W.L. (1989) 'What's the right stuff for tomorrow's leaders?', *The New Zealand Principal*, **4**, 2, July, pp. 9–12.

Goff, P. (1989) 'Address to NZEI conference', Wellington, August.

Hanson, E.M. (1979) *Educational Administration and Organizational Behavior*, Boston, MA, Allyn and Bacon.

Learning for Life (1988) White Paper on Education and Training Beyond the Age of Fifteen, Wellington, Government Printer.

Mitchell, T.R. (1982) *People in Organizations: An Introduction to Organizational Behavior*, New York, McGraw-Hill.

Performance Indicators in Schools (1988) Consultation Document, London, Chartered Institute of Public Finance and Accountancy.

Peters, T.J. and Waterman, R.H. (1982) *In Search of Excellence*, New York, Bantam.

Renwick, W.L. (1983) 'Accountability: A tangled skein', opening address, Third New Zealand Educational Administration Society Conference, Auckland.

Snook, I. (1990) 'The principal: Manager or professional leader?', *The New Zealand Principal*, **5**, 1, April, pp. 5–7.

Stewart, D. and Prebble, T. (1985) *Making It Happen*, Palmerston North, Dunmore Press.

Tannenbaum, A. (1968) *Control in Organizations*, New York, McGraw-Hill.

Taskforce to Review Education Administration (1988) *Administering for Excellence* (The Picoe Report), Wellington, Government Printer.

The Quality of Teaching (1986) Report of the Parliamentary Education and Science Select Committee, Wellington, Government Printer.

Today's Schools (1990) Report to the Minister of Education, Wellington, Government Printer.

Tomorrow's Schools (1988) White Paper on the Reform of Education Administration in New Zealand, Wellington, Government Printer.

Torrington, D. and Weightman, J. (1989) *The Reality of School Management*, Oxford, Basil Blackwell.

Van Fleet, D. (1988) *Contemporary Management*, Boston, MA, Houghton Mifflin.

Weick, K. (1976) *Organization: A Guide to Problems and Practice*, London, Harper and Row.

4 Effective Schools: An International Perspective

Larry Sackney

The effective schools movement is now almost two decades old. At the core of the movement is the belief that 'schools can make a difference.' It challenges the assumption that differences among schools have minimal effect on student academic achievement.

During the intervening years we have witnessed the continued search for effective schools variables, development of implementation models and policy directives. With the establishment of the International Congress for Effective Schools (ICES) in 1988, the movement now has an international focus.

At the same time, the effective schools bandwagon has had its share of critics. Much of the criticism by those who prefer goals related to social transformation (Giroux and McLaren, 1986), has centred around the significance of the criteria of effectiveness. There has also been considerable scepticism about whether the effective schools reforms can be implemented and what it is that school effectiveness researchers have discovered (Holmes, 1989, p.3).

This chapter is about the implications of research into school effectiveness at the school, district and international levels. The chapter also outlines policy determinants for effective schools and a model for school improvement based on collaborative cultural notions.

History of School Effectiveness

The conventional view in the late 60s and early 70s was that it was impossible to identify important, school-based characteristics that were clearly beneficial to student learning outcomes. The belief was that the primary determinant of achievement outcomes was family background as measured by socioeconomic status (SES) and ethnicity. High SES students did well in school while disadvantaged students, especially minorities, did poorly. In essence, the conclusion was that 'schools did not make a difference.'

Miller (1983), in an historical analysis of the effective schools research, contends there were a number of different phases that influenced the movement. During the 1950s and 1960s structural-functionalism dominated sociological theory. The focus of research in this paradigm was on social class and social mobility. The conclusion was that schools accounted for very little difference in achievement once family background and social class characteristics were accounted for. Simply put, some schools were better than others because of the mix of students.

A second strand of research, known as the status maintenance literature, examined the relationships among social class, measured ability, schooling and occupational status as an adult. Many of these studies provided evidence for the meritocratic tradition (Miller, 1983, p. 17).

The studies that had the greatest impact on the effective schools movement were the Coleman *et al.* (1966) and Jencks *et al.* (1972) studies. The studies concluded that the major factor in achievement differentials both between schools and within schools resulted from family background. Schools had little impact on achievement once race and SES were controlled. These studies could be thought of as the first major school effects research and the progenitor of the effective schools studies that followed.

The Effective Schools Research

While the previous research was 'down beat', the research on school effectiveness is basically hopeful. Using a different research paradigm (interpretive and qualitative) researchers have been able to isolate attributes that differentiate more from less effective schools. Essentially the conclusion of this research is that 'schools make a difference.'

It would be easy to conclude that the findings of the effective schools research contradict the findings of Coleman *et al.* (1966), Jencks *et al.* (1972) and others. However, the new studies look at other variables. Secondly, the new studies do not find that there are overall large differences in achievement existing among schools. Most studies find a 10–30 per cent variance due to school differences, with most tending towards the lower end. There are many excellent reviews of the effective schools research (for example, Austin, 1979; Clark *et al.*, 1980; Edmonds, 1979; Purkey and Smith, 1983) and it is not the intent of this chapter to duplicate that effort.

Whereas the previous research (for example, Coleman *et al.*, 1966) has tended to entail large survey-type studies, the effective schools research has looked at different variables and has often used qualitative methodologies to discover them. Essentially, the sample sizes are small and the studies tend to focus on case studies, 'outlier' schools, and programme evaluation approaches.

These initial studies tended to focus on atypically successful schools. Prototypic of the atypical case studies is Weber's (1971) study of four successful inner-city elementary schools. He found eight characteristics typical to these schools: (i) strong instructional leadership; (ii) high expectations on the part of staff; (iii) positive atmosphere; (iv) strong emphasis on reading; (v) additional reading personnel; (vi) use of phonics; (vii) individualization; and (viii) careful evaluation of pupil progress. Similarly, the Phi Delta Kappan (1980) case study of eight exceptional schools found the importance of goal focus on academic excellence and basic skills achievement, effective discipline, and instructional leadership, among others.

The Brookover *et al.* (1979) and Brookover and Lezotte (1979) studies showed that social psychological factors affecting learning vary widely from school to school and that much of this variation is independent of SES and ethnicity. An analysis of the factors revealed that teacher expectations and evaluations were related to achievement.

A British study by Rutter *et al.* (1979) of twelve inner-city London high schools using a four-year (4 variable) longitudinal analysis suggests that staff attitudes, behaviour, and academic focus produce an overall ethos that is conducive to achievement. Other results included classroom management that kept students actively engaged in learning, firm discipline, use of rewards and praise, a physical environment that is conducive to learning and effective monitoring practices.

A second strand of research used the 'outlier' approach. Most of the studies employ regression analyses of school mean achievement scores, controlling for socioeconomic factors. Based on the residual scores, highly effective (positive outliers) and highly ineffective (negative outliers) are identified and then assessed by surveys or case studies to determine the reasons for the outcomes.

Typical of this strand are the Lezotte and Passalacqua (1978) and Austin (1979) studies. Lezotte and Passalacqua, after controlling for SES, found that the school attended explains 16 per cent of the variance. The more pervasive common elements are better control or discipline and high staff expectations for student achievement.

Perhaps the best known list of correlates is that suggested by Edmonds (1979). Based on his own research and his extensive review of other studies, Edmonds suggested five effectiveness characteristics: (i) strong instructional leadership; (ii) high expectations for all students; (iii) an orderly, work-oriented climate; (iv) priority focus on instruction; and (v) frequent monitoring. These five characteristics have become the generic set for many school improvement efforts.

A third strand of school effectiveness research is programme evaluation. Typical of this research is the Armor *et al.* (1976) study. They attempted to identify school and classroom policies that were successful in raising reading scores of minorities. Their results suggested the following characteristics as being associated with increased reading performance: (i) teacher sense of efficacy and high expectations; (ii) maintenance of orderly classrooms; (iii) high levels of contact with the home; (iv) ongoing teacher in-service; and (v) principals who engage in leadership roles.

Purkey and Smith (1983), in summarizing the results from programme evaluation studies, contend that the results are generally consistent. 'Most schools with effective programmes are characterized by high staff expectations and morale, a considerable degree of control by the staff over instructional and training decisions in the school, clear leadership from the principal or other instructional figure, clear goals for the school, and a sense of order in the school' (p. 438).

An additional aspect of the broader conception of school effects is that of delivery of instruction by teachers. McLaughlin and Marsh (1978) conclude that the most powerful association with achievement is teacher efficacy, the degree to which teachers perceive themselves able to make a difference in the learning of students. Rosenholtz (1989) found that in high consensus schools teachers shared goals, beliefs and values that led them to a 'more ennobling vision that placed teaching issues and children's interest in the forefront, and that bound them, including newcomers, to pursue that vision' (p. 39). Additionally, she found that in 'moving' schools there was more staff collaboration, greater teacher commitment and less teacher uncertainty than in 'stuck' schools.

Effective Schools Research in Context

According to Wimpelberg *et al.* (1989) the effective schools research constitutes two eras. The first is characterized by explicit concern for equity. This was the search for urban elementary schools where achievement gains were unusually high (for example, Brookover *et al.*, 1979; Edmonds, 1979; PDK, 1980; Weber, 1971). These studies were conducted in urban ghetto areas and the results produced five main correlates: goal focus/mission, safe and orderly climate, strong instructional leadership, high expectations and close monitoring/alignment of instructional programmes.

The second era focused on the efficiency basis. At this point context became important (for example, Cuban, 1983; Rowan *et al.* 1983). Wimpelberg *et al.* (1989) contend that context became important because there were differences between urban elementary schools and secondary schools. Typical of this research is that of Hallinger and Murphy (1985). The introduction and exploration of context differences among schools and their relationships to effectiveness shifted the focus from equity to efficiency. Finally, it should be noted that the effective schools research is a subset of the school effects research, which is generally more concerned with macro-level analyses of the impact of schooling on social class and occupational mobility. The effective schools studies, on the other hand, tend to focus on the micro-level characteristics and structures within the school which account for differences between schools.

Various researchers are now calling for a further shift in focus (for example, Wimpelberg *et al*., 1989). This aspect will be dealt with in a later section of this chapter.

Effective Schools Research in Developing Countries

In that much of the research has been done in North America and Europe, how transferable is the effective schools research to developing countries? Will what works in Latin America be necessarily effective among African or South-east Asian countries?

Farrell (1989), in his review of the literature on school effectiveness for the developing countries, concludes that the research cannot be transferred directly from the developed to the developing countries. Whereas in the developed countries out-of-school factors (SES) explain more of the variance in student achievement, such is not the case for developing countries. In Chile, Farrell found that the difference in test scores between elite private schools and the public schools of the nation were entirely explained by the difference in the students' home backgrounds and that key schools-related factors had a greater effect upon the learning of the poor children.

Heyneman *et al*. (1978), in a Philippines study, concluded that the availability of testing and reading material were important. There is some indication, although sparse, that the availability of textbooks allows teachers to assign homework and thus increase student achievement.

Farrell (1989) in reviewing the sparse research literature available in developing countries concluded that the 'best bets' for improvement were: availability of testing and reading materials, library size and activity, years of teacher training and in-service opportunities. The latter activities can be explained in that in many developing countries primary teachers rarely have more than a grade 8 education themselves. He advocates that primary teachers should have junior-secondary and junior-secondary teachers should have a university degree. Thus the importance of in-service training for the purposes of skill development becomes obvious. Another variable that Farrell advocates as a good bet is the duration of the instruction programme. He feels that if children in developing countries would spend more time in school the achievement levels would rise, although similar conclusions could be made in developed countries.

Other promising bets for improvement according to Farrell were provision of desks, availability of instructional media, provision of facilities and nutrition and feeding programmes. The scale of resource availability in developing countries is considerably different from that of developed countries. The provision of desks and adequate buildings, which is a minimal condition for effective teaching, is therefore less likely to be at a satisfactory level.

While Farrell does not reject the findings of the effective school research from the developed countries, he does contend that developing countries have many more basic issues with which to contend. Thus the payoff from the above attributes may be considerably greater.

Criticisms of the Effective Schools Research

The effective schools research has not been without its critics (for example, Buttram and Carlson, 1983; Purkey and Smith, 1983; Ralph and Fennessey, 1983; Firestone and Herriott, 1982; McKenzie, 1983).

A major criticism is the narrow and relatively small sample sizes used for intensive study. In many cases fewer than a dozen schools comprised the sample. Consequently, the possibility exists that the characteristics identified may be chance events. The lack of sample representativeness also raises the question of generalizability of results.

A second criticism has been in the identification of 'outlier' schools. If the partialing out effects of social class and home background are weak, differences in school characteristics will be confounded.

A third criticism has to do with multilevel effects on school achievement. The problem of units of observation and units of analysis (for example, classroom vs school vs district) may mask differential effects. Cohen (1983) points out that the greatest differences among students are measurable within schools, not between them. Thus how the researcher makes sense of the data becomes crucial. There have been attempts by individuals such as Murnane (1981) to rectify this deficiency with some degree of success.

A fourth criticism, according to Purkey and Smith (1983), is the inappropriate comparison of 'high' and 'low' schools (p. 432). Their contention is that unless schools can make a quantum leap in effectiveness, it may be more appropriate to compare effective schools with average schools.

Additionally, there has been criticism that the research has been essentially correlational rather than causal. Thus we do not know whether the characteristics have equal potency or whether some contribute to effectiveness more than others. The research also does not tell the practitioner whether all of the characteristics have to be implemented simultaneously and in what order.

Although there has been criticism of specific studies and methodologies used, Purkey and Smith (1983) contend that 'there remains an intuitive logic to the findings of the above research' (p. 439). Critics have not dismissed the research as being useless or irrelevant; most simply caution that the use of five, seven or twelve key variables may not work as expected in many schools, and may in fact be counterproductive in some schools. What is required are suggestions on how to combine the ingredients.

Next Phase for Effective Schools Research

Wimpelberg *et al.* (1989) contend that we need to move to a third phase of effective schools research. They state:

> The future of effective schools studies will be greatly enhanced if advocates begin to place their work in a larger arena that is equally sensitive to context factors and shares a dual interest in the improvement of schooling for poor children (equity) and the improvement of everyone's schooling, constrained by limitations on fiscal resources (efficiency). (p. 88)

They advocate, as have others (Purkey and Smith, 1983; Renihan and Renihan, 1989), a research agenda that is context sensitive and related to issues of leadership, parental involvement, cumulative resources, and multi-level effects. These include questions such as:

(i) How do principals allocate time in more and less effective schools?
(ii) How does parental involvement impact on effectiveness?
(iii) How do incentive structures and resource allocations impact on effectiveness?
(iv) What proportion of student achievement in schools can be attributed to classroom, school and district level decisions?
(v) What are the differences between average and effective schools?
(vi) How have effective schools become effective?
(vii) How can we institutionalize effectiveness practices?
(viii) Are there rural, urban, and suburban developmental effectiveness differences among schools?
(ix) How do organizational structures impact on effectiveness?

Moreover, there is the need for a causal ordering of variables: are some school factors more important than others? Longitudinal, quasi-experimental research designs are needed to determine causality and to explicate complex interrelationships among the variables. In particular, studies of the type conducted by Mortimore *et al.* (1988) that utilize multivariate analysis are needed.

Educational Policy and District Involvement

How best to implement the effective schools research has been perplexing for both researchers and practitioners. In many instances there is strong support for improvement efforts at the district level, but scepticism on the part of teachers and principals. There are a number of reasons for this scepticism (Sackney and Wilson, 1987). Firstly, many teachers and principals see the movement as 'another educational bandwagon.' Secondly, many teachers and principals perceive that most implementation models require too much effort. Thirdly, some educators have yet to be convinced of the efficacy of the school effectiveness research. Finally, many teachers and principals perceive these programmes as being top-down designed more closely to monitor and control their work.

The literature on school renewal and change seems to be of two minds. One view is that schools are self-directed and that change is a continuous process. According to this view, those working in the schools should be left to their own devices (for example, Barth, 1990). The other view is that school renewal must come from the top. For many the bureaucratic metaphor is fraught with problems.

A more recent view (Riffel, 1987; Sackney and Wilson, 1987) calls for a developmental approach to school improvement. According to this view, the system establishes clear expectations that schools must improve, but a great deal of autonomy is given to the school in choosing the direction it may wish to pursue. In other words, empowerment is a condition for improvement.

In reviewing the recent research on school district involvement, Seashore (1989) concludes that the district has an important contribution to make to school improvement. In particular, the school district has the following roles to play in improvement efforts: system building (visioning and goal setting); setting broad policies (designing a school effectiveness process); stimulating (providing access to new ideas); enabling (staff development); supporting (technical and moral); and buffering (from distractions) (p. 164). Thus, superintendent pressure and support are critical in maintaining the innovation over time. She also noted that the roles played by urban and rural superintendents are considerably different. The rural superintendent has much more of a key role to play in comparison to the urban superintendent who tends to work through others.

LaRocque and Coleman (1989) found that school districts that were able to promote school improvement had a system ethos which encouraged renewal (p. 70). The district ethos had six foci: learning, accountability, change, caring, commitment and community. Effective school districts hold schools accountable for academic and other kinds of success. Additionally, an emphasis on teacher and principal accountability via supervision is a staple system behaviour (Bridges, 1986; Murphy *et al.*, 1985; LaRocque and Coleman, 1989).

Finally, in 'moving' districts superintendents tended to model the way whereas in 'stuck' districts superintendents did not do so (Rosenholtz, 1989). 'Moving' superintendents took responsibility and proactive measures to improve the performance of teachers and principals alike. 'Stuck' superintendents, on the other hand, tended to blame others for the ills of the schools.

The research literature on educational policy for school effectiveness seems to conclude that policy has an impact on school success. Both Rosenholtz (1989) and Holmes *et al.* (1989) argue that school effectiveness is affected through the quality of the linkages between policy and the intended beneficiaries of that policy. There is, however, an alternative paradigm for institutionalizing the efforts of school effectiveness research, which will be outlined in the following section.

A Theory of Collaborative School Cultures

The collaborative culture notion of school improvement has been suggested by many writers (Deal and Kennedy, 1982; Purkey and Smith, 1983; Firestone and Wilson, 1985; Rosenholtz, 1989; Sackney and Wilson, 1987; Leithwood and Jantzi, 1990). The cultural notion rests on a conception of schools that links process with context.

The appropriateness of the collaborative school culture notion is supported by literature derived from organizational theory (for example, Schein, 1985; Ott, 1989) and change theory (for example, Fullan, 1982). Collaborative school culture assumes that consensus among the staff of a school is more powerful than overt control. The notion of empowerment assumes that such cultures not only foster the types of student outcomes that are valued by educational reformers but also stimulate continuous professional growth among teachers (Rosenholtz, 1989).

Culture can be viewed as how the work of the schools gets done. As such, culture is socially constructed, symbolically maintained and transmitted, and therefore susceptible to change. Schein (1985) suggests that the shared elements of culture are derived through a learning process based on experience, problem-solving, anxiety-avoidance and validation. On this basis, 'something can become part of the culture only if it works' (p. 18).

Schools have been described as 'loosely coupled' (Weick, 1976; Meyer and Rowan, 1978). Their technology is relatively soft and teachers are generally isolated in their classrooms (Lortie, 1975). The cultural model attempts to resolve the dilemma which is thus posed by loose coupling (Purkey and Smith, 1983). It assumes that changing schools requires changing norms, behaviours and attitudes. As such, a cultural approach is premised on consensus among staff; it attempts to build agreement on specified norms and goals.

Central to the concept of a collaborative culture is the more equitable distribution of power for decision-making among members of the school (Leithwood and Jantzi, 1990). Additionally, such an environment promotes collaborative planning, collegiality, supportiveness and an atmosphere that fosters experimentation and creativity. Use of improvement teams is one approach employed by many schools.

At the same time, a collaborative school culture does not deny the leadership role of school principals. Leithwood and Jantzi (1990) in a recent study on how principals can help reform school cultures advocate a 'transformational' leadership approach. They state: 'Principals have access to strategies which are "transformational" in effect, and hence, assist in the development of collaborative school cultures' (p. 30). This entails a change in staff members, individual and shared understanding of their current purpose and practices, and 'an enhanced capacity to solve future problems, individually and collegially' (p. 30). Rosenholtz (1989) concludes that collaborative cultures increase the teachers' professional self-esteem and ultimately student achievement.

Leithwood and Jantzi (1990) suggest that principals use six broad strategies to influence school culture: develop shared goals to foster a shared technical culture; use a variety of bureaucratic mechanisms to stimulate and reinforce cultural change; foster staff development activities; engage in direct and frequent communications about cultural norms, values and beliefs; share power and responsibility with others; and use symbols and rituals to express cultural values (p. 22).

Rarely in an isolated professional culture will teacher assumptions, norms, values and beliefs be challenged by significantly more ambitious visions of what is possible. Rosenholtz (1989) notes that when teachers conversed in either moderate or low consensus schools, they tended to stress students' failings instead of triumphs. In high consensus schools, by contrast, 'shared goals, beliefs, and values led teachers through their talk to a more enabling vision that placed teaching issues and children's interests in the forefront, and that bound them, including newcomers, to pursue that vision' (p. 39). Principals and superintendents have an important role to play in this regard.

Our own work (Sackney, 1990) would tend to support this approach. It is within a collaborative culture that people come to define their own realities and a set of shared assumptions about appropriate behaviour and attitudes, for it is within the school that meanings of work are exchanged, negotiated and modified through discourse with others. Leadership provides the impetus for such activities.

Conclusion

This chapter attempts to provide a broad brush approach to the status of the effective schools research and practice. It is suggested that the effective schools research is a useful step forward. However, the adoption of a specific set of characteristics for all schools may be counterproductive in some schools. Much more research needs to be done on how we combine the ingredients in different settings.

The greatest strength of the effectiveness literature is that it has collated a number of effectiveness attributes that appear to be international correlates of desired school outcomes. Sufficient research evidence is now available to suggest that there can be a degree of confidence in the results (see Creemers *et al.*, 1989).

The central problem facing the movement today is one of implementation. How does one institutionalize school improvement? This review suggests a developmental and collaborative cultural approach; however, much more research is required to substantiate this direction. Theoretically and intuitively what we know about change and adult learning suggests this is an appropriate way to go. Perhaps Rosenholtz (1989) captures the state of the movement best: 'we are just beginning to understand how schools' social organization can be altered in ways to make teaching a more professional activity' (p. 206). It is within 'moving' schools that we should look for future advance towards effective schooling.

References

Armor, D.J. *et al.* (1976) *Analysis of the School Preferred Reading Program in Selected Los Angeles Minority Schools*, Sant Monica, CA, Rand.

Austin, G.R. (1979) 'Exemplary schools and the search for effectiveness', *Educational Leadership*, **37**, 1, pp. 10–14.

Barth, R.S. (1990) *Improving Schools From Within*, San Francisco, CA, Jossey-Bass Publishers.

Bridges, E.M. (1986) *The Incompetent Teacher*, London, Falmer Press.

Brookover, W., Beady, C., Flood, P., Schweitzer, J. and Wisenhaber, J. (1979) *School Social Systems and Student Achievement: Schools Can Make a Difference*, New York, Praeger.

Brookover, W. and Lezotte, L. (1979) *Changes in School Characteristics Coincident With Changes in Student Achievement*, East Lansing MI, Institute for Research on Teaching, Michigan State University (ERIC Document Reproduction Service No. ED 181005).

Buttram, J. and Carlson, R. (1983) 'Effective school research: Will it pay in the country?', *Research in Rural Education*, **2**, 2, pp. 73–78.

Clark, D., Lotto, L. and McCarthy, M. (1980) 'Factors associated with success in urban elementary schools', *Phi Delta Kappan*, **61**, pp. 467–70.

Cohen, M. (1983) 'Instructional management and social conditions in effective schools' in Odden, A. and Webb, L.D. (Eds) *School Finance and School Improvement: Linkages for the 1980s*, Cambridge, MA, Ballinger, pp. 17–50.

Coleman, J., Campbell, E., Hobson, C., McPartland, J., Mood, A., Winfield, F. and York, R. (1966) *Equality of Educational Opportunity*, Washington DC, Government Printing Office.

Creemers, B., Peters, T. and Reynolds, D. (1989) (Eds) *School Effectiveness and School Improvement*, Amsterdam, Swets and Zeitlinger.

Cuban, L. (1983) 'Effective schools: A friendly but cautionary note,' *Phi Delta Kappan*, **64**, pp. 695–6.

Deal, T.E. and Kennedy, A.A. (1982) *Corporate Cultures: The Rites and Rituals of Corporate Life*, Reading, MA, Addison-Wesley.

Edmonds, R. (1979) 'Effective schools for the urban poor' *Educational Leadership*, **37**, pp. 15–24.

Farrell, J.P. (1989) 'International lessons for school effectiveness: The view from the developing world' In Holmes, M., Leithwood, K. and Musella, D. (Eds) *Educational Policy for Effective Schools*, Toronto, OISE Press, pp. 53–70.

FIRESTONE, W. and HERRIOTT, R. (1982) 'Prescriptions for effective elementary schools don't fit secondary schools', *Educational Leadership*, **40**, pp. 51–3.

FIRESTONE, W.A. and WILSON, B.L. (1985) 'Using bureaucratic and cultural linkages to improve instruction: The principal's contribution', *Educational Administration Quarterly*, **20**, 2, pp. 7–30.

FULLAN, M. (1982) *The Meaning of Educational Change*, Toronto, OISE Press.

GIROUX, H. and MCLAREN, P. (1986) 'Teacher education and the politics of engagement: The case for democratic schooling', *Harvard Educational Review*, **56**, 3, pp. 213–38.

HALLINGER, P. and MURPHY, J. (1985) 'Instructional effectiveness and school socio-economic status: Is what's good for the goose, good for the gander?' paper presented at the annual meeting of the American Educational Research Association, Chicago, April.

HEYNEMAN, S., FARRELL, J. and SIPULVEDA, M. (1978) *Textbooks and Achievement: What We Know*, Washington DC, The World Bank.

HOLMES, M. (1989) 'School effectiveness: From research to implementation to improvement' in HOLMES, M., LEITHWOOD, K. and MUSELLA, D. (Eds) *Educational Policy for Effective Schools*, Toronto, OISE Press, pp. 3–30.

HOLMES, M., LEITHWOOD, K. and MUSELLA, D. (1989) (Eds) *Educational Policy for Effective Schools*, Toronto, OISE Press.

JENCKS, C., SMITH, M., ACLAND, H., BANE, M., COHEN, D., GINTIS, H., HEYNS, B. and MICHELSON, S. (1972) *Inequality: A Reassessment of the Effect of Family and Schooling in America*, New York, Basic Books.

LAROCQUE, L. and COLEMAN, P. (1989) 'Quality control: School accountability and district ethos' in HOLMES, M., LEITHWOOD, K. and MUSELLA, D. (Eds) *Educational Policy for Effective Schools*, Toronto, OISE Press, pp. 168–91.

LEITHWOOD, K. and JANTZI, D. (1990) 'Transformational leadership: How principals can help reform school cultures,' paper presented at the annual meeting of the American Educational Research Association, Boston, April.

LEZOTTE, L. and PASSALACQUA, J. (1978) 'Individual school building: Accounting for differences in measured pupil performance'. *Urban Education*, **13**, pp. 283–93.

LORTI, D. (1975) *Schoolteacher: A Sociological Analysis*, Chicago, University of Chicago Press.

MCLAUGHLIN, M. and MARSH, D. (1978) 'Staff development and school change,' *Teachers College Record*, **80**, 1, pp. 69–94.

MCKENZIE, D.E. (1983) 'Research for school improvement: An appraisal of some recent trends,' *Educational Researcher*, **12**, pp. 5–17.

MEYER, J. and ROWAN, B. (1978), 'The structure of educational organizations' in MEYER, M. *et al.* (Eds) *Environments and Organizations*, San Francisco, CA, Jossey-Bass.

MILLER, S.K. (1983) 'The history of effective schools: A critical overview,' paper presented at the annual meeting of the American Educational Research Association, Montreal.

MORTIMORE, P., SOMMONS, P., STOLL, L., LEWIS, D. and ECOB, R. (1988) *School Matters*, Berkeley, CA, University of California Press.

MURNANE, R.J. (1981) 'Interpreting the evidence of school effectiveness,' *Teachers College Record*, **83**, pp. 19–35.

MURPHY, J., HALLINGER, P. and PETERSON, K. (1985) 'Supervising and evaluating principals,' *Educational Leadership*, **43**, 2, pp. 79–82.

OTT, S.J. (1989) *The Organizational Culture Perspective*, Pacific Grove, CA, Brooks/Cole Publishing.

PHI DELTA KAPPAN (1980) *Why Do Some Urban Schools Succeed? The Phi Delta Kappan Study of Exceptional Urban Elementary Schools*, Bloomington, IN, Phi Delta Kappa.

PURKEY, S. and SMITH, M. (1983) 'Effective schools: A review,' *Elementary School Journal*, **83**, pp. 427–52.

RALPH, J. and FENNESSEY, J. (1983) 'Science or reform: Some questions about the effective schools model,' *Phi Delta Kappan*, **64**, pp. 689–94.

RENIHAN, F. and RENIHAN, P. (1989) 'School improvement: Second generation issues and strategies in CREEMERS, B., PETERS, T. and REYNONDS, D. (Eds) *School Effectiveness and School Improvement*, Amsterdam, Swets & Zeitlinger, pp. 365–76.

RIFFEL, A. (1987) 'A developmental perspective on school improvement,' *The Canadian Administrator*, **26**, 4, pp. 1–5.

ROSENHOLTZ, S.J. (1989) *Teachers' Workplace — The Social Organization of Schools*, New York, Longman Inc.

ROWAN, B., BASSET, S. and DWYER, D. (1983) 'Research on effective schools: A cautionary note,' *Educational Researcher*, **12**, pp. 24–31.

RUTTER, M., MAUGHAM, B., MORTIMORE, P. and OUSTON, J. (1979) *Fifteen Thousand Hours: Secondary Schools and Their Effects on Children*, Cambridge, MA, Harvard University Press.

SACKNEY, L.E. (1990) 'School renewal and the school audit,' paper presented to the International Congress for Effective Schools, Jerusalem, Israel.

SACKNEY, L. and WILSON, K. (1987) 'Alternative rural school improvement models: developmental and cultural perspectives,' paper presented to the annual conference of CSSE, Hamilton, Ontario.

SCHEIN, E.H. (1985) *Organizational Culture and Leadership*, San Francisco, CA, Jossey-Bass.

SEASHORE, L.K. (1989) 'The role of the school district in school improvement' in HOLMES, M., LEITHWOOD, K. and MUSELLA, D. (Eds) *Educational Policy for Effective Schools*, Toronto, OISE Press, pp. 147–67.

WEBER, G. (1971) *Inner-city Children Can Be Taught to Read: Four Successful Schools*, Washington, DC, Council for Basic Education.

WEICK, K. (1976) 'Educational organizations as loosely coupled systems,' *Administrative Science Quarterly*, **21**, pp. 1–19.

WIMPELBERG, R., TIDDLIE, C. and STRINGFIELD, S. (1989) *Educational Administration Quarterly*, **25**, 1, pp. 82–107.

5 The Professionalization of Teachers

Kevin A. Wilson

What is teaching? It has been variously called a craft, an art, a science, a set of techniques, labour, or some admixture of these. Teaching has also been touted as one of the oldest professions, but such a declaration is more easily defended on the basis of the importance of teachers' work than on the nature of what teachers do or the effects of their efforts. The purpose of this chapter is to examine some of the things that can and have been said about the professionalization of teachers. Has progress been made in moving teachers to a status which could be granted the approbation of professional? How should one proceed with a consideration of these matters? Scheffler (1960) writes: 'Educational discourse, in sum, embraces a number of different contexts, cutting across the scientific, the practical, and the ethical spheres, which lend a variety of colours and emphases to ostensibly common notions' (p. 5).

The Meaning of Profession

Consideration of the professionalization of teachers can be discussed in a number of contexts, including those cited by Scheffler. We could add other contexts and for the sake of this chapter choose to include the social, the cultural, and, to some extent, the political. Before getting to those considerations, it might be helpful to consider what we mean by the terms profession and professionalism by making reference to a prior question which Soltis (1968) suggests has to do with '... an examination of the idea of definition itself ...' (p. 3). In other words, if definitions are drawn and used as though there are different kinds of definitions, we should be aware of these differences especially if the differences affect the nature of our discourse. In recent times, the term 'profession' has been used in reference to so many different occupations that the original meaning has been all but lost. How the term is used, Wittgenstein (1953) would say, is an appropriate way of finding out what the term means. Perhaps both things, the ubiquitousness of the term and how one comes to use it and understand it, help to emphasize that a discussion about 'the professionalization of teachers' involves an investigation of what people mean by that expression. Such an investigation is, at base, a philosophical task.

Scheffler (1960) is helpful here. He declares that there are very significant variations in the ways in which terms in education are used, and therefore defined. He contrasts the precision of definitions associated with the building and confirmation of scientific theory with the less precise definitions used in general discourse about educational matters. He calls the latter 'general definitions' and argues that they are different because the context in which a term is defined and the intention we have in mind when we set out a particular definition makes such definitions distinctive. He suggests that there are three distinguishable types; he gives an explanation of their distinctiveness and he gives them particular names (pp. 11–35). The first kind of definition he labels as 'stipulative' because he sees one class of definitions as those where the writer asks that a term's given meaning be accepted for the duration of a particular discourse. This sense of a definition conveys the notion that the meaning attributed to it is not set out as necessarily exhaustive, nor is it the meaning that may be usually associated with it, but it will be a convenient meaning which will help the purpose of the discourse. The chief purpose of the stipulative definition then is instrumental, as a means to an end. The second class of definitions he calls 'descriptive' because this kind purports to indicate how a term has been used in the past, or in other words to explicate its usual meaning. Here the intention is associated with giving a conventional and perhaps an acceptable and even the most authentic meaning because it describes the phenomenon well. He says: 'For beyond formal and pragmatic considerations, descriptive definitions may be called to account in respect of the accuracy with which they reflect normal predefinitional usage' (p. 16). The third class of definitions he calls 'programmatic', in part because a definition of this kind '... is acting as an expression of a practical program ...' (p. 19), but perhaps more directly, the distinguishing feature of this form of definition is the ascription of values and norms which introduces the senses of should and ought to the meaning intended. To summarize, he differentiates between meanings in the following way:

> The interest of stipulative definitions is communicatory, that is to say, they are offered in the hope of facilitating discourse; the interest of descriptive definitions is explanatory, that is, they purport to clarify the normal applications of terms; the interest of programmatic definitions is moral, that is, they are intended to embody programs of action. (p. 22)

It may be useful then to start our discussion with this kind of framework. In doing so, one should recognize that while it may be possible to distinguish conceptually among types of definitions, their separation may not always be that straightforward. For the purposes of this chapter, lists of criteria which purport to set out the salient features of a profession will be considered as stipulative definitions. Second, discussions about the present state of teaching as a profession will be treated from the perspective of descriptive definitions. Third, current debates, and programmes of action will be regarded from the standpoint of programmatic definitions.

Stipulative Definitions of a Profession

When writers set out to consider the concept of profession, they seldom proceed far without giving a list of the criteria considered central to an understanding of the concept. The list may be as lengthy as the ten items set out by Horton (cited in Blackington III & Patterson, 1968, p. 17) or as short as the three given by Carr and Kemmis (1986, pp. 7–8). In any event, the discussant is, on most occasions, stipulating a particular meaning of ‘profession’ for the purpose of explicating some other ideas, including the thoroughness or the precision with which the criteria are able to make good sense of the idea. When ‘profession’ is applied in the more traditional and formal senses, the term is intended to identify a few rather than many occupations and much is made of the uniqueness of the functions performed by ‘professionals’. But there is more. These groups of individuals are generally acknowledged as members of a ‘real’ profession because a particular set of criteria can be stipulated which not only seems to describe them well, but also sets them apart from the pretenders. What then are the characteristics of a ‘real’ profession? An extensive list includes at least the following: (i) practice is based on a body of knowledge which is continually refined through scholarly and systematic inquiry; (ii) acquisition of this body of knowledge requires a lengthy period of formal preparation; (iii) the practice is beyond the competence of individuals not so schooled; (iv) entry to the preparation programme is highly selective; (v) the form of preparation involves socialization into the professional role which is aimed at developing a strong commitment to service as a member of the profession; (vi) upon completion of the requirements of the programme, members are accepted into the profession and allowed to practise autonomously; (vii) members of the profession acknowledge and undertake to adhere to particular standards of behaviour and practice; (viii) unacceptable behaviour by members is dealt with by peers, not outsiders, through censure or removal of the right to practise; (ix) the work of the members is regarded as crucial to the well-being of society.

Carr and Kemmis (1986) argue that the essential features of a profession can be summarized as:

> ... [F]irst, that the methods and procedures employed by members of a profession are based on a body of theoretical knowledge and research .... [S]econd ... that the overriding commitment of their members is to the well-being of their clients .... Thirdly, to ensure that

> they can always act in the interest of their clients, members of a profession reserve the right to make autonomous judgments free from external non-professional controls and constraints. (p. 8)

While these are but three criteria, other items contained in longer lists are implicit. Each version is an attempt to stipulate essential features of callings where the members have some exclusivity over certain knowledge and skills that are used not in self-interest but in the interest of others. On the basis of these stipulations, certain groups are granted particular and special status; but the stipulations have other uses. They are referred to in disputes before the courts, they are used by some to seek and justify levels of compensation, and they may be employed to make comparisons among groups. For example, Carr and Kemmis use theirs as the basis for dismissing teaching as a profession (p. 8). They defend such a conclusion by explaining how the teacher-student relationship is not as it is for the professional-client, that the teacher lacks autonomy, and the teacher has a limited rather than an extensive role in representing the community. Any of the many stipulative definitions of the term 'profession' are useful in explicating meaning and in addressing instrumental matters, as Scheffler (1960) suggested, but we need to turn to another kind of definition if we wish to understand more of the reality of teaching and the teacher's role.

Descriptive Definitions of Teaching

In considering ways of describing teaching as a profession, there are several approaches that might be employed. One way is to look at the tasks or the role of the teacher, another is to review the extent to which the practice of teaching rests on a body of theoretical knowledge, and a third example is to consider the contextual factors of teaching. We will begin by considering the role of the teacher.

The Role of the Teacher

How does the role of the teacher measure up as a profession? Broudy (1972) considered that the notion of the 'professional teacher' is, in his words, 'a mischievous illusion' (pp. 39–67). This position was argued by indicating that the expectations for a teacher who measures up to the standards set out for a professional classroom teacher are almost impossible to achieve and that if any are properly prepared to achieve this lofty and noble status they should account for no more than about 10 to 15 per cent of the group. Broudy considers that the rest might be trained as rule-followers who would deal with didactics, which he defines as '... any instruction in which the contents can be made explicit and in which the criteria for successful learning are objective' (p. 60). Why does Broudy suggest that for most teachers the attainment of professional status is well nigh impossible? Is the role such that it is unmanageable? What then are the expectations held for teachers? The expectations might be thought of as statements about how the teacher is prepared, whom the teacher represents, and how the teacher carries out the role.

The preparation of teachers

First, the teacher is called upon to have more than a modicum of knowledge, of several kinds. A generous measure of liberal education is seen as an essential foundation so that the teacher can properly represent the elements of society that ought to be reproduced. This kind of knowledge is then coupled with more specialized knowledge in the chosen teaching areas. Together these form the justification for a teacher to claim some right to educate, indeed, for the critics of teacher training programmes, they are justification enough. The education fraternity would add other kinds of 'foundational' knowledge like those dealing with the links between education and society, and the nature of learning and learners. The knowledge acquired through general or liberal education and the foundational knowledge could be acquired by many people, so the acquisition of certain kinds of knowledge seems not sufficient to set teaching apart. Most preparation programmes now include the additional item of teaching practice carried out in a clinical situation or in regular classrooms. So in various ways, through trial and error, by the apprenticeship method, or through thoughtful attempts to link the knowledge acquired in the lecture room with the reality of the classroom, beginning teachers engage in a rite of passage which has the potential to be both helpful and rigorous. But is it so? The premise of the Holmes Group (a consortium of Deans of some major research universities in the United States) is a resounding no. Their commentary on the present contribution of formal preparation programmes to the professionalization of teachers is an indictment of current practices (The Holmes Group Report, 1986). So, even in one of the most affluent countries of the world, teaching cannot measure up to the hallmarks of a profession. However, 'hope springs eternal' and the Holmes Group advocates some steps to begin the process of real reform.

The teacher as agent

The teacher is expected to assume a special role as an agent who represents well the best interests of the parents, the community and the society. What is usually intended here is not merely the perpetuation of features of the past for their own sake, but the transmission of knowledge, values and skills which have relevance for the successful continuation of a society. As we think about these delegated duties or obligations, some of the complexity confronting the teacher begins to emerge. For example, we are fond of declaring, with some justification, that no classroom of youngsters is homogeneous with respect to ability, attitude, needs and preferences. We can hardly expect their parents to be any more homogeneous with respect to the expectations and sometimes demands they would place before the teacher on behalf of their children. If a consensus among parents appears difficult to imagine, it is even more problematic when one considers the difficulty of a teacher trying to represent the opinions and interests of the community, let alone the society.

Proper representation of the community and the society may be straightforward when there is social and cultural stability and therefore continuities between the schooling of the young and the roles they will assume as adults. But the adequacy of this representation becomes difficult in the absence of these stabilities. For example, the egalitarian features of a democracy and the rapidity of change in a 'post-industrial' society are influences which create discontinuities. The former influence supports social equality aims which, if properly reflected in a society, encourage the assumption of roles not by tradition but by individual preferences. At times, some of these preferences may be constrained by social pressures and customs, but as more of these constraints are removed, there will be more variation in personal preferences, not all of which can be represented by the teacher.

Influences found within some societies also compound the situation. Dramatic and sometimes quicker than expected shifts in the structure of the labour force make the connection between the school and the workplace tenuous at best. What compounds the teacher's attempts to shape students' schooling appropriately is not merely the unpredictability of the students' future role in society, but also the variety of alternatives that others advocate to deal with that uncertainty. People who represent the futurists project amazing changes and challenges for all members of society in the next millennium (Toffler, 1980, Naisbitt, 1982, Benjamin, 1989). Teachers have every right to feel humbled by the prospect of acting as society's agents in dealing with these challenges.

The teacher's attempts adequately to represent the community and the society might be somewhat more manageable under some forms of sociopolitical arrangements. Such arrangements may make more clear what the teacher should represent. However, the validity, potency and strength of that representation seem difficult to sustain without extreme forms of surveillance and monitoring. Under such rigid controls, the opportunity to exercise autonomy and professional judgment is severely limited.

In whatever setting the teacher works, the adequate and acceptable representation of the parents, the community, and the society is extremely difficult. How does a teacher respond to this complexity? One response may be to treat learning episodes as ends in themselves and to measure the success of a teacher's efforts by how much, how well, and how efficiently students have learned and to set aside obligations of the teacher acting as an agent for others. This response puts the teacher into a 'rule-following' mode and gives teaching the appearance of a craft more than a profession.

Classroom roles

Hoyle (1969) set out what he says is an incomplete list of 'sub-roles of teachers' because of lack of research into the classroom behaviour of teachers (pp. 59–60). Even so, he lists thirteen items additional to 'the representative of society' notion referred to above. He suggests that the sub-roles can be divided into two sets: 'One set corresponds with the major functions of instruction, socialization, and evaluation. The second set is concerned with motivating pupils, maintaining control, and generally creating an environment for learning' (p. 50). Hoyle's observations draw attention to another kind of complexity confronting the teacher. He points out that, most of the time, the teacher is not able to enjoy the exclusivity of a single professional-client relationship for two reasons. First, the teacher has twenty to thirty clients clamouring for attention and, second, the teacher is beset with a multiplicity of role demands. Again it seems that the professionalization of teaching is thwarted.

Knowledge About Teaching

Probably all attempts to stipulate the criteria of a profession include reference to a body of knowledge on which practice is based. One could be generous about teaching and say 'Whatever the approach, the strategies employed, and the relationships generated, the choice is related to one or more of the theoretical constructs that may or may not be consciously identified' (Stiles, 1974, p. 1). Of course there are a number of people who feel comfortable with the notion that teaching is based on a body of knowledge which has and is being refined, but others are not. Tom (1984), for example, calls the research undertaken to build such a body of knowledge, 'at best, inconclusive, at worst barren' (cited in Gage, 1989). In gentler times, Kaplan (1964) described a theory as:

> ... a symbolic construction ... thus contrasted both with practice and with fact ... the device for interpreting, criticizing, and unifying established laws, modifying them to fit data unanticipated in their formulation, and guiding the enterprise of discovering new and more powerful generalization. (pp. 295–7)

However, this view is no longer automatically popular; indeed it is exceedingly unpopular because it represents a paradigm associated with the logical positivists. The language of both the critics and the observers has been harsh. Gage (1989) speaks of 'Raging during the 1980s, the Paradigm Wars resulted in the demise of objectivity-seeking quantitative research on teaching — a victim of putatively devastating attacks from anti-naturalists, interpretivists, and critical theorists' (p. 4). The nature and forms of these criticisms cannot be explored in detail here; suffice it to say that consensus among scholars about the substantive knowledge base of teaching does not seem possible at this time. Teaching or learning episodes are seen as too elusive, too idiosyncratic, too discontinuous, too inappropriate and too trivial for *theoretical* [my emphasis] study in the Kaplan sense.

If the professionalization of teachers depends on the development of 'a specialized knowledge and means of verifying claims to knowledge that enable them to perform this function with an economy unique to that individual or group' (Blackington III and Patterson, 1968, p. 21), the goal seems to be in a state of suspended animation. It seems likely that the wranglings of the scholars will proceed for some time in the form of argumentation about paradigms, but schooling will continue and the matter of professionalization may be helped by the practitioners as they go about their daily business. As Hawkins (1966) remarked: 'there have often been times in the history of science when the personal knowledge of practitioners was significantly deeper than anything embedded in the beliefs and writings of the academically learned' (p. 3).

While the paradigm wars are raging, some are looking for other ways to respond. Schon (1987, chapter 1) is one of them. He characterizes the malaise around paradigms as predictable because we have been searching for the wrong things in the wrong places. In effect, he suggests that the technical rationality of the scholars may be helpful in elucidating some of the problems of professional practice, but the rules so derived may be fewer and less important than we would like. He sees the practitioner confronting 'indeterminate zones of practice — uncertainty, uniqueness, and value conflict — [which] escape the canons of technical rationality' (p. 6). He then argues that because of this the practitioner needs to inform his/her practice by reflection which he talks about as 'reflection-in-action'. The practitioner becomes professional and remains so not according to how well he/she applies knowledge learned *a priori*, but how well he/she recognizes and uses additional and significant knowledge from the context of practice. In a similar vein, Leinhardt (1990) suggests that although there are problems to overcome, there are some ways of 'capturing [the] craft knowledge of teaching' (p. 20). The author makes reference to what Schwab (1971) and Shulman (1987) have called the wisdom of practice and suggests that the certification assessment procedures now in place test the general, mostly theoretical knowledge acquired in preparation programmes but not the 'particular knowledge of [the] related craft' (p. 20). The thesis of Leinhardt's paper is that there is a significant knowledge base which should and can be derived from the wisdom of practice and which complements the knowledge base derived from theory. The directions envisaged in the work of both Schon and Leinhardt indicate some promise in lifting the knowledge base of teaching into the realm of respectability. These ideas suggest that the reality of teaching has to be taken into account, which leads to a consideration of the settings in which teaching takes place.

Contexts of Teaching

Up to this point, the discussion has been general in nature and not too much related to any particular time or place. But when we examine some different contexts of teaching, we are forced to look at more particular factors that may affect the professionalization of teachers. The contextual factors which affect teachers are numerous and they usually present themselves in such a disorderly mixture that it is an oversimplification to try and single out particular examples as representative. While recognizing that risk, it may be useful to make mention of several interesting and perhaps unusual contexts that seem to be having a direct effect on the conduct of schooling and perforce the role of the teacher as a professional. Reference will be made to: organization for schooling, pressures of growth, and popular movements in education.

Organization for schooling

Changes in school organizations are not uncommon; indeed, Wildavsky (1979) says that 'no one can accuse local educators of inertia; they are always in motion, tinkering with the organization of their schools' (p. 79). Recent changes in the organization of education in Australia (Watt, 1989) and New Zealand (Macpherson, 1989) could hardly be called tinkering. Up until the 1970s, the state systems of education in Australia could be characterized as having a centralized form of governance. Since that time, several states, perhaps most noticeably the state of Victoria, have moved to a governance system featuring local control and much more decentralized decision-making. Watt (1989) says 'Victorian public schools [publicly funded], already under a much higher degree of local control ... are currently being pushed towards total control over resources and staffing ... Radical devolution of power over schooling is obviously in the air' (p.19).

One of the several reasons advanced in support of this devolution was the vesting of more power in the teachers' hands. One could see justification for this in the spirit of enhancing the professionalism of the teaching force. Watt's article and a recent study reported by Chapman (1988) seem to call such a conclusion into question. In particular, Chapman found that involvement in decision-making about matters educational was not generously shared among the members of school staffs. Rather, in many cases, the centres of influence were found in traditional places, with people who had organizational responsibility, with the men and with teachers with seniority. Not only were women underrepresented, but some felt dissuaded from striving for greater involvement because their efforts were not taken seriously by men. Because we usually associate competence with professional worthiness, it is disturbing to find Chapman setting down the following as one of her conclusions:

> the evidence of this study strongly suggests that in some schools ... social acceptance may be of greater significance than relevant intellectual competence and expertise in determining whether a particular

> staff member is nominated and subsequently elected to a decision making committee. (p. 68)

The thesis developed by Watt (1989) also deals with the outcomes from placing great stock in the devolution of power to the teachers. He claims that there is evidence to show that schooling now is not more relevant, appropriate and better than that which existed under the centralized system of governance. Indeed, he points to a number of weaknesses which seem to have occurred because the upper and middle management groups have been removed. Watt suggests that lack of coordination between elements of the system is causing inequities and inefficiencies and that the effects are worrisome. He calls for a careful reconsideration of devolution and makes the following plea:

> In a radically decentralized system, who is to be concerned for the interests of all children, and particularly of those whose parents and neighborhoods lack the education, the experience and the personal and political power to advance their interests effectively in a deregulated, competitive environment? (p. 27)

Perhaps the professional needs some kind of infrastructure independent of his/her own role before professional practice can flourish. Removing the bureaucracy altogether may create what the functionalists called 'unanticipated consequences' (Merton, 1940). A number of studies following on from Scott (1965), including those reported by Hall (1968), and Firestone and Wilson (1985) indicate that so-called bureaucratic norms and professional norms may create a healthy web of tension in an organization. In several of the Australian states, and more latterly New Zealand, major policy initiatives which stripped away power and authority from centralized structures and simultaneously granted power and authority to local bodies were implemented with dispatch. It may be too soon to ascertain the lasting effects of devolution on the professionalization of teachers.

Pressures of growth

For a different kind of context, we turn to an African country, Kenya. Simiyu (1990) points out that primary school enrolment in Kenya expanded from about 890,000 students in 1963 (the year of independence) to about 4.8 million in 1986. Over the same period, the number of primary schools increased from 6058 to 13,392 and the total number of primary teachers increased from 22,727 to 142,807. In percentage terms, the increases are about 440 per cent for students, 120 per cent for schools, and 530 per cent for teachers. The growth in secondary school enrolment looks even more dramatic: from about 30,000 students in 1963 to almost 460,000 in 1986. The number of secondary schools increased from 151 to 2485, and the total number of teachers from 1602 to 22,296. These increases are about 1400 per cent, 1500 per cent and 1300 per cent, respectively (p. 12). These growth rates are staggering by the standards of developed countries and they have created tremendous pressures. On the one hand, such a rapid growth has caused a financial crisis for the Government which has instituted an unusual scheme for increasing available funds: the teachers of Kenya are required to contribute a fixed portion of their salary to school building funds (Eisemon, 1988, p. 30). On the other, the need for such a large number of additional teachers in the span of one generation has resulted in the employment of a high proportion of untrained teachers. According to Ministry of Education statistics for 1986 (cited by Simiyu, 1990, pp. 13–14), about 30 per cent of the primary teachers and 40 per cent of the secondary teachers were untrained.

Other African countries have also had to respond to rapid growth of their educational systems. Tanzania tackled the problem by recruiting large numbers of primary school leavers and having them teach half-time and study half-time. A similar case has been cited in Lesotho. Mohapeloa (1982) indicates that about a third of the primary teachers were untrained and he goes on to say that as a result the status of teachers has fallen quite sharply (p. 144). Shabaan (1990) reports that the salaries of teachers in Kenya are so low that many 'operate illegal classes in the evenings, weekends and during school holidays and charge fees [to earn extra money]' (p. 6). For the foreseeable future, it seems that the employment of unqualified teachers will be a permanent feature of a number of the educational systems in Africa. Predictable effects resulting from these conditions include the difficulty of attracting and retaining people, and low teacher satisfaction. The professionalization of teachers in the developing world might involve improved initial training and attention to teaching conditions. It is clear that a preoccupation with the niceties of this or that paradigm have no primacy at the moment; much more fundamental things are needed to support the education of students.

Popular movements in education

It seems that education is constantly in a state of becoming. Change and innovation were catchwords not so long ago, but they have been overtaken by phrases like the 'effective schools movement', 'organizational culture', 'teacher empowerment', and the latest term in vogue, 'restructuring'. All of these 'movements' have a couple of things in common. They are all school-based and the importance and centrality of the teacher's role is emphasized. One of them that seems to have had particular relevance for the professionalization of teachers is the effective schools movement, which was discussed in the previous chapter.

The effective schools movement, as Sackney noted, received quite a fillip in the 1970s when a number of writers (Weber, 1971; Frederickson, 1978; Rutter, *et al.*, 1979; Brookover and Lezotte, 1979; Edmonds, 1979) raised points of view about school effects which were felt to call into question the conclusions reached by Coleman (1966). Much of the school effectiveness literature contains several recurring themes: first, schools can be identified that produce unexpectedly better results on measures of schooling than other schools with like circumstances; second, schools which are comparatively better comprise a set which seems to have more characteristics in common than it has differences; third, the characteristics that are shared by 'more effective' schools might be helpful in improving 'less effective' schools. Although there are variations on the theme, the teachers were seen to be a latent and powerful source that could be tapped to energize the operation of the school. In places where school improvement efforts were attempted, teachers reported a greater sense of satisfaction and accomplishment (Wilson, 1988). In many cases, the teachers' roles were enlarged to encompass much more than the tasks associated with the classroom. They had opportunities to work collaboratively in developing the school's mission, establishing school-wide priorities, and forming action plans. Although teachers were also engaged in many familiar routines, they seemed to carry out their tasks with greater zest and a renewed sense of purpose. Perhaps they felt more professional about their work. What else is being advocated to enhance the professionalization of teachers?

Programmatic Definitions of Teaching

In the 1980s a great deal of interest has centred around the notion that has been labelled 'empowerment of teachers'. Maeroff (1988) suggests 'a blueprint for empowering teachers' (pp. 473–7). He advocates such a process by claiming it is essential if schools are to improve. The three key areas in which he argues that 'teachers can be lifted' are: 'their status, their knowledge and their access to decision making' (p. 473). His suggestions sound like an attempt to make teachers feel more professional so that they might become more professional. More focused efforts, on the process of teaching particularly, are those advocated by people like Glickman (1989) who sees possibilities through a particular kind of supervision.

> Supervision must shift decision making about instruction from external authority to internal control .... Teachers are the heart of teaching. Without choice and responsibility, they will comply, subvert, or flee: and motivation, growth and collective purpose will remain absent. (p. 8)

Here again is an interest in developing professionalism. Empowerment, restructuring, or whatever, the school reform movement seems to be shifting to this new emphasis. Are these programmes that give hope for the professionalization of teachers?

Something that began in Australia, at least a decade ago, is just now being touted in the United States as a major struggle between pressures for 'top-down reform and standardization of practice [and] local control of schools, school-based management, shared decision making, parent participation, and teacher professionalism' (Wise, 1990, p. 57). Wise clearly favours the latter set of pressures and suggests that this outcome would have a very beneficial effect on the professionalization of teachers. He goes on to set out a programme of six steps which he claims ought to lead to teacher professionalism (pp. 57–60). In summary, the steps are as follows:

> The first such change is to reform teacher education ... Step two is the reform of teacher licensing and certification ... Third, we must restructure schools to promote teacher participation in decision making ... The fourth change needed is the reform of teacher organizations ... the long-term welfare of the unions rests on a better balancing of union and professional responsibilities ... Fifth, we need to reform accountability in schools ... Last, but not least, we need to motivate people to want to become teachers by reforming working conditions and salaries. (pp. 58–9)

Not surprisingly, as Wise elaborates the list of items, he makes reference to many of the stipulations that others, like Lieberman (1956), have used. More recently, Soltis (1985) expressed similar sentiments as he dared 'to dream of an ideal school' (pp. 321–2).

What can we conclude about the professionalization of teachers? To return to Scheffler (1960), stipulative definitions of a profession outline reasonable, perhaps admirable, qualities for teachers and teaching. From the descriptions of the realities of teaching, one has to conclude that it is not easy to attribute professional status to teachers. But educators are an optimistic lot; programmes are being advocated which have promise for enhancing the professionalization of teachers.

These programmatic definitions might be associated with another sentiment outlined by Finn (1990, pp. 584–92). He suggests that Kuhn's (1970) analysis is helpful in clarifying the distinction between education as a process and education as a product. Finn (1990) suggests that we have to return to a much more serious consideration of education as a product, as 'the result achieved, the learning that takes root when the process has been effective. *Only* if the process succeeds and learning occurs will we say that education *happened*' (p. 586). Perhaps this is the only way we can properly address the professionalization of teachers. Only if the process of professionalization occurs will we say that it happened.

References

Benjamin, S. (1989) 'An ideascape for education: What futurists recommend, *Educational Leadership*, **47**, 1, pp. 8–14.

Blackington III, F.H. and Patterson, R.S. (1968) *School Society and the Professional Educator*, New York, Holt, Rinehart and Winston.

BROOKOVER, W.B. and LEZOTTE, L.W. (1979) *Changes in School Characteristics Coincident with Changes in Student Achievement*, Michigan State University (ERIC Document Reproduction Service No. ERIC ED 181 005).

BROUDY, H.S. (1972) *The Real World of the Public Schools*, New York, Harcourt Brace Jovanovich.

CARR, W. and KEMMIS, S. (1986) *Becoming Critical*, London, Falmer Press.

CHAPMAN, J. (1988) 'Decentralization, devolution and the teacher: Participation by teachers in the decision making of schools', *Journal of Educational Administration*, **26**, pp. 39–72.

COLEMAN, J.S. *et al.* (1966) *Equality of Educational Opportunity*, Washington, US Government Printing Office.

DE ZOYSA, R. (1986) 'A letter from England: Professionalism and education', *Phi Delta Kappan*, 67, pp. 607–9.

EDMONDS, R.R. (1979) 'Some schools work and more can,' *Social Policy*, **9**, pp. 28–32.

EISEMON, T.O. (1988) *Benefiting from Basic Education, School Quality and Functional Literacy in Kenya*, Oxford, Pergamon Press.

FAFAUNWA, A.B. and AISIKU, J.U. (Eds) (1982) *Education in Africa: A Comparative Survey*, London, Allen & Unwin.

FINN, JR., C.E. (1990) 'The biggest reform of all', *Phi Delta Kappan*, **71**, pp. 584–92.

FIRESTONE, W.A. and WILSON, B.L. (1985) 'Using bureaucratic and cultural linkages to improve instruction: The principal's contribution', *Educational Administration Quarterly*, **21**, pp. 7–30.

FREDERICKSON, J.R. (1975) *School Effectiveness and Equality of Educational Opportunity*, New York, Carnegie Corporation.

GAGE, N.L. (1989) 'The paradigm wars and their aftermath: A "historical" sketch of research on teaching since 1989', *Educational Researcher*, **18**, 7, pp. 18–25.

GLICKMAN, C.D. (1989) 'Has Sam and Samantha's time come at last?', *Educational Leadership*, **46**, 8, pp. 4–9.

HALL, R.H. (1968) 'Professionalization and bureaucratization', *American Sociological Review*, **33**, pp. 92–104.

HAWKINS, D. (1966) 'Learning the unteachable' in SHULMAN, L.S. and KEISLAR, E.R. (Eds) *Learning by Discovery: A Critical Appraisal*, Chicago, Rand McNally, pp. 3–12.

KAPLAN, A. (1964) *The Conduct of Enquiry: Methodology for Behavioral Science*, San Francisco, CA, Chandler.

KUHN, T.S. (1970) *The Structure of Scientific Revolutions* (2nd edn), Chicago, IL, University of Chicago.

LEINHARDT, G. (1990) *Capturing Craft Knowledge in Teaching*, Educational Researcher, **19**, 2, pp. 18–25.

LIEBERMAN, M. (1956) *Education as a Profession*, Englewood Cliffs, NJ, Prentice-Hall.

MACPHERSON, R.J.S. (1989) 'Radical administrative reforms in New Zealand education: The implications of the Picot Report for institutional managers', *Journal of Educational Administration*, **27**, pp. 29–44.

MAEROFF, G.I. (1988) 'A blueprint for empowering teachers', *Phi Delta Kappan*, **69**, pp. 473–7.

MERTON, R.K. (1940) 'Bureaucratic structure and personality', *Social Forces*, **23**, pp. 405–15.

MOHAPELOA, J. (1982) 'Education in Lesotho' in FAFUNWA, A.B. and AISIKU, J.U. (Eds) *Education in Africa: A Comparative Survey*, London, Allen and Unwin, pp. 140–61.

Naisbitt, J. (1984) *Megatrends*, New York, Warner Books.

Rutter, M., Maughan, B., Mortimore, P., Ouston, J. with Smith, A. (1979) *Fifteen Thousand Hours: Secondary Schools and Their Effects on Children*, Cambridge, MA, Harvard University Press.

Scheffler, I. (1960) *The Language of Education*, Springfield, IL, Charles C. Thomas.

Schwab, J.J. (1971) 'The practical: Arts of eclectic', *School Review*, **79**, 4, pp. 493–542.

Schon, D. (1987) *Educating the Reflective Practitioner*, San Francisco, CA, Jossey-Bass.

Scott, W.R. (1965) 'Reactions to supervision in a heteronomous professional organization', *Administrative Science Quarterly*, **10**, pp. 63–81.

Shabaan, M. (1990) 'Issues and recent trends on development of education in African Commonwealth countries', unpublished manuscript, University of Saskatchewan, Saskatoon, Canada.

Shulman, L.S. (1987) 'The wisdom of practice: Managing complexity in medicine and teaching' in Berliner, D.C. and Rosenshine, B.W. (Eds) *Talks to Teachers: A Festschrift for N.L. Gage*, New York, Random House, pp. 369–86.

Simiyu, J.H.G.W. (1990) 'Vocational and technical education and training in Kenya: Case studies of two exemplary youth polytechnics', unpublished Master's Thesis, McGill University, Montreal.

Soltis, J.F. (1968) *An Introduction to the Analysis of Educational Concepts*, Reading, MA, Addison-Wesley.

Soltis, J.F. (1985) 'Imagine a school ...', *Phi Delta Kappan*, **66**, pp. 321–2.

Stiles, L.J. (Ed.) (1974) *Theories for Teaching*, New York, Dodd Mead.

The Holmes Group (1986) *Tomorrow's Teachers: A Report of the Holmes Group*, East Lansing, MI, The Holmes Group.

Toffler, A. (1980) *The Third Wave*, New York, Bantam Books.

Watt, J. (1989) 'Devolution of power: The ideological meaning', *Journal of Educational Administration*, **27**, pp. 19–28.

Weber, G. (1971) 'Inner-city children can be taught to read. Four successful schools', Occasional Paper no. 17, Washington, DC, Council for Basic Education.

Wildavsky, A. (1979) *Speaking Truth to Power: The Art and Craft of Policy Analysis*. Boston, MA, Little Brown.

Wilson, K.A. (1988) 'A report of the school effectiveness project conducted in the Kinistino School Division 1984–1987', Regina, SK, SSTA Research Centre.

Wise, A.E. (1990) 'Six steps to teacher professionalism', *Educational Leadership*, **47**, 7, pp. 57–60.

Wittgenstein, L. (1953) *Philosophical Investigations*, Oxford, Blackwell.

6 Equity and Cultural Diversity

M. Kazim Bacchus

The first part of the chapter will focus on the issue of equity. It will examine conflicts which often result from the pursuit of greater equity through the rapid expansion of the educational services, and those which are likely to arise from efforts geared towards maintaining or improving the quality of the existing educational services.

The second part will concentrate on the role of education in preserving cultural diversity in multicultural societies and the conflicts which the pursuit of this goal is likely to generate with efforts directed towards achieving a greater degree of social cohesion or national integration. These two issues are quite closely linked since the pursuit of equity itself often has, as one of its goals, national unity which is sometimes incorrectly seen as the opposite side of the coin to cultural diversity.

The final part of the chapter will examine, although briefly, ways in which *schools* might help with the achievement of these two goals. It will also indicate the importance of the contribution which other social institutions must make if the efforts by the schools in this direction are to be successful.

The Issue of Equity

Over the past three decades equity has been of increasing concern to educational policy makers especially in the developing countries. For example, Davies (1986), in a review of the national planning documents of a number of these countries, found that educational inequality was a key consideration of their governments. As she noted 'virtually all developing countries make some reference to equality and egalitarianism in their policy statements or policy documents'. This issue will probably continue to increase in importance because, while Western education has traditionally been an instrument of upward social mobility for children of poorer families, it has also been helping to reproduce social and economic inequality in these societies. This is becoming even more marked as some of the developing countries begin to produce more educated individuals than their economies can readily absorb. As this happens ascriptive factors seem to be reappearing in occupational selection, even though now, in conjunction with educational achievement.

Different Meanings of the Concept of Equity in Education

Despite the growing concern over the issue of equity in education there are differences in perception among educational policy makers as to how education can contribute to the achievement of this goal. For some, equity is synonymous with the more equal provision of educational opportunity for all sections of the population while for others education helps to achieve equity through its contribution to the goal of a more egalitarian society. The Government of Fiji (1985), for example, attempts to combine these two goals in its Ninth Development Plan (1986–90) where it stated that a major national objective is 'to promote a more equitable distribution of the benefits of development' and one of the ways by which it hopes to do this is through equalizing educational opportunity by eventually making twelve years of education available for every child in the country.

However, among educational policy makers and administrators the relationship between equity and education is now seen to refer to a range of concerns including a *more equitable distribution of educational resources* throughout a country, and a *greater equality of learning outcomes* among those who happen to be attending the nation's schools.

Sources of Educational Inequality

There are a number of sources of inequality in education including rural/urban, regional, sex, class and cultural differences and to achieve greater equity these various sources of inequality would normally have to be overcome together, especially since they are usually closely inter-linked. However, from the evidence which is currently available, it seems that the policies aimed at reducing these inequalities are not likely to have the same outcomes for all societies, even though individual countries can learn very much from the experience of each other in this field.

Increasing Concern for Equity in Education

Even before the present outpouring of educational policy statements and national planning documents mentioning this need for greater equity in education, the governments of the economically less developed countries (LDCs) had become concerned with this issue, tended to see education as a basic human right and expressed a commitment to provide some level of education for all their children of school age. This can be observed in the recommendations of the Addis Ababa, the Santiago and the Karachi conferences held under the auspices of UNESCO in the 1960s. More recently there have been concerted efforts by an increasing number of these countries, though with different degrees of success, to universalize primary education as the essential first step in the achievement of this goal.

Such efforts were started long before these countries were aware of the findings (Psacharopoulos, 1973, 1982) that the rate of return on primary education was higher than that on any other level of the educational system. In other words concern for equity rather than just economic returns was the major consideration in the decision by most LDCs to attempt to provide some amount of primary education for all. At the post-primary level educational policies pertaining to the proportion of primary school children who could proceed to secondary schools have varied tremendously depending on the economic resources of the country and its perceived need for higher level manpower. In some cases such as Tanzania less than 2 per cent of primary school pupils are able to proceed to secondary school while in other countries such as Zimbabwe and Fiji there is a policy which aims at a 100 per cent transition rate between these two levels of schooling. But despite these different policies one sees that here too the desire is to provide all students with an equal opportunity to compete for these scarce educational resources at the post-primary levels.

Therefore, where selection occurs for education after the primary stage, it is increasingly being made on the basis of achievement rather than the economic ability of parents to pay for such education. It is true that the outcomes often fall far short of expectations and the concern is usually directed at equalizing opportunities by which means the beneficiaries become increasingly unequal, in terms of the rewards they eventually receive as a result of their education. But nevertheless there is no doubt that most LDCs share some common commitment to achieve greater equity in the provision of their educational services.

Conflict Between Equity and Quality in Education

However, these efforts at achieving greater equity in the distribution of educational services, even by universalizing primary education, have been accompanied by a number of problems. Foremost among these is the conflict which has arisen over the issue of improving the quality of the education that is currently offered in schools as against further expansion of the existing educational facilities. The suggestion is sometimes made that instead of 'spreading the butter thinly' by attempting to provide educational services in 'every nook and corner' of a country, especially in the context of the severe resource constraints, the overall educational returns might be greater if say, the additional funds were used to increase the quality of education now offered to the 60–80 per cent of the present population of school age, who are already enrolled in schools. The issue has been coming more to the forefront because it is now being recognized that, where attempts are made to extend educational services to these marginal groups, especially if they live in the more remote areas of the country, the per capita costs are often very high and the response usually poor, judging by the retention rates and the learning outcomes among these children as compared with those in the more populated areas of the country.

But the suggestion to sacrifice the goal of equity because it seems to conflict with that of educational efficiency is short-sighted for a number of reasons. To begin with the universalization of primary education (UPE) is the first and most crucial step towards achieving equality of educational opportunity. Secondly, it can be an important factor in helping to increase social stability and reduce discontent, especially among the educationally deprived groups in a society. Education is increasingly being seen by all groups in the developing countries, especially among those with little or no capital resources, as the most important factor in their own economic and social improvement. Hence the denial of even primary education to any section of the population for any length of time cannot be conducive to long term social and political stability, especially when this facility is already being enjoyed by a large section of the citizenry. Further social stability, to which UPE is likely to contribute is a 'sine qua non' of long term economic development.

Another fact is that, as available evidence indicates, the returns on primary education are greater that those from any other level of the educational system. This means that, from an economic point of view, it might even be worthwhile, in a situation in which funds are limited, to transfer resources from other levels of the educational system in order to universalize primary education. So the universalization of primary education is likely to contribute concurrently to both equity and economic productivity.

Changing Existing Administrative Practices in Education to Achieve Equity

Despite the importance of a policy of UPE as a step in furthering the goals of equity, one has to examine further the assumption, often implicitly made, that there is an essential conflict between efforts at increasing equity and those geared towards improving the quality of education. It is obvious that all efforts at achieving equity in education would call for additional resources, whether it be the allocation of extra funds to education or the reallocation of resources between the different sectors of the educational system. But an important contribution might also be made by some imaginative thinking which challenges some of the current assumptions about the processes by which qualitative improvements in education can be made. For example, it is usually accepted that in developing countries, improving the quality of teachers through providing them with higher levels of formal education and training is crucial to any effort at raising the quality of education in the schools. Beeby (1966) devoted his whole book on *The Quality of Education in Developing Countries* virtually to making this point.

Yet, when one is faced with the choice of allocating additional resources that might become available to education, either to the training of more untrained teachers or providing instructional aids such as reading materials in situations in which these are very limited or non-existent, the decision is often not an easy one. In fact indications are that, in such situations, the returns in terms of learning outcomes, are likely to be greater if the money is spent in providing good quality reading materials rather than going for the obviously more expensive route of increasing the percentage of trained teachers in the schools. However, if curriculum materials are to be put in the hands of teachers who are untrained and not very highly educated they have to be substantially different from those prepared for use by teachers who are better educated and trained. In other words the use of cheaper but well prepared and appropriate inputs into the educational process, as part of the strategy to have a more equitable distribution of educational facilities in a country, might not necessarily conflict with efforts to maintain or improve the quality of education.

Another factor that has to be considered in efforts to achieve a more equitable distribution of education among the various regions of a country is the impact of the administrative structures which are devised to help achieve this goal. For example, in attempts to find additional resources for education outside those traditionally available from the central government, some countries have attempted to encourage community participation in the financing of education which has led to increasing pressures for decentralizing the control of education. But here there are forces pulling in the opposite direction. While increased community financing of education might assist with the local expansion of educational services it is also likely to exacerbate regional inequalities and hence result in a less equitable distribution of educational opportunities in a country, particularly between the different ethnic groups where regional and ethnic inequalities happen to coincide. This, for example, seems to have been happening in countries such as Papua New Guinea (Bray, 1984). Therefore to implement a policy of decentralization, and at the same time not run the risk of exacerbating educational inequalities between regional and ethnic groups, which can be detrimental for national integration, the decentralization has to be accompanied by such compensatory policies as equalization payments or special allowances for qualified teachers to work in the more remote parts of a country.

We also have to consider by possibility that the poorer utilization of educational facilities by some groups might be due to a variety of underlying factors — cultural, economic and educational — which existing administrative practices and organizational structures in education might have failed to take fully into consideration. It cannot be assumed that this results simply from the lack of appreciation of the value of education by these groups. True, there have been many efforts made to overcome some of the problems, including the establishment of schools in fairly sparsely populated communities, the provision of transportation and boarding facilities along with free tuition and scholarships for children whose parents are unable to pay for their education. The Government of Fiji (1985) has, for example, reported that it has been making 'special efforts ... to uplift the standards of Fijian and rural education' (p. 136) by the use of some of these measures.

While the popular responses to such steps have been fairly heartening, for any substantially greater degree of success to be achieved in bringing these marginal or underrepresented groups more within the ambit of the existing educational system and its provisions, a few innovative approaches might have to be used. For example, one of the factors contributing to the low academic performance of some students is not only their poor home backgrounds, both from an economic and an educational point of view, but also the irrelevance of the curriculum materials used in their instructional programmes. This even happens when the materials are produced locally because they are usually developed for and based on the experiences and environments of the children living in the more accessible or populated areas of the country, especially the cities. Because of this they are often quite unsuitable for use in what are sometimes vastly different environments of the more remote rural areas.

Also the level of poverty of some of these marginalized groups makes them less able and often reluctant to bear the opportunity cost of sending their children to school, especially at times of the day or the year when it is most convenient to the teachers and the administrators and not necessarily to the local population. But quite often the existing administrative arrangements in education fail to take this factor into consideration.

While this is a common situation in the LDCs it is not unknown in the economically more developed countries (MDCs) where efforts are also being made to provide educational services which would be more effectively used by groups previously underrepresented in schools. I recall the experiences narrated to me by two teachers — a husband and wife team — who went out to work among the native population in the North West Territories in Canada. The parents of the children were at first quite reluctant to send their children to school but eventually did so, as a 'favour' to the new teachers, who seemed to them to be very friendly individuals. But when the trapping season came the parents moved away to the trapping grounds, taking their children with them and leaving the teachers with their empty schools. Not to be outdone the teachers packed up the motorized mobile home which they had, followed the children and attempted to conduct classes during the day for the young ones and in the late afternoon and evening for the older children after their trapping duties for the day were completed.

But then they received a stern note from the Superintendent of Education informing them that they must return to their school forthwith since the regulations did not permit them to conduct classes away from the premises officially provided by the Government for that purpose. It was not simply a case of the Superintendent lacking an understanding or not being sympathetic to the educational needs of the native population. It was more an example of how organizations like Government Departments of Education are not flexible enough to handle situations which do not exactly fit into the traditional administrative patterns. For administrators the safest line of action is usually to try to refer to the 'normal' situation in which the existing regulations would clearly apply. Even if there were no children in the school building, as happened in this particular case, the official regulations were not being infringed.

This kind of reaction is also quite common in developing countries, whether one is dealing with nomadic peoples like the Masai in East Africa or even with more settled populations who, when the planting or the reaping seasons come along, are unable to send their children to school with any degree of regularity. Our school systems are usually not structured to cope with such situations. In fact administrators have always tended to take existing organizational structures and sometimes even the current administrative arrangements as given and expect the local population to reorganize their ways of living to fit in with these patterns. In contexts like these administrators need to be prepared to modify the ways according to which our organizations are expected to work, by starting with a different approach, ie. taking the people's way of living as a given and then structure the organizations around this fact so as to make it possible for the children to make use of the facilities at times and in places which are most convenient to them.

In fact when the need arises, what administrators or policy makers tend to do, is to recommend the use of the state control mechanism to produce from the population the kind of behaviours which they expect, or consider as 'normal'. For example, they are more likely to see the answer to the problem of irregular attendance as the introduction of a compulsory education ordinance which allows them to specify the hours and the times of the year when schools would be open and then expect the population to adapt their life-styles in order to conform to these regulations.

The point here is that if equity in education is to be made a more attainable goal then administrators and policy makers have to be prepared to be more flexible in the kind of practices and organizational structures which they develop in order to provide education, especially for these marginalized groups. In doing this they would need to take more fully into consideration the life-styles and constraints which such groups might be facing in their efforts to send their children to school. Indeed there are administrators who are increasingly becoming aware of the importance of such flexibility in their efforts to achieve equity, not only in the provision but also in the utilization of educational services. But these are far too few in number.

Equity of Outcomes

However, as indicated above, the issue of equity in education is not only concerned with the provision and utilization of educational services but also with learning outcomes. Here we return to the suggestion that curriculum materials developed for the instruction of pupils must be relevant to their own experiences and environment. The important point is that the special needs of the various groups in the society have to be taken into account if we are also hoping to achieve more equitable academic outcomes in terms of students' performance.

Greater consideration of the factors which affect the learning outcomes among children even at the primary school level is important for a number of reasons. In most LDCs, a secondary education is a crucial factor in determining a student's future life chances, but admission to secondary schools is still very selective. And the key that often unlocks the admission door to these schools lies in the academic performance of the students at the primary school stage.

Therefore special attention needs to be directed at efforts aimed at overcoming the hurdles which adversely affect the academic performance of primary school students, if the policy of using education as a means to equalize 'life chances' of different groups in the society is to materialize. This is partly why an increasing number of developing countries like Fiji, Guyana, Jamaica and others, some with the assistance of the Van Leer Foundation, have extended their concern, to the provision of facilities for early childhood education in the hope that such a step would help to equalize the chances which students from lower socioeconomic backgrounds have in passing the secondary schools selection examination. Whether or not this is the most appropriate strategy to achieve such a goal is another matter. But one of the concerns of educational administrators interested in the role which education can play in achieving greater equity must be not only to ensure, a more equitable distribution of secondary educational facilities, but also to equalize the opportunities among all groups in the society of gaining access to these institutions. And the same would apply to entry into tertiary level educational institutions.

Limitations of Educational Policies in Achieving Greater Equity of Outcomes

Nevertheless, despite the various efforts by policy makers and administrators to secure a more equitable distribution of educational resources, there are many factors, some much more difficult to overcome than others, which affect the achievement of this goal. For example, all the selection strategies for secondary and tertiary education which have been tried and which are based on students' achievement at some competitive examination have resulted in certain groups maintaining an advantage over others, in terms of their securing entry into such institutions. And this has proved to be an almost universal phenomenon, one which is very difficult to overcome.

For example, in Jamaica in 1957 the Government decided to break the traditional dominance which certain groups had in terms of their children's access to secondary schools because of the parents' ability to pay the cost of this education (Woolcott, 1984). It attempted to do this by increasing substantially the number of Government awards to these schools and made them available on the basis of the students' performance at a competitive selection examination which all pupils seeking entry into secondary schools had to take. To implement the scheme one of the most eminent psychometricians from the United Kingdom was recruited to advise on selection procedures which it was hoped would be as unbiased and non-disciminatory as possible.

Despite the precautions that were taken the outcome was that children from the upper social-economic groups, who in Jamaica were mainly from among the 'coloureds' and others with a 'fair' skin complexion, tended still to be heavily overrepresented among those selected for secondary education in comparison with those from the black population. The Government considered that this was still not an equitable outcome and later decided to make further changes in its policies to ensure that there was a greater representation in the secondary schools of children from black families who were economically the more disadvantaged group. Since most of the children with a fairer complexion, and hence from the higher income groups, were entering for the secondary schools selection examination from the private schools or the 'prep' divisions of some of the secondary schools, which generally had higher academic standards than the Government primary schools, the decision was made to allocate 70 per cent of all secondary school places to students attending the latter schools.

There were two outcomes of this decision which ran counter to the intentions of the Government to achieve a greater degree of equity in the allocation of secondary school places. First, a substantial number of parents from the higher socioeconomic groups began to send their children, at least for a year or so before the selection examination, to the Government primary schools so that they would be among those competing for the 70 per cent of the secondary school places. This shift not only reestablished these children's chances of entering the secondary schools but also meant that those who had remained in the private schools still had 30 per cent of these awards for which they competed. The outcome was that, while the chances of the black children getting into secondary schools did increase, it still fell short of what the Government intended when it imposed the 70:30 ratio for secondary school admission. Through the strategies which they used the higher socioeconomic groups were able to maintain much of their traditionally higher representation in the secondary schools, as compared with the lower class black population.

But despite this, the number of black children from the lower socioeconomic groups in the society who won secondary school places increased. However a new problem arose. The academic performance of these children from the lower socioeconomic groups, judged by their success at the GCE examinations was lower than for those who were previously selected on an open competitive basis only. So it meant that, for the same expenditure, the 'efficiency' of the secondary schools, measured in terms of the number of GCE 'O' and 'A' level passes which their students were able to secure, had fallen. This occurred despite the fact that there was no evidence of any relaxation by the teachers of their efforts to assist these pupils. In fact many of the teachers even worked harder in an effort to maintain the level of passes which their schools had achieved in previous years at these external examinations.

This is a problem which often faces multicultural societies in their quite understandable efforts to equalize educational opportunities among the educationally more disadvantaged ethnic groups, especially at the post-primary levels. Malaysia for example, operates a quota system in favour of the rural indigenous population who are said to be particularly underrepresented in the post-secondary educational institutions. But laudable as this objective is, it can result (as was seen in the case of secondary schools performance in Jamaica) in lower levels of academic attainment among the students selected for further education on the basis of quotas. In addition this method of allocating places in educational institutions challenges the meritocratic principle which educational systems tend to emphasize and could, unless other corrective measures are taken, have adverse effects on the goal of national integration and national unity in a 'plural' society. In summary, therefore, the efforts to achieve greater equity in the distribution of post-primary educational opportunities among various ethnic groups or regions in a country can result in a decrease in the academic output of educational institutions as measured by the important index of examination results used in most societies.

In addition to efforts aimed at equalizing academic outcomes education policy makers need to give more attention to the ways in which education can increase its employment outcomes which, as Paul Willis (1986) notes, can be 'the final inequality'. Many LDCs have been expanding student outputs from their educational systems, especially at the secondary and post-secondary levels, at a rate much faster than the increase in job opportunities for which these graduates have traditionally aspired, resulting in growing numbers of educated unemployed. This can have adverse effects on the rate of economic growth, on social stability and on the relationships between major ethnic groups in a 'plural' society. It is therefore becoming more of an issue to which educational policy makers have to turn if they are hoping to increase the contribution which education can make towards equity and at the same time social stability and harmony between the various groups in the society. There have been a number of efforts at coping with this problem but these have either been ineffective or marginal in their impact, partly because the solution is often seen in local rather than in national and even international terms. However, if the role of education in increasing equity is to be enhanced there would be a need to examine more critically the deeper causes of this problem and to come up with broader policy alternatives which are likely to be more effective than the present narrower solutions that have been and are being attempted.

Education for Cultural Diversity

Let us now look at the second goal of education to which this chapter directs attention, ie. the contribution which education can make towards maintaining cultural diversity and the implication this has for ensuring a certain degree of social cohesion among the various groups that might make up the nation state, particularly in multicultural societies.

'Basic' Institutions

Every society, irrespective of the fact that it might be comprised of different cultural groups, needs its members to have a minimum core of shared or common values and beliefs along with the facility of communicating with each other. If groups who are living side by side within a nation state have no such common institutions which transcend sectional interests to bind them or to bring them together and create some degree of national unity then ethnic and regional polarizations are more likely to develop and these can be potentially divisive. This has been the case in many culturally 'plural' societies where different ethnic groups have remained sharply segmented, with the result that sectional hostilities have frequently broken out, threatening the long-term social and economic development of the society. Further this even minimal level of consensus is necessary if the various groups in a society are to develop the realization that, even though they might be trying to achieve different goals, these should, in the long run, be recognized as complementary, if together they are to enhance the development of the nation. In other words a certain degree of inter-group cohesion and unity are needed in any society to ensure its long term stability and reduce the possibility of conflict among its various cultural sub-groups.

These 'basic', 'key' or 'national' institutions should ideally be shared on a common basis by all the citizens, be cross-cutting in their membership and relate equally to all sections of the population. For example, all individuals and groups need to have equal access to the political, legal and economic institutions which are some of the 'key' institutions in any society. Further the institutions must not only be accessible to all but they should also be open to everyone on *an equal basis*. If this does not happen the society would virtually have a policy of apartheid in operation. In addition the population should have the knowledge and skills to permit them to make full use of these institutions as they see fit so that these are not commandeered by one or more sections of the society at the expense of the others. These 'key' or 'national' institutions therefore play an important role in developing a degree of cohesion, unity, and solidarity among the various ethnic groups that make up a culturally 'plural' society.

'Local' Institutions

In addition multicultural societies must, in their institutional structures, recognize the importance for their different cultural groups to retain aspects of their own cultural heritage in order to meet their specific psychocultural needs. Such institutions include the religion, the music, the dances and other art forms, the language and other aspects of their cultural systems. These 'local' institutions as they are often referred to, must be encouraged because they give to the members of these particular groups a sense of 'rootedness' in the overall society and a feeling that they enjoy the respect of other groups, rather than being culturally dominated by one or more of them. In other words a culturally 'plural' society must provide for the vibrant development of at least these two types of institutions — those which attempt to integrate the society at a 'national' level and those which allow the different ethnic groups to express themselves in their own cultural medium and ways.

It is often argued that the development of these two sets of institutions can increase the divisive tendency in a society and retard the emergence of a sense of nationhood. Because of this it is sometimes suggested that 'local institutions' that serve the needs of particular cultural groups should give way to the more inclusive type of institutions which operate on a more universalistic basis. This process can be described as one of 'cultural assimilation' or more correctly, in Carnoy's (1974) phrase one of 'cultural imperialism'. But this is a short-sighted policy, more likely to bring conflict between the different groups since the various ethnic minorities would be inclined to see such efforts as one of 'cultural genocide' for them. Also such a view misinterprets the relationship that can develop between 'national' and 'local' institutions in a society.

First, instead of being conflicting they can be complementary, with each contributing in its own way to national solidarity and to the overall harmony of the society. Secondly, any attempt to suppress the cultural aspirations of any group, especially if that group is large enough to react effectively, is likely to be socially very disruptive and costly to the society as a whole, including the dominant group also, as we see in South Africa today. Further, this policy is not likely to be successful, judging from the fact that after years of colonial domination, which many developing countries experienced, they have, since their independence, tried to assert their own cultural identity. Thirdly the assumption that the cultural expressions of sub-groups should be suppressed and be replaced by the culture of the dominant group in order to achieve national integration is one which totally disregards the human rights of individuals and groups.

'Broker' Institutions

However, for 'plural' societies to retain their vibrancy which comes from their multiculturalism they need to find ways and means not only of strengthening both their 'national' and their 'local' institutions but also of extending bridges between these two types of institution through the use of what is sometimes known as 'broker' institutions such as schools and the educational system in general.

The Role of the School in Maintaining Cultural Diversity

The success of the efforts aimed at encouraging cultural diversity in a society and at the same time maintaining harmony between various cultural groups would depend very much on the formulation of a comprehensive set of national policies, and concrete steps being taken concurrently, to achieve greater equity in the society. In other words, these goals of equity and cultural diversity are most likely to be achieved if they are pursued together and success would depend on the support of overall social, political and economic measures. But once the total policy has been accepted and measures are being taken towards its implementation, the education system can then play an important supportive role to such efforts.

Within this context schools can assist not only in the development and strengthening of both 'national' and 'local' institutions but also in helping to increase the awareness and understanding by the different groups in the society of each other's culture and value systems. This it does by increasing the level of articulation between 'national' and 'local' institutions. The alternative to this approach which could create many social problems, often leading to political instability, is for the dominant group to attempt to use the school culturally to homogenize the various ethnic groups which make up a 'plural' society and get them to accept its cultural system as the only one which is 'respectable' and therefore should be 'universalized' within the society.

It is because of the realization of the possible contribution which schools can make to the achievement of the goals of cultural diversity within national unity, that education policy makers and administrators have been exploring ways and suggesting policies and programmes which would help them to achieve the above mentioned objectives, ie. to develop in the future citizens, irrespective of their particular cultural group membership,

(a) a common core of values and support for the 'key', 'basic' or 'national' institutions which ideally would embody these values;
(b) the knowledge and skills which would prepare youngsters eventually to participate fully in the workings of these 'key' institutions;
(c) respect for, and appreciation of, the cultural traditions of the other groups who form part of these multicultural societies. It is in the performance of this role that schools act as 'broker' institutions.

This type of political function of education is readily acknowledged (c.f. Milburn and Herbert, 1974). Schools are more likely to be effective in this task if there is substantial congruence between the reality of how these institutions work and what is taught to the pupils about them.

Let us look back at these three roles of the schools mentioned above. Schools and other educational institutions use a variety of approaches in attempting to develop among future citizens a sense of national solidarity, national unity or belongingness to a single nation state. For example, they help students to understand the workings of these 'key' or 'national' institutions, to develop necessary skills, knowledge and dispositions to participate in these institutions and above all to accept the idea that they operate with essential fairness to all. There is evidence that one of the main outcomes of schooling is that it passes on these universalistic values which contribute towards social integration and the development of a sense of national unity among the various groups in the population (Dreeben, 1968; Coleman, 1973).

One of the more well-known strategies is through the use of a common or core curriculum which exposes all students to these values and the 'hidden curriculum' which further reinforces them. Another means is through the language policy which is often adopted in education. Despite the linguistic diversities which might exist in a multicultural society there is usually an attempt to educate the younger generation in a common language which would better prepare them to communicate effectively with each other. A latent function of this ability of the citizens to understand and speak to each other in a common language is also to contribute to the development of a sense of national unity, social cohesion or belongingness to a single nation state. However this policy might not always be easy to implement when the numerical strength of each language group is substantial, as, for example, in India.

In addition to inculcating in children these universalistic values, schools in multicultural societies, as was indicated before, also need to help develop an awareness and sensitivity among all students to the more particularistic elements of the culture of the various ethnic groups that form part of the nation state. This would help to ensure that 'local' institutions do not continue to be seen as separatist, mutually exclusive and potentially antagonistic or subversive to national unity but as essential elements in the social fabric of a culturally 'plural' society.

There are many ways in which schools can help to increase the degree of articulation between 'local' and 'national' institutions. For example, schools might attempt to help their pupils acquire a basic understanding of the religious beliefs and practices not only of the numerically dominant group but of all other groups in the society. However, the specific aspects of, say, the religious practices of a group will have to be taught in the 'local' institutions which each group might establish for this purpose such as Sunday schools, madrasas, etc. Another example is again the language policies adopted in schools in multicultural societies. While for the sake of national integration, schools might be assigned the task of passing on a common language to all groups so as to make it possible for them to communicate easily with each other they should also provide the opportunity for the various cultural groups, where their numbers make it possible, to learn their own language because of its importance for their overall cultural survival. So while a single national language might be an important integrating force in a society it does not mean that the languages of the various cultural groups should be ignored by the school system. And here Fiji presents an outstanding example of a country that recognizes the importance of language in the maintenance of cultural diversity. The number of examinable languages has been increasing over the years and now includes, or will soon include, Hindi, Urdu, Tamil, Telegu, Arabic, and Chinese.

Another area to which attention needs to be given if schools are to develop as effective 'broker' institutions is in the training of teachers to work in communities whose cultural systems might be quite different from their own. Teacher training has been increasingly focusing on the classroom performance of pupils and earlier efforts at developing among trainees, a recognition of the importance of the links between the school and its community has, over the years, been gradually deemphasized. But if schools are to play this broker role effectively it means that the teachers themselves would also need to develop a better understanding of the communities from which the schools draw their pupils. This would, therefore, involve a shift in the focus of most teacher education programmes since teachers can only effectively work with various cultural groups in the successful education of their children if they themselves have a sound understanding and appreciation of the culture of these communities.

Finally, as educators we need to remind ourselves that schools *alone* cannot successfully perform the task of achieving equity and diversity and developing greater harmony between the different ethnic groups in the society, by attempting to increase individuals' awareness of each other's cultures and value systems. They can only play a supporting role in this task. It is ultimately the effective openness of the political, economic and other 'national' institutions of the society, on an equal basis to all its member groups, which would finally determine the success of any attempt to achieve equity and social stability and at the same time maintain cultural diversity in 'plural' societies. For example, education has been, and probably still is, an important instrument of upward mobility and determinant of income in the developing countries. But this relationship does not hold equally well for all groups in a 'plural' society and the degree to which factors such as race, ethnicity or other non-achievement variables modify this relationship depends very much on how the unequal economic and political power are distributed in the overall society.

Therefore, unless the various groups in a culturally 'plural' society have access to and share in an equitable manner the political economic and other resources of the country then the schools would not be very effective in trying to achieve the goals of equity and cultural diversity. There are, in the long run, two possible outcomes of the relationship between the various groups in a multicultural society. Either a situation develops in which some groups become economically, politically and culturally dominated while the dominant group continues to assign a greater part of the national wealth and other tangible or intangible but nevertheless crucial resources such as effective political power to itself, or the dominated groups rebel against the existing system and attempt to change it radically or in some cases, even overthrow altogether the existing social order. On this point it would be useful to recall the continuing controversy among social scientists as to whether the major ethnic groups in a 'plural' society could live and work together in harmony or whether, as Smith (1965) asserts, 'no peaceful change' or long term harmonious relationship between them can be achieved because the various 'sections have nothing in common except involvement in economic and political relations which are essentially antagonistic' (Smith, 1966).

Admittedly social cohesion and the maintenance of cultural diversity in a 'plural' society is not easy to achieve. But the chances of securing a peaceful and harmonious relationship between these various groups would ultimately depend on the overall steps taken by the ruling or dominant group to achieve greater equity including, as was mentioned above, a more equitable sharing of economic and political power and other scarce resources by the various groups that make up these societies. Failure to move along in this direction also, would create continued dissatisfaction and disharmony among the groups who are disadvantaged as far as the allocation of these resources are concerned. And it is only when this becomes a policy which is accepted by the nation and actively pursued throughout its many institutions that the schools and other educational institutions would be able to maximize their contribution in helping to achieve equity and preserve cultural diversity in these societies.

Acknowledgement

This chapter is based on a Keynote Address delivered by Professor Bacchus during the Fiji Phase of the 1986 International Intervisitation Programme in Educational Administration, which was subsequently published in *IIP '86 Record of Proceedings*, edited by Dr. Wayne L. Edwards. Reproduced by permission.

References

Beeby, C. (1966) *The Quality of Education in Developing Countries*, Cambridge, MA, Harvard University Press.

Bray, M. (1984) *Educational Planning in a Decentralized System: The Papua New Guinea Experience*, Sydney, Sydney University Press.

Carnoy, M. (1974) *Education as Cultural Imperialism*, New York, McKay.

Coleman, J. (1973) 'Educational and political socialization' in Bell, C. (Ed) *Growth and Change*, California, Dickenson Publishing Co.

Davies, L. (1986) 'Policies on inequality in the third world', *British Journal of Sociology of Education*, 7, 2, pp. 191–204.

Dreeben, R. (1968) *On What is Learned in Schools*, Mass., Addison Wesley.

Government of Fiji (1985) *Fiji's Ninth Development Plan 1986–90: Policies, Strategies and Programmes for National Development*, Suva, Government of Fiji.

Milburn, G. and Herbert, J. (1974) *National Consciousness and the Curriculum: The Canadian Case*, Toronto, OISE Press.

Psacharopoulos, G. (1973) *Returns to Education: An International Comparison*, Amsterdam, Elsevier Scientific.

Psacharopoulos, G. (1982) *Rates of Return to Investment in Education Around the World*, London, LSE Higher Education Unit.

Smith, M.G. (1965) *The Plural Society in the British West Indies*, Los Angeles, CA, University of California Press.

Smith, R.T. (1966) 'People and Change', *New World, Guyana Independence Issue*, Georgetown, New World Group of Associates.

Willis, P. (1986) 'Unemployment the final inequality', *British Journal of Sociology of Education*, 7, 2, pp. 155–69.

Woolcott, J. (1984) 'Class conflict and class reproduction: An historical analysis of the Jamaican educational reforms of 1957 and 1962', *Social and Economic Studies*, **33**, 4, pp. 51–99.

Comment

William G. Walker

While the developments described above do reflect Ansoff's key words: paradox, ambiguity and risk, and while Dewey's 'unstable star' is obviously shining brightly, it must be admitted that in the chapters there is an air of excitement, of change, of challenge about education in the Commonwealth which exceeds anything we have seen hitherto.

It is, of course, possible to highlight the tensions, the economies, the negatives, but the experience of over 2000 years of written history tells us that educational extremes do not last. In classical dialectical terms, the thesis is followed by the antithesis and ultimately by the synthesis — and our synthesis looks promising.

The data and opinions presented in the five chapters above suggest that something like an educatively desirable synthesis is emerging in that large part of spaceship Earth occupied by the Commonwealth. This does not imply that all countries, states or provinces have found ideal solutions (that would be impossible) or have found common solutions (that would be counter-productive), but it does imply that there is an important element of autonomy, confidence and security in most countries' educational policy making which was by no means so noticeable two or three decades ago.

Obviously the 'professionalization' of teachers *is* improving, judging from almost any way the term is defined; obviously teachers and administrators *are* accepting more autonomy and accountability in spite of their initial suspicions and unease; obviously 'excellence', perhaps as locally interpreted, *is* being sought. Moreover, the 'bean counting' excesses of the early effective school movement have not gained a firm hold in the Commonwealth at large, and there may be more awareness of equity issues, particularly in a multicultural context.

An interesting aspect of the reports leading to the reform described in the chapters is that a great deal more rationalization and professionalism is being demonstrated in strategic planning. For example, those systems that have long been recognized as being unduly centralized are moving in the direction of decentralization, those perhaps unduly decentralized towards a measure of centralization. Furthermore, the men and women leading such movements tend to be much better prepared for their tasks. As pointed out earlier, there has been an explosion in the education and training of educational administrators (though admittedly a much larger explosion is greatly to be desired!).

The level of sophistication of educational leadership has risen immeasurably since the 1960s, and this has been reflected in attendances at conferences, enrolment in university courses and writing for professional journals.

It has been said that it is never safe to generalize too much about the Commonwealth. As one who, from 1960 onwards, has been intimately but objectively involved with educational administrators from all parts of the Commonwealth, I find great satisfaction in the improvements that have occurred and in the growth that has indubitably been achieved.

As the teachers and administrators of our still-young Commonwealth look to the fast-approaching year 2000 I am reminded of Wordsworth's words on the eve of the French Revolution,

> Bliss was it in that dawn to be alive
> But to be young was very heaven.

Section 3

Key Administrative Roles

Introduction

Robin H. Farquhar

The chapters in this section describe and analyze the nature of certain crucial roles in the practice of educational administration in a variety of Commonwealth countries — their historical evolution, responsibilities and constraints, progress and problems, current issues and future prospects. The intention is to gain a good understanding not only of how each role has developed and where it is going, but also of why and what factors seem to account for these developments. In this way it is expected that something can be learned about the distinctive nature of each country concerned and about the similarities and differences among various parts of the Commonwealth.

Toward these ends, the focus in the following chapters is limited to two of the most significant roles in the practice of educational administration — the school principal or headteacher (the 'building level' administrator) and the school superintendent or education officer (the 'district-level' administrator). For each of these two roles five and four countries respectively have been selected to represent a reasonable cross-section of Commonwealth members. Notwithstanding the specific role focus of each chapter, the authors have been encouraged to refer, if and as appropriate, to other relevant roles and institutions in terms of their functions and relationships to the position on which each chapter concentrates.

It is hoped, then, that the specific focus on roles and countries in this section of the book will contribute to improved understandings of both educational administration and the Commonwealth.

Part A

The School Principal/Headteacher

7 The School Principal in Australia

Judith D. Chapman

Education in Australia is constitutionally the responsibility of the six states (New South Wales, Queensland, South Australia, Tasmania, Victoria and Western Australia) and the two territories (the Northern Territory and the Australian Capital Territory). Within each state or territory, Government education is controlled by the state Ministry or Department of Education which is headed by a Chief Executive or Director General.

Although education is primarily a state responsibility, since the 1970s the Commonwealth Government has played an increasingly important role. This role has been expanded since the Australian High Court ruled that Commonwealth financial aid to non-Government schools was constitutionally valid. As a result approximately 25 per cent of Australian students now attend non-Government schools. The largest proportion of non-Government schools are Catholic schools which are administered by the Catholic Education Commission of each state. The remainder are independent schools which frequently operate under the auspices of one of the Protestant churches.

Major Developments in the Evolution of the Role of Principal

Australia was established in the late eighteenth century as a colony of Britain. It was not surprising, therefore, that in the Government systems of education established in Australia in the late nineteenth century, the system of administration strongly followed the traditions of the British Civil Service. Thus, administration came to be characterized by a high degree of centralized control, a clearly defined hierarchy of authority, and an extensive set of regulations designed to ensure uniformity and fairness in the provision of resources and services, together with efficiency and accountability in the management of schools. Under these arrangements, all major decisions, both professional and managerial, were made by senior officers of the Education Department of each state. The State Education Departments prescribed curriculum, enrolment procedures, and school organization. Schools were evaluated annually by inspectors. The Principal acted as an agent of the Department, implementing policies and decisions made by officials in the central office.

Over the past two decades, however, there has been an erosion of this bureaucratic tradition. Since the end of the Second World War, immigration from Europe, and more recently from the Middle East and Asia, has transformed Australia from a previously Anglo-Saxon dominated society. Respect for diversity, matched by a concern for equity and participation which has been evident in broader social and political change, has been reflected in the educational reform effort.

Since 1972, a distinctive rhetoric centred around democratization has characterized reform in Australian education. The Commonwealth-sponsored Karmel Report (1973), considered among the most influential documents in the history of post-war education in Australia (Ashenden and Gallagher, 1980), established one of its principal values as the 'devolution of responsibility to schools':

> The Committee favours less, rather than more, centralized control over the operation of schools. Responsibility should be devolved as far as possible upon the people involved in the actual task of schooling, in consultation with the parents of the pupils whom they teach and at the senior levels with the students themselves. (Karmel, 1973, p. 10)

The Karmel Report proposed a multi-faceted response to the difficulties perceived to exist in Australian education at that time. Among its recommendations were:

* an erosion of the monopoly of the state bureaucracies (largely through the establishment of the Commonwealth Schools Commission);
* a move towards decentralized and more personal styles of educational management; and
* a refurbishment of school syllabi and teaching styles, stressing relevance, child centredness, personal development and more humane relationships between staff and students.

An era of reform and renewal of Australian schools emerged with the establishment of the Commonwealth Schools Commission in 1973.

Collaborative school-level decision-making and the transformation of the quality of the educational experience through the improvement and development of school-based personnel was highlighted in a series of reports from the Schools Commission. Reports such as *Educational Leadership for Responsive*

Schools (1985) emphasized the images of 'adaptive', 'innovative', and 'responsive' schools characterized by leadership teams, collaborative school-based decision making, and local community involvement. To facilitate change in these directions the Commonwealth tied grants for specific projects to the evidence of such participatory processes and leadership styles.

With education being primarily a state responsibility, however, it was pressures at the state level which ultimately determined change in administrative structure and management. Throughout the 1970s, educational policymakers and system administrators in many states recognized that they could no longer provide effective administration for rapidly expanding and increasingly complex school systems and thus began to consider alternative forms of system organization and school administration. The most far-reaching changes in this regard were to be found in the state of Victoria.

In 1972 it became the Victorian Government's policy to decentralize administrative arrangements pertaining to education. This decentralization process had two dimensions. One was associated with the creating of regional directorates and the other with the granting of increased authority to the principals of schools. Principals became responsible for budgeting and accounting for equipment, furniture, and fuel. In addition they became responsible for determining staffing needs for instruction, support services, and administration. The withdrawal of the Board of Inspectors also resulted in principals becoming responsible for the maintenance of staff discipline, reporting on unsatisfactory teachers and the maintenance of school standards.

In 1976 the enactment of the Education (School Councils) Act added another dimension to the principalship. The Act reflected a new direction in government policy — the devolution of authority from the bureaucracy of the Education Department to the *community* of the school. Whilst the Principal remained ultimately responsible for the determination of the school's educational policy, members of the school community as represented on the council were, for the first time, given statutory authority to advise the Principal on the development of that policy. Whereas in the past there was only limited interaction between the school and its community, after the passing of the Act it became the Councils' responsibility to ensure effective interaction, initially through the wider use of school facilities in the community's recreational, cultural and continuing education activities.

The passing of the Act, however, found many principals opposed to the reforms. The threat of more open structures and increased accountability, the suspicion that Council members might use control over finance to become involved in the day-to-day running of the school, the fear of ideological influences and the loss of their recently gained but not inconsiderable autonomy, caused disquiet to many principals (Fitzgerald and Pettit, 1978). Initially, despite the changes in structure and function introduced by the Act, some principals at least, through their control of the Council agenda, their linguistic skills in persuading and influencing councillors, and their monopoly of information about the day-to-day operation and internal administration of the school, were able to ensure their dominance in relationships with council members (Gronn, 1979).

In 1981, however, a White Paper on *Restructuring the Education Department* recognized some of the problems that had been encountered in the implementation of the original School Councils legislation, and in 1981 and the first part of 1982 there were massive system-wide structural changes consistent with the White Paper's recommendations. In the midst of these changes, however, a new Government came to power. This Government established as a major objective a shift in the focus of education to the school level. Particular emphasis was placed upon:

* general devolution of authority and responsibility to the school community;
* collaborative decision-making processes in schools;
* a responsive bureaucracy, with the main function of serving and assisting schools;
* effectiveness of educational outcomes; and
* the active redress of disadvantage and discrimination.

In line with these priorities the State Minister of Education released a statement on the 'Role of Principals'. While reiterating the central role played by principals in the life and work of the school, the statement emphasized that 'this important leadership function is to be exercised in cooperation with the School Council and the staff of the school'. Contemporaneously the Education Act was amended to provide that 'the School Council shall determine the general education policy of the school within guidelines issued by the Minister'.

Changes were also made to the composition of School Councils to provide for a higher proportion of teacher representation. These amendments placed a new emphasis on local responsibility and shared decision-making in educational policy matters.

In 1984, the role of the School Council was extended further with the introduction of School Council involvement in the selection of principals and deputy principals. Aspirants to the Principal position or principals wishing to transfer among schools were now confronted with an entirely new procedure for selection and appointment based on an attempt to match the particular background, qualifications and values of the applicant to the particular needs of the school as identified by members of its community. In the same year, and as a result of negotiations between the unions and the Department, it was announced that within each school Administrative Committees were to be established to offer advice to the Principal on the implementation of the Industrial Agreement and on general school operations. Whilst principals retained the right of veto on the Administrative Committees, reasons were to be given for any advice that was disregarded. Such changes in emphasis, policies, organizational structures, and styles of management have had a significant impact on the reconceptualization of the Principal's role.

The New Conception of the Role of Principal

Within a context of economic restraint and fewer resources for education, the Principal has found him/herself working with new values, new decision-makers and a new set of management decisions and responsibilities. In this context the Principal is no longer able to see him/herself as the authority figure, supported and at times protected by system-wide and centrally determined rules and regulations. Instead the Principal must become a coordinator of a number of people representing different interest groups within the school community, who together will determine the direction the school is to follow. In the words of the past president of the Victorian Primary Principals' Association, 'The Principal now becomes relocated from the apex of the pyramid to the centre of the network of human relationships and functions as a change agent and resource' (Wilkinson, 1983). The transition to this new conception of the Principal's role, however, has not been without difficulty.

In the traditional, highly centralized systems of Government education, considerable power and authority had resided in the bureaucratic position of school Principal. In the process of devolving more decision-making to the school level, this bureaucratic authority was severely eroded.

Initially, the most extreme response to the changed bases of the Principal's power and authority was to interpret the decreasing importance attached to bureaucratic position as a complete diminution of the Principal's power (Chapman and Boyd, 1986). Although clearly this was not the case, the situation for principals was a paradoxical one. Whilst principals became more visible and accountable to their local communities, they remained the system's most senior officers in the schools. This dual responsibility carried with it considerable role ambiguity. On the issue of accountability, for instance, many more traditional principals continued to defer to the central legal authority, steadfastly guarding their claim to 'ultimate' responsibility in the school; others queried, 'Who is the master to be?'

Not surprisingly, the confusion of principals confronting this issue was exacerbated during the early stages of decentralization when they perceived their newly-created councils or school-based committees as inexperienced and uninformed and when they found the central office transformed by new administrative arrangements and changed personnel who were possibly unknown and perhaps unable and/or unprepared to offer the support provided in the past by the 'centre'. The sense of isolation engendered by this situation was likely to become particularly acute on legally contentious issues or on problems that could involve industrial action.

Moreover, at the same time as the expanded role of 'councils' and other school-based decision-making committees were operating significantly to limit the principals' decision-making discretion, the principals' decision-making arena was being expanded as they were being asked to make decisions in response to new sets of questions. In answering these questions, however, principals were working with new groups of people, new participants in the decision-making process. Having been schooled in traditions where principals were expected to be prime sources of authority and decision making at the school level it is not surprising that many principals did not possess the skills to adapt to the new decision-making and management style that was required.

Of course, unless principals had been properly prepared to facilitate participative decision-making, it was inevitable that they would encounter problems in managing the conflict which would arise when attempts at collaboration failed. Diminished bureaucratic authority and external support made it harder for principals to deal with such situations. Vexing too was the problem for many principals of balancing collaboration with supervisory duties. Many principals found it difficult to discipline a teacher in one context, with regard to student supervision for example, and then work again with that teacher on another matter in a collaborative setting.

Collaborative school-based management, as a result, has dramatically altered the nature of the principal's professional life. In addition to changed relationships with 'the system' and with staff, principals are forced to assume a more public role, interacting with people in the wider community, forging links with the school and its environment. While such activities contribute to a more varied and fragmented professional life than that experienced by principals in the past, they may also contribute to a greater incidence of stress.

Despite these pressures, however, there is evidence that principals are adapting to this new conceptualization of their role. In a study of the factors influencing principal effectiveness in a decentralized and devolved system, Chapman (1987) found that overall principals have a more positive, rather than negative, attitude to the changes that have impacted on their role in recent years. A decade after the first major changes towards collaborative school-based management, factors which were perceived by principals as having the highest positive influence on principal effectiveness were those which related to increasing parental involvement in schools, encouragement at schools to take greater responsibility in developing educational policies and practices, and successful implementation of consultative and participatory approaches to decision-making and management. The factors which showed the most negative perceptions were all factors which tended to make the achievement of effective school-based decision-making more difficult, in particular the limited resources to support initiative and change at the school level and the tension in relationships between the school and the central and regional administration.

The successful adaptation to the new conceptualization of the principalship was found to be based on each Principal's ability to respond to personal and professional challenges in a period of significant change, the creation of adequate support structures to assist principals in their adjustment, the provision of professional renewal for incumbents of the principalship, and the improvement of procedures for the preparation of aspirants to principal positions.

Prospects for the Future

Throughout the late 1970s and early 1980s in Australia, leading educational theorists, researchers, and policy makers promoted the notion that a school that was relatively autonomous, self-appraising, and aware of its own strengths and weaknesses was most able to address problems of quality. In Australia, the effective implementation of this notion required a radical reshaping of the relations between the centre and the periphery of the education system and consequently a revision of the principles governing the organization, operation, and management of schools. In this chapter, the implications of this reshaping for Australian school principals have been explored. In recent times, however, there has been pressure to move towards specific, direct, and short-term approaches to 'quality' issues.

As we enter the decade of the 1990s in Australia, the current educational debate is being conducted in a context of alarm regarding the state of the economy and national competitiveness. The 'language of crisis and mobilization in the face of threats to national survival' (Angus *et al.*, 1990) as highlighted in reports such as the QERC report (Quality of Education Review Committee, 1985) reflects the concerns of politicians and policy makers operating in an economic context which has forced federal and state governments to question the nature and cost of the existing educational services. Associated with these pressures has been an increased demand for public accountability, and the emergence of a new group of interests and agencies which, with their own assessments of education and training needs arising from structural changes in the economy, industry, and the international economic environment, have driven the educational debate towards a redefinition of the main objectives and outcomes of education from a fundamentally utilitarian and instrumental philosophy.

In response, the Commonwealth Government of Australia has moved towards placing greater emphases on setting quality targets and providing the means to attain them, monitoring the implementation of the appropriate strategies, and conducting appraisals of performance. In the immediate future, the challenge facing the principals of Australian schools is to resolve the dilemmas and the unquestionable tensions which exist between the past emphasis on improvement through school-based decision-making and management and the emerging political pressure for centrally determined quality control.

References

Angus, L., Poole, M. and Seddon, T. (1990) 'Pressures on the move to school-based decision making and management' in Chapman, J.D. (Ed) *School Based Decision Making and Management*, London, Falmer Press.

Ashenden, D. and Gallagher, M. (1980) *The Political Context in Australian Schooling — Discussion Paper*, Canberra, ACT Schools Authority.

Chapman, J. (1987) *The Victorian Primary School Principal: The Way Forward*, Report to the Victorian Primary Principals Association.

Chapman, J. and Boyd, W. (1986) 'Decentralization, devolution and the school principal: Australian lessons on statewide educational reform', *Educational Administration Quarterly*, **22**, 4, Fall.

Fitzgerald, R. and Pettit, D. (1978) *The New Schools Councils*, Burwood Monograph Series No. 3, Burwood State College.

Gronn, P. (1979) 'The politics of school management', unpublished doctoral thesis, Monash University.

Karmel, P. (1973) *Schools in Australia*, Canberra, Australian Government Printer.

Wilkinson, V. (1983) 'Presidents' Report', *Primary Principals*, VPPA, **1**, 19.

8 Headteachers in England and Wales

Ray Bolam

Introduction

The purposes of this chapter are threefold: first, to outline the salient and significant features of the contemporary role of headteachers in the light of its historical development and recent research; second, to highlight the main impact of the Government's education reform strategy on school management and headteacher training; and finally, to raise some key issues which are of wider professional concern.

In British schools the key person with school management responsibilities is the Headteacher; others include the Deputy Heads, Heads of Department in secondary schools and certain teachers with specialist responsibilities in primary schools. All such people, including the headteachers, have a classroom teaching function but, unlike ordinary classroom teachers, they are responsible for a management function outside the classroom which has direct implications for other teachers in the school. Thus, they have some managerial responsibility for one or more of the following task areas: the school's overall policy and aims; its decision-making and communication procedures; the curriculum; the staff; the pupils; material resources; external relations; and the processes of maintaining, developing and evaluating the work of the school. On this working definition there are at least 130,000 staff with a management function in primary, middle, secondary and special schools in England and Wales. They include approximately 30,000 headteachers, 40,000 deputy headteachers, and 70,000 department or section heads.

Five further background features of the situation in England and Wales are worth highlighting. First, appointments to headships and deputy headships are made by school governors, some of whom represent political parties, following a process of advertising in professional journals and the national press. Second, applicants for such posts are not required to have completed an accredited course in school management and administration (since accredited courses, as such, do not exist), but are judged on the basis of their previous experience and on their performance in a selection interview. Third, there is a trend towards management by teams of senior staff, including the Head, particularly in secondary schools, which affects job specifications and training needs. Fourth, women are significantly underrepresented in senior positions in all types of school. Fifth, most heads are members of one of two national professional associations — the National Association of Head Teachers (NAHT) or the Secondary Heads Association (SHA) — while many continue their membership of a teachers' association like the National Union of Teachers (NUT) or the National Association of Schoolmasters and Union of Women Teachers (NAS/UWT).

The Developing Role of the Headteacher

Headteachers have had a unique position since the mid-nineteenth century (Bernbaum, 1976) which marked the transition from the head who was master of the boys and who employed auxiliaries as servants to that of the chief of staff of a group of teachers. The archetypal public school head in the mid-nineteenth century was Thomas Arnold of Rugby who reformed the school by emphasizing the importance of Christianity in the formation of morals and character. During the third quarter of the nineteenth century, financial pressures drove public school governors to appoint heads who had to act as entrepreneurs if their schools were to survive in the education 'market' and who thus became the dominant figures, deciding on the number and quality of the teaching staff, the size of the pupil intake and the overall image of the school. Following the 1902 Education Act many smaller grammar schools accepted the capitation grant from the Central Board of Education and thus became subject to inspection which imposed new constraints on heads' autonomy. Also, from 1902, local education authorities exercised considerable control over elementary schools and later on over secondary modern schools. By the 1960s, with the advent of large comprehensive schools, the role of the head was becoming increasingly managerial but the nineteenth century public school and twentieth century grammar school traditions continued to influence the leadership styles of many secondary heads and the ways in which they organized 'their' schools.

Systematic and large-scale research into the roles and tasks of headteachers is a relatively recent phenomenon. Hughes (1976) studied seventy-two secondary heads and distinguished between their chief executive and leading professional roles, illustrating well the tensions involved in trying to carry out both administration and teaching. It is no accident that the term 'headteacher' is the preferred one: virtually all heads continue to teach for some of their time and, in primary schools, for the major part of their time. Lyons (1974) used diary and other data to study the ways in which the heads of sixteen large secondary schools managed twenty-one major, recurring administrative tasks (for example, compiling the timetable). He concluded that the way the school was structured (for example, into upper, middle and lower schools) largely determined the pattern of task allocation but that all heads faced the same problems of having little or no time in the school day to handle these tasks and of being compelled to work in a fragmented situation which involved constant interruptions by apparently urgent and unpredictable tasks and crises.

Morgan *et al.* (1983) carried out an extensive study of the procedures used by LEAs to appoint secondary headteachers. Only one of the eighty-five LEAs surveyed provided a general job description for their heads so the researchers used an analytic framework with four major task areas: educational, conceptual and operational management, leadership and human relations management, and external accountability and community relations. A critical factor in a headteacher's selection is that three interest groups are normally involved: LEA officers (professionals), elected members of the LEA Education Committee (local politicians), and the school's governing body (parents and lay community representatives). The researchers concluded that the procedures adopted were extremely weak. Characteristically these procedures did not use explicit elimination criteria, relate evidence of candidate performance to job criteria, treat candidates equally or weigh all the evidence to make considered, systematic decisions. Selectors were likely to treat internal and female candidates differently, engage in bargaining and trade-offs and allow image stereotypes and taken-for-granted values to rule their decisions. In a follow-up action-research study the same researchers produced some recommended procedures but there is little evidence that these have been adopted. Moreover, given that, in future, headteacher appointments will be made by the school governors of each school, the need for better selection procedures is now even more important.

Two recent studies have confirmed and extended the findings of earlier researchers about what secondary heads actually do. Hall *et al.* (1986), using an ethnographic approach, concluded that headteachers' days were indeed fragmented, with interruptions themselves being interrupted, that they were highly people-intensive and that they encompassed a range of often complex tasks. Classroom teaching was often their longest sustained task whereas scheduled meetings made up only a small proportion of their day. However, intensive study of four heads led to the conclusion that each of them adopted a different approach to leadership and management and to the assertion that 'variety remains the chief characteristic of how secondary headship is practised in England and Wales today' (p. 213). Weindling and Earley (1987) carried out a national study of 188 new secondary heads and case studies of sixteen schools, concentrating on the ways in which heads managed change. Early initiatives by the new heads were concerned with organizational matters (for example, arrangements for consultation and communication), with promoting the school's image (for example, links with local newspapers and the community) and with laying the foundations for longer-term change (for example, a curriculum review working party). Of the several hundred changes in which the sixteen case study schools were engaged, the vast majority were initiated by the heads, some were externally driven (for example, by the LEA) and only a few were initiated by teachers. By the end of their second year 60 per cent of the national sample said they had been unable to achieve all they wanted, usually citing staff resistance as the main reason. The study was not concerned with experienced heads and this, together with the impact of the recent spate of national initiatives, suggests that the picture of the typical head is somewhat different.

All of the research evidence summarized above refers to secondary schools. There are far fewer research studies of primary schools and most of them are small-scale, offering limited scope for generalization. Coulson (1990) reviewed available research and concluded that it confirmed the dominant role of headteachers in primary schools, the fragmented nature of their work pattern, and the widespread existence of a paternalistic leadership style but with a preference by teachers for a style which combines consultation with clear direction. Wallace (1988) identified several significant, distinctive features of the role of heads in small, mainly rural, primary schools: they themselves had rarely been deputy heads, they often had full teaching loads but only limited secretarial support, the school had a very high profile in a rural community, pupils were taught by a small number of teachers with necessarily restricted expertise, and classes had pupils covering a wide age range. Nias *et al.* (1989) concluded from their participant observation study of six primary school cultures that heads felt a powerful sense of ownership of 'their' schools and expected to determine their philosophies. They set great store by their own teaching role as a way of communicating this and also used public occasions like morning assembly to reinforce their views of the schools' ethos. They were almost obsessively fascinated by their schools, spending a great deal of time talking to their staff and simply getting around the schools; in consequence, they were accepted as members of the staff teams and thus had a dual role — team leader and member; at best, they acted as educative leaders, stimulating and challenging their colleagues.

There has long been concern about the effectiveness of headteachers as institutional leaders. Her Majesty's Inspectorate concluded from their study of *Ten Good Schools* that:

> What they all have in common is effective leadership and a climate that is conducive to growth ... without exception the most important single factor in the success of these schools is the quality of leadership of the head. (DES, 1977, p. 36)

Two major research studies carried out in Inner London have provided illuminating evidence. The secondary schools study (Rutter *et al.*, 1979) concluded that the following factors were associated with effective schools: strong positive leadership with decisions taken at senior level, but teachers' views represented; high expectations; a recognized set of discipline standards with an emphasis on reward, praise and appreciation; checks that staff set homework and an awareness of staff punctuality; staff involvement in joint planning in subject departments; consistency of aims and values; teachers share in the high expectations, and know that their views are considered before senior management makes decisions; and a positive school ethos — an amalgam of all the above effective processes, plus care and decoration of the school, availability of drinks and telephones for pupils, and pupil participation in assemblies and meetings. The junior schools study (Mortimore *et al.*, 1988) concluded that the following factors were important correlates of effectiveness: purposeful leadership; heads involved in curriculum planning and ensuring that teachers keep records, which they discuss with teachers; heads intervene selectively to influence teaching strategies, and plan teacher attendance at in-service courses to meet the schools' needs; involvement of deputy heads in policy decisions on, for example, the allocation of classes and budget; consistency among teachers — all teachers follow curriculum guidelines in the same way, demonstrating unity of approach; parental involvement — the school is an open-door establishment, where parents feel welcome, help in classes, on outings and with fund-raising, and attend meetings; positive climate — the school's atmosphere is pleasant, with greater emphasis on praise and less on punishment; clubs and outings are organized for pupils; and a positive climate for teachers, who have non-teaching periods for planning. These two sets of findings are broadly consistent with those from other developed countries, including the caveat that leadership factors account for a much smaller proportion of student achievement differences than do social class factors. Nevertheless, the part played in explaining between-school differences by leadership is large enough to provide encouragement to headteachers and to raise important questions about their preparation and training.

National Reform and Management Training

Major changes in the role of headteachers are being generated from the Government's education reform programme which is embodied in the 1986 and 1988 Education Acts. The main components of this programme include: a National Curriculum plus national testing and examinations; school governors and headteachers to be responsible for the local management of schools (LMS), including the budget and the hiring and firing of staff; the opportunity for schools to opt out of LEA control; Government-imposed, national salaries, conditions of service and career-ladders for all teachers; a national teacher appraisal scheme which includes classroom observation; school-level budgets for staff development plus five school closure days available for training each year ('Baker days'); and regular monitoring and evaluation of school performance by LEA inspectors.

These changes have the following features: the establishment, for the first time, of a framework of national objectives, standards and priorities, hitherto the responsibility of schools and LEAs; the redistribution of power by decentralizing as many decisions (for example, on finance and the hiring and firing of staff) as possible to the school level and by requiring local education authorities to act as 'enabling' implementation agencies and to evaluate the outcomes of school level decision-making within the framework of national objectives and standards; the creation of a market-oriented culture for schools whereby clients (parents) are empowered (via governors, open enrolment, published assessment scores and the possibility of opting out of LEA control) to choose which schools to support and whereby schools are compelled to compete with each other for their clients and thus, in theory, to raise their teaching and learning standards by using their financial, human and physical resources most cost-effectively; and the requirement that LEAs should hold school heads and governors accountable for the planning and delivery of the national objectives and standards by evaluating and inspecting their work according to specified performance indicators.

This massive reform programme is being phased in over approximately five years and thus the main task for all headteachers and their senior staff is to manage the implementation of a complex package of multiple, radical changes while simultaneously maintaining ongoing work. Most fundamental are the managerial changes associated with the introduction of financial delegation to schools and of the new powers for governors, together known as local management of schools. The Headteacher and governors will, under this scheme, be responsible for the school's budget and for the recruitment, appointment, payment and dismissal of the staff. Headteachers and governors are adopting several strategic management techniques for managing their delegated financial budgets and their new powers over school-level decisions about priorities and policies. These include various methods of school self-management, institutional review and development and performance measurement (for example, McMahon *et al.*, 1984). However, schools vary in their capacity to cope. For example, Muse and Wallace (1988) reported on an interview study of twelve primary heads, chosen by their LEAs as effective leaders, about the implications of the Education Reform Acts for their roles. The heads were operating successfully in difficult conditions: large classes in small classrooms, impressive work displays in depressingly unpainted surroundings, relative isolation from LEA advice and support, lack of communication between schools, and deputy heads who were unable to provide much help because of full teaching loads. Moreover, despite a commitment to the implementation of the national reforms, most did not normally plan or manage strategically and were therefore likely to need considerable training and support.

Since 1987, management training has been established as a national priority in the Government's Training Grant Scheme. It is now an even higher priority because the sheer scale and pace of the current educational reforms mean that the main task facing headteachers and teachers is the management and implementation of multiple change. The government has acknowledged this, first, by setting up a Task Force to identify the implications for management training and development (Styan, 1989) and, second, by requiring each LEA to adopt a systematic approach to management development along the lines advocated by the National Development Centre for School Management Training (McMahon and Bolam, 1990). However, recent evidence suggests that the impact of the Education Reform Acts is overwhelming and distorting the efforts of LEAs to adopt such a systematic approach to management development (Wallace and Hall, 1989) by causing them to deal with current and immediate training needs in a piecemeal fashion.

Some Key Issues

In this final section, some of the major issues facing headteachers are summarized with reference to three categories: managing change, the new education culture and implications for the profession. Contextually, it is worth reflecting on the continuing, long-term importance of headteachers in the national cultural life: most of today's headteachers and deputy headteachers will still be in post in the twenty-first century, educating students and future teachers, some of whom will live and work in the twenty-second century. Although such projections are not new, the escalating pace of social, political and technological change in the recent past and the foreseeable future does place a particularly heavy burden on today's headteachers.

The most pressing general problem now facing headteachers is the need to manage the implementation of multiple changes of a fundamental nature. While a large part of the agenda for change arises directly from current Government policies, much does not. Information technology is now impacting significantly on schools. The political changes in Europe caused by the planned opening up of the European Community countries in 1992 are already producing substantial innovations in school curricula and will no doubt produce even more as the full implications of the political changes in Eastern Europe become clear. A second part of the changed agenda is attributable to the policies of successive governments: the effect of lack of investment in school buildings, books and equipment over many years are now only too apparent; the system faces a chronic shortage of teachers with many London schools regularly sending classes home because they have no teachers and part-time schooling now being seriously discussed as a stop-gap solution; sustained criticism of educational standards and of teachers by politicians and the media over the last fifteen years, however justified or unjustified, together with a significant drop in teachers' salaries in real terms have manifestly undermined morale; the added pressures of the Government's education reform strategy have produced an abnormally high level of stress, alcohol addiction and drug abuse by teachers; and in consequence of all of these factors, teacher recruitment and retention are very poor, especially in cities. The third component on the headteachers' change agenda does arise directly from the reform programme described previously above, which certainly poses technical and managerial problems of considerable scale and complexity, especially when they are set in the context of the first two sections of this changed agenda.

Yet in many ways it is the new culture of schools which poses the most fundamental challenge to headteachers and teachers alike. This new culture is the cumulative product of the various elements in the reform programme but it is essentially the result of the attempt to transform schools into competitive, market-oriented, entrepreneurial organizations, analogous to small commercial companies. In this context, the head is seen as the Chief Executive, answerable to governors who are in the role of a board of directors. Alongside this has come an increasing emphasis on industrial style techniques, like the nationally imposed conditions of service and job descriptions, appraisal, performance indicators and, on the horizon, site-level pay bargaining rather than the present system of national pay agreements. The implications of this profound cultural shift are only slowly becoming evident as the reform programme moves into the implementation stage. Many of today's headteachers were trained in the sixties when equality, cooperation and child-centred teaching were the underpinning political and professional values of comprehensive schools and Plowden-style primary schools. These and similar values must now be rethought in the light of the new culture.

Inevitably, this is leading many people to ask what kind of teaching profession is wanted. Traditionally, headteachers and teachers have been allowed by society to exercise considerable professional autonomy. It was no accident that such notions as child-centred learning, school-based curriculum development and school-focused in-service training were born and nurtured in this professional culture. The nationally imposed curricula, assessment and conditions of service are, arguably, contributing significantly to the deprofessionalization of teaching, and run the serious risk of transforming teachers into bureaucratic functionaries. Headteachers and their deputies are undoubtedly receiving increasing attention, and possibly status, in the form of relatively higher pay and greater emphasis on their training needs. The price to be exacted may well be the adoption of an exclusively managerial or executive role and the jettisoning of their leading professional role, together with an overall reduction in the autonomy of the profession. Whether or not these changes will lead to better teaching and learning remains to be seen.

References

Bernbaum, G. (1976) 'The role of the head' in Peters, R.S. (Ed) *The Role of the Head*, London, Routledge and Kegan Paul.

Coulson, A. (1990) 'Primary school headship: A review of research' in Saran, R. and Trafford, V. (Eds) *Research in Education Management and Policy: Retrospect and Prospect*, London, Falmer Press.

DEPARTMENT OF EDUCATION AND SCIENCE (1977) *Ten Good Schools*, London, HMSO.

HALL, V., MACKAY, H. and MORGAN, C. (1986) *Headteachers at Work*, Milton Keynes, Open University Press.

HUGHES, M.G. (1976) 'The professional as administrator: The case of the secondary school head' in PETERS, R.S. (Ed) *The Role of the Head*, London, Routledge and Kegan Paul.

LYONS, G. (1974) *The Administrative Tasks of Heads and Senior Teachers in Large Secondary Schools*, Bristol, University of Bristol, School of Education.

MCMAHON, A. and BOLAM, R. (1990) *School Management Development and Educational Reform: A Handbook for LEAs*, London, Paul Chapman.

MCMAHON, A., BOLAM, R., ABBOTT, R. and HOLLY, P. (1984) *Guidelines for Review and Internal Development in Schools: Primary and Secondary School Handbooks*, York, Longman for the Schools Council.

MORGAN, C., HALL, V. and MACKAY, H. (1983) *The Selection of Secondary School Headteachers*, Milton Keynes, Open University Press.

MORTIMORE, P., SAMMONS, P., STOLLE, L., LEWIS, D. and ECOB, R. (1988) *School Matters: The Junior Years*, Wells, Open Books.

MUSE, I. and WALLACE, M. (1988) 'Effective primary headship: Looking to the future', *Education 3–13*, October, pp. 22–6.

NIAS, D.J., SOUTHWORTH, G. and YEOMANS, R. (1988) *Understanding the Primary School as an Organisation*, London, Cassell.

NIAS, D.J., SOUTHWORTH, G. and YEOMANS, R. (1989) *Primary School Staff Relationships: A Study of School Culture*, London, Cassell.

PETERS, R.S. (Ed) (1976) *The Role of the Head*, London, Routledge and Kegan Paul.

RUTTER, M., MAUGHAN, B., MORTIMORE, P. and OUSTON, J. (1979) *Fifteen Thousand Hours, Secondary Schools and Their Effects on Children*, London, Open Books.

STYAN, D. (1989) *School Management Task Force: Interim Report* (mimeo 23 pp.), London, DES.

WALLACE, M. (1988) 'Innovation for all: Management development in small primary schools', *Educational Management and Administration*, **16**, 1, pp. 241–50.

WALLACE, M. and BUTTERWORTH, B. (1987) *Management Development in Small Primary Schools*, Bristol, NDCSMT, University of Bristol, School of Education.

WALLACE, M. and HALL, V. (1989) 'Management development and training for schools in England and Wales: An overview', *Educational Management and Administration*, **17**, 4, pp. 163–75.

WEINDLING, R. and EARLEY, P. (1987) *Secondary Headship: The First Years*, Windsor, NFER-Nelson.

9 The School Principal in India

Chaman L. Sapra

Introduction

School education in India is mainly provided through schools run by the state governments, local bodies and private agencies.[1] The schools managed by private organizations include both aided and unaided schools. The latter category of schools are also called public schools or independent schools.[2]

This chapter examines the profiles of the school principals in India with special reference to recruitment policies and selection procedures, roles and functions, professional preparation and training, constraints under which the school heads have to operate and the problems they are confronted with. The chapter also attempts to make predictions about their future roles.

Recruitment Policies and Selection Procedures

Recruitment policies and selection procedures have much to do with the efficiency of the school headship. It may, therefore, be pertinent to analyze them in the context of schools managed by different agencies.

Sapra (1983) in his study reports that in almost all states,[3] while the heads of primary and middle schools are promoted from the ranks of teachers on a 100 per cent basis, the headmasters of high schools and principals of higher secondary schools are appointed not only from among the teachers by departmental promotion but also by direct recruitment. According to that study, the quota of direct recruits, however, varies from 25 per cent in some states to 50 per cent in others. Of the total number of all posts, including those of school principals, 15 per cent are reserved for Scheduled Castes (S/C) and 7.5 per cent for Scheduled Tribes (S/T),[4] corresponding to their proportions in the total population of the country. Age and qualifications are also relaxed in their cases.

Selection of direct recruits for schools managed by the state governments and local bodies is made by the State Public Service Commissions through open competition, while departmental candidates are promoted on the criterion of seniority-cum-fitness/merit by the Departmental Promotion Committees.[5] All those teachers who are promoted as principals on the basis of seniority may not have administrative acumen. In fact, this is what Bhouraskar (1964) found in his study. He reports that a majority of the educational administrators (principals, education officers) who entered government service as teachers and were promoted as administrators on the basis of their length of service had no aptitude for administration. If that be so, it may be a double loss to the educational system in the sense that the teaching profession loses a very good teacher who has no taste for administration and the teacher, in turn, after his/her promotion as administrator, makes a total mess of administration.

In regard to the selection procedures and practices in private-aided schools and public schools, job requirements for the heads of these schools are more or less the same as for the heads of Government schools, the only exception being that in the case of public schools sufficiently long experience in a public school as a Housemaster or a Vice-Principal, or in any other senior position with a strong aptitude for extra-curricular activities, is an additional essential requirement. The selection to the post of Principal in private-aided schools is made through open competition by the selection committees appointed by their own managing committees with representation from the State Department of Education. The boards of governors of public schools also constitute their own selection committees for selecting their school principals through open competition, but in their cases the State Department of Education is not represented.

Roles and Functions

The school Principal in India has to play multifarious roles. He/She has to be a good teacher, a good manager, a competent academic supervisor, an efficient professional leader, and an astute public relations officer.

While the above-mentioned roles are common for all principals working in schools managed by different agencies, in actual practice a gap has always been noticed between the assigned roles and their actual behaviour and also in the relative emphases placed by them on different roles. Obviously, this is due to variations in the backgrounds of individual principals and the environments in which they have to work.

The author interviewed a cross-section of teachers, principals, education officers, senior students, parents and community leaders in Delhi to elicit their opinions about the actual roles performed by the principals of higher secondary schools run by the Delhi Administration and private management. On the basis of this empirical study it was found that, while twelve periods were allotted to a Principal for classroom teaching, not more than 25 per cent of the principals fulfilled this requirement. About 70 per cent of them taught only six periods a week, while the remaining 5 per cent did not teach at all.

The supervisory role was also being performed by a large majority of these principals in a perfunctory manner. This role was confined only to observational visits to classes in session — unscheduled in most cases, scheduled in some, and by invitation in none — and checking of teachers' diaries. The leadership aspect of stimulating teachers to improve teaching and diary writing was found to be a weak feature. Staff meetings, individual conferences, orientation and induction as instruments of teachers' growth and specific in-service education techniques such as action research, inter-class visitation, and inter-school visitation, also found little place in the school life.

Almost all the responding principals mentioned that whenever changes were made in the school curriculum and textbooks, they deputed their teachers to the seminars, workshops, and training programmes organized by the National and State Councils of Educational Research and Training from time to time to provide orientation for them to the new curricula and textual materials. However, most of the principals confessed that the transfer effect of newly-acquired knowledge and skills by the teachers through these programmes into the classrooms was minimal because of lack of appreciation of the curricular changes by the principals themselves, large size of classes, and paucity of funds required for purchasing teaching aids for operating the new curriculum.

A large majority of the principals admitted that they were not able to play their roles as academic supervisors and professional leaders effectively because most of the time they were engrossed in administrative routine, accounts matters, and public relations work. According to them, they had to spend a lot of their time and energy dealing with pulls and pressures for admissions, attending to routine correspondence, and making the teaching and non-teaching staff work in the absence of a work culture in the country. Most of these principals took pains to explain how teachers had become politicized and how difficult it was to get work from them. Almost all the teachers were engaged in private tuition after school hours until late in the night with the result that they were left with little energy to work in schools during daytime. Even to make them take their classes regularly, when they were present in schools, had become a formidable task for the school principals in both government-run and private-aided schools. Then the teachers had a feeling of 'over security' in service. Frequently, the principals and management had failed in their legal battles to remove defaulting teachers. It is not too much to assume that what is true of the Delhi school principals may also be true of most of the school principals in other parts of the country.

No discussion of the role of the school Principal in India would be complete unless the Indian social ethos and its changing genre are also reviewed. Singh (1984) in his study of *The Teachers in India* depicts the Indian social ethos as follows:

> Broadly speaking, the typical Indian ethos has certain distinctive features. It is outwardly democratic, has an elected polity and a good

> deal of freedom of the press. In short, it has all the trappings of a democratic society. But beneath this superficial slogan-mongering level, lies real India — unchanging, feudalistic or paternalistic and class-ridden. The authoritarian set-up of our society with its hypersensitivity towards caste-distinctions makes a mess of policy decisions ... In other words, the nature of Indian society is ambivalent and is, therefore, not conducive for a clear-cut, systematic delineation of our social ethos. It is confusing, contradictory and unabiding.

Given this kind of social ethos it is not surprising to find that the leadership style of most of the school principals in India is authoritarian. In those few progressive schools where the school principals have adopted a democratic leadership style, studies have shown that the results have been encouraging in many respects. Ezekeil (1966) in her study observed that democratic school administration facilitated improved communication, fostered initiative and creativity, and broadened understanding on the part of all concerned. Sharma (1971) in his study concluded that democratic leadership contributed to good organizational climate and there was a significant positive relationship between organizational climate and school academic index. Shukla (1984) in his study reported that highly desirable educational leadership was reflected in more favourable attitudes by teachers towards their jobs and vice-versa.

Major sociopolitical changes in post-independent India, which have literally overtaken other changes, have also added a new dimension to the existing roles of the present-day school Principal. The monopolistic economy and social groupings are now being counteracted by public-owned industries and the public-supported corporate sector, and by the uplifting of the deprived sections of society through granting them their rights which had been denied to them for centuries. In other words, in economy and society, a set of new relationships is replacing the old one. The present-day school principals have not only to unravel, interpret and implement the changing socioeconomic reality by shedding the old attitudes and value patterns and replacing them with new, more constructive and meaningful concepts and values, but they also have to inspire their teachers and students to do the same.

Professional Preparation and Training

Pre-service and pre-induction training of school principals in India is conspicuous by its absence, and their in-service training, which is only of recent origin, leaves much to be desired. The starting point in the process of professional development of school principals through in-service training is to carry out a formal needs-assessment. But unfortunately, no such exercises are being undertaken by the institutions that are responsible for organizing in-service education programmes for heads of schools in this country. In-service education programmes are, therefore, of such a general type that the school principals do not feel much interest. They attend these programmes because they are sponsored by their managements.

On requests received from the *Kendriya Vidyalaya Sangthan* (Central School Organization) and *Navodaya Vidyalaya Samiti*, the National Institute of Educational Planning and Administration (NIEPA) has been organizing in recent years in-service training programmes for their principals. These programmes were designed on the basis of job requirements of principals or, in other words, taking their perceived needs rather than their felt needs into consideration.

Recently, the *Kendriya Vidyalaya Sangthan* started its own training wing for the training of its teachers and school principals. NIEPA faculty have been participating in these programmes as guest instructors. NIEPA also conducts training programmes for the training of trainers from the training wing of the *Kendriya Vidyalaya Sangthan* and also from the State Councils of Educational Research and Training and State Institutes of Education. Since 1986, the National Council of Educational Research and Training (NCERT) has been organizing orientation programmes for the heads and teachers of primary and secondary schools during summer vacations covering about half-a-million teachers and heads every year. The main purpose of these programmes has been to orient them to various facets of the National Policy on Education (NPE) 1986 and to enable them to perceive their role in the implementation of NPE. The training inputs, in terms of training modules and faculty, for heads of schools in these programmes were provided by the NIEPA.

Constraints and Problems

The role of the school Principal in India is becoming increasingly complex and challenging, sometimes even frustrating, because of a variety of problems that have to be faced and the suddenness with which these problems emerge and become critical. Some of these problems and constraints have already been discussed in a previous section. To understand the roles and functions of the Indian school Principal in their proper perspective, it is necessary to highlight some other constraints and problems that must be confronted.

In recent years, there has been immense growth of 'trained' teachers who acquired their teaching degrees through correspondence courses or from sub-standard teacher training institutions run on commercial lines, particularly in the states of Andhra Pradesh, Karnataka, Kerala, and Maharashtra. The school principals have to run schools with these teachers of very poor quality in terms of both knowledge in subject-content and pedagogy. Since principals have no say in the appointment of these teachers, they are virtually thrust upon them. These teachers are mainly responsible for lowering standards in the schools, for which the school principals are generally blamed.

Another constraint is that, unlike their counterparts in the UK, Canada and other Commonwealth countries in the West, the school principals in India have no freedom in matters of curriculum, textbooks and evaluation procedures. All these are predetermined for them by the State Departments of Education and State Boards of Secondary Education to which their schools are affiliated. In view of this constraint, most of the school principals lose all initiative and turn out to be routine administrators.

Still another constraint is that the delegation of administrative and financial powers at the school Principal level is minimal. Even purchase of furniture for schools is centralized in almost all states and union territories. In fact, experience in the union territory of Delhi shows that there have been shifts from centralization to decentralization to recentralization in the purchase of furniture for schools in the last two decades.

The school Principal in India also does not receive any academic support from the supervisory officers of the State Departments of Education, who are designated differently in different states (such as inspectors of schools, district education officers, block education officers, extension officers (education), etc.). These officers are so engrossed in para-academic and non-academic activities that they do not find time to go for supervisory visits to schools within their jurisdictions, despite a specific provision having been made in the Education Codes/Acts of all states and union territories to this effect. There has been a huge backlog of inspection over the years in all states.

Decentralization of school administration to the local bodies in some states has also created a variety of problems for the heads of schools. Inamdar (1971) in his study reported that one of the problems faced by the headmasters/principals of schools in rural India as a result of the transfer of administration of primary and secondary schools to the *Zilla Parishads* (District Councils) in Maharashtra was the widespread interference of the non-official members of these bodies in the frequent transfer of teachers, especially during the academic session. This had resulted in dislocation of the stable and smooth functioning of schools. Victimization of the heads and teachers of schools by the authorities of *Panchayati Raj Institutions* (local bodies) had also been reported in Rajasthan in a study undertaken by Iqbal Narain (1972) which revealed that a number of headmasters and teachers had been dismissed out of political motives.

Another problem that the school principals in India have to face is that their efficiency is generally measured on the basis of performance of their students in the external examinations. This indicator appears to be erroneous on many counts. Firstly, external examinations are not the true measure of educational standards. Secondly, success in external examinations depends upon the socioeconomic backgrounds of students attending a particular school; if a school has students from higher socioeconomic brackets, as is generally the case in a public school, the examination results will be better as compared with another school (managed either by government, local body, or private trust), where a large majority of students belong to lower socioeconomic strata of society, including a substantial number of first generation learners. Finally, a school is responsible not only for the mental development but also for the physical and moral development of students. Again, it is not the only place where learning of all kinds takes place; there are many other sources of learning which are equally important. For instance, the powerful modern media of communication — the press, radio, television and the cinema — can mould an individual's character more than any teacher or school Principal could even hope of moulding and shaping it. Obviously, therefore, the school principals and teachers cannot be held responsible for intellectual and moral standards of their students, if society fails to check the negative influences of mass media.

Another serious constraint is the woeful inadequacy of training facilities for the school principals in India which hinders their professionalization. A reference to this has already been made in the relevant section. To reduce the gap between the assigned roles and actual behaviour of the school principals and to enable them to play their roles more effectively, institutional arrangements for providing them with training (both pre-induction and in-service) will have to be expanded at all levels (*viz*. national, state, district, and block).

According to the Fifth All-India Educational Survey (1989), single-teacher schools constituted 27.96 per cent of the total number of primary schools in the country as at 30 September 1986. All these schools are located in rural areas. The single teacher in such a school must combine personally all the roles and functions of a head as well as a teacher. Multigrade teaching is the major problem, apart from the problems of managing physical and material resources and keeping liaison with the community.

Still another serious constraint is that a large number of primary and middle school heads, particularly in rural areas, work in schools where basic minimum facilities are not available. The Fifth All-India Educational Survey (1989) reveals that 13.5 per cent of the primary schools and 4.11 per cent of the middle schools in the country are without buildings. These schools are run in open space, tents, or thatched huts. Most of these schools and some other schools do not even have blackboard and chalks, let alone other teaching aids.

A Look to the Future

The role of the school Principal in India will undergo a sea change in the 1990s in the wake of changes that are taking place and/or are likely to take place in social, political, and technological domains. In the emerging social scenario in this country one finds that the cultural values are changing so fast that a generation gap is developing. The present generation has seen the application of science and technology to solve human problems; its members are growing up with television and other media which expose them to the larger world with all its diversity of culture and view; they have seen humanity experience release from earth into space; and they are living with the prospect of complete automation in the near future with all its attendant impacts on living styles and value systems. With the rapid development of communication media, youth no longer gets its cues from carefully monitored messages from adults at both school and home. The young are creating their own reality out of the messages they receive from different sources.

Besides, many of them are experiencing a feeling of alienation that comes with imposition of certain ideas by elders. They are drifting into peer groups where relationships are more satisfying and communication is possible. In some extreme cases, they are becoming split personalities torn between the traditional and modern values and are even taking to drugs.

This generation gap is likely to expand if the school principals and teachers do not play their roles effectively to bridge the gap well in time. They can do so only if they are able to come close to the experience of youth, only if they themselves can continuously narrow the gap between their own cultural background and the present, without alienating themselves from the earlier generation and the authority system of society.

On the political front, there has been a tremendous revival of faith in education in India as a means of building and rebuilding society. As a response to social need, the New Education Policy was formulated in 1986 following a critical assessment of the existing situation. Also, there was a marked increase in the allocation of outlays for education during the Seventh Five-Year Plan.

As a result of strong political will and technological developments, education in India will undergo a revolutionary change in the coming years. The changes in its educational system will be pervasive indeed. They will include changes in the content of the subject fields (for example, modern maths, new physics, etc), the explosion in knowledge in every field, changes in the methodologies of teaching (team teaching, micro-teaching, etc), new technology (use of television and computers), new insights from research in the social and behavioural sciences (for example, sociology, psychology, systems theory, etc), and new ideas about education.

This last change really is the result of the changes in the other areas and of the changes in society. The goal of individualization has long been consciously held by educators in this country but it could not be realized because of large-sized classes. Similarly, there has been awareness of the principles of immediate knowledge of results and reinforcement, but it was an elusive goal under the circumstances found in India's schools. Another example is the knowledge of the need for multisensory experiences for which there was little opportunity to apply. Developing technologies are bringing many of these goals within reach now. All these changes portend new roles for the country's school principals and teachers.

Examination of the emerging trends reveals a very different education for the future where the learners will become responsible for their own learning and the school principals and teachers will become facilitators helping the learners to understand their needs, plan and execute their activities, and evaluate the results. Learning activities will be individual at times; at other times, they will be carried out in groups. It is apparent that more and more of the content learning in future will be on an individual basis with students drawing on all the media in the learning system as they need them. Teachers will guide, diagnose, and advise; in response to demonstrated need, some will of course instruct part of the time. But the notion that the teacher is the fountain of knowledge will be discarded. At the heart of each school there will be a learning resources centre to which students will go to collect the needed information or develop the needed skills. Keeping this scenario in view, the new roles of the school principals will be to augment the resources of the learning resources centre on a continuing basis to meet the needs of students, to acquire hardware and arrange for its repair and maintenance, and to arrange for in-service training of teachers to prepare them to face subtle, multifaceted and numerous challenges posed by new technologies and the shift in focus from instructing to facilitating self-learning by students.

NPE 1986 also has some implications for the role of school principals in terms of removing certain constraints in their role performance in some cases and in assigning new roles in others. These implications are presented below.

NPE 1986 envisages decentralization of educational administration through setting up of District Boards of Education (DBEs), District Institutes of Education and Training (DIETs) as academic wings of DBEs, and establishment of school complexes as well as Village Education Committees (VECs). DIETs will foster the professionalization of the heads of primary and middle schools (heads of secondary schools are outside the purview of DIETs) through in-service training which has so far been a neglected area. The heads of these schools will be able to play their role as professional leaders more effectively by arranging professional development for their teachers through DIETs at regular intervals. School complexes will contribute to the overall improvement of quality of education in schools within each complex through sharing of resources and will also lead to improvement in academic supervision — a role neglected by both the supervisory officers of the State Departments of Education and heads of schools, mainly due to time constraints. VECs through microplanning at the grassroots level within the framework of multilevel planning will help accelerate the pace of quantitative expansion of education. In microplanning, the heads and teachers of schools will have to take on the new role of preparing education plans at the village level in cooperation with the local communities.

Planning at the institutional level for purposes of institutional self-evaluation and renewal is also contemplated in all schools within each school complex, where the head of the lead school of the complex will have an important role to play by way of providing guidance to the heads and teachers of satellite schools within that complex in the preparation of institutional plans and by assuming responsibilities of coordinating and monitoring the implementation of these plans at the complex level so as to take timely corrective action to remove the bottlenecks, if any.

Some other policy directives in NPE 1986 that will help obviate the problems of heads of schools and enable them to play their role more effectively include provision of minimum threshold facilities to all the primary schools and conversion of single-teacher primary schools into two-teacher schools in the country under the scheme 'Operation Blackboard' as well as provision of autonomy to the selected colleges and designation of the National Council of Teacher Education (NCTE) as a statutory body. Though NPE 1986 is silent about the extension of the concept of autonomy to schools, it will not be surprising if some schools are also made autonomous on a selective basis. Even at present there is a provision for autonomous schools in the Delhi School Education Act (1973) and the Education Codes/Acts of some other states. Already a very few autonomous schools have come into existence in the country. The heads and teachers of these schools have been given freedom to choose the subject matter, teaching methods, instructional materials, and evaluation procedures which they consider will be most suitable for their students. If the concept of autonomous colleges and schools is widely implemented across the country, the National Testing Service envisaged in NPE 1986 will take care of inter-school and inter-college differences in standards. The NCTE, with statutory status, will acquire teeth to review the working of existing teacher training institutions in the country and withdraw recognition from those which do not fulfil the prescribed norms. All teacher training institutions, both old and new, will have to be accredited by the NCTE in future. This will provide the heads of schools with properly trained teachers and relieve them from one of their greatest anxieties.

NPE 1986 envisages two other reforms which will require the heads of schools to take on new roles. One of these is provision of education to children with motor handicaps and other mild disabilities in common with normal children in general schools. This will require the heads of primary schools not only to arrange for procurement of necessary equipment and materials but also to get the teachers reoriented to deal with the special difficulties of the handicapped children. The other reform pertains to the vocationalization of education at the 'plus two' stage in general higher secondary schools. In the policy document, it is targeted to divert 10 per cent of students enrolled in general higher secondary schools to the vocational stream by 1990 and an additional 15 per cent by 1995. Introduction of vocational courses in general higher secondary schools will require the principals of these schools to provide for vocational and educational guidance services, to arrange for the construction of sheds for workshops, to arrange for procurement of equipment for workshops, to approach the concerned institutions for the training of teachers in vocational courses, to get instructional materials prepared in these courses, and (most important of all) to establish linkages with the production units in the vicinity of their schools. The latter role is crucial in the sense that any amount of practical training in the simulated classroom situation will not be as effective as training on the shop floor of industry by the master craftspersons.

Linkages with the production units will also be essential from another viewpoint in that the equipment provided to schools would become obsolete and need replacement after every two to three years because of rapid technological advancements, the cost of which will be staggering.

The symptoms of stress due to role expansion are becoming visible among the school principals in India. Nevertheless, despite the heavy odds against which they have to work, they will probably be able to measure up to the challenging tasks ahead through proper management of their time among different roles, sharing of responsibilities with their senior teachers, increasing professionalization of the school principalship, and other relevant measures contemplated in NPE 1986 to obviate their difficulties in role performance.

Notes

1 The central government also runs some of its own schools such as *Kendriya Vidyalayas* (central schools) to cater to the educational needs of the children of its transferable employees, providing education through the media of English and Hindi, to get over the problem of regional languages becoming the media of instruction in different states and making inter-state migration of students impossible, and *Navodaya Vidyalayas* to offer quality education to the bright students from rural areas. The overall management of these schools rests with the central government-sponsored autonomous organizations called the *Kendriya Vidyalaya Sangthan* (Central School Organization) and the *Navodaya Vidyalaya Samiti*, respectively. Besides, *Sainik School Society*, a sponsored body of the Ministry of Defence, runs *Sainik Schools* and the Ministry of Railways as well as public sector undertakings like the Steel Authority of India, Bhabha Atomic Research Centre, etc, have their own networks of schools for the wards of their employees.

2 Public schools or independent schools in India are patterned on the model of public schools in Britain. These schools are English-medium schools and charge very high tuition and other types of fees, which only the well-to-do parents can afford. The schools are, therefore, dubbed as 'elite' schools. Although these schools do not receive any grants from the Government, they are recognized by the State Boards of Secondary Education for preparing their students for high and higher secondary school examinations. Of late, due to a craze for English-medium schools, there has been a proliferation of 'public' schools in urban and semi-urban areas, which are proprietary in nature.

3 The Republic of India consists of twenty-five states and seven union territories. Union territories are areas that are directly administered and financed by the central government.

4 The terms 'Scheduled Castes' and 'Scheduled Tribes' are used in India to denote statutorily defined socially and economically disadvantaged groups.

5 For higher secondary schools located in union territories, the principals under direct recruitment quota are selected by the Union Public Service Commission (UPSC). For departmental candidates also, who are promoted as principals, concurrence of the UPSC is necessary.

References

Bhouraskar, S. (1964) 'A new approach to the philosophy of educational administration', unpublished PhD thesis, Vikram University.

Ezekeil, N. (1966) 'Teacher participation in school administration in Greater Bombay', unpublished PhD thesis, Bombay University.

Government of india, Ministry of Human Resources Development, Department of Education (1986) *National Policy on Education*, Chandigarh, Government of India Textbooks Press.

Government of India (1973) *The Delhi School Education Act*, Delhi, The Controller of Publications.

Inamdar, N.R. (1971) *Educational Administration in the Zilla Parishads in Maharashtra: A Pilot Study*, New Delhi, ICSSR.

Narain, I. (1972) 'Rural local politics and primary school management' in Rudolph, S.H. and Rudolph, L.I. (Eds) *Education and Politics in India — Studies in Organization, Society and Policy*, Delhi, Oxford University Press, pp. 148–64.

NCERT (1989) *Fifth All-India Educational Survey*, New Delhi, NCERT, p. 12.

Sapra, C. (1983) 'Recruitment policies and selection procedures for heads of schools and inspection/supervisory officers in different states', unpublished research report, New Delhi, NIPEPA.

Sharma, M.L. (1971) 'Organizational climate of schools and academic achievement', *Indian Journal of Psychometry and Education*, **2**, 1 and 2, pp. 15–22.

Shukla, P.C. (1984) 'A study of educational leadership in relation to teachers' attitudes', *EPA Bulletin*, **7**, 1 and 2, pp. 15–23.

Singh, R.P. (1984) *The Teachers in India*, New Delhi National Publishing House, pp. 86–7.

10 The School Headteacher in Kenya

Jotham O. Olembo and Samuel S. Maneno

Headteachers play a key role in the management of education in the Republic of Kenya. They are the frontline administrators and have been involved in educational administration for a period of a little over a century. Pioneer headteachers were missionaries.

Christian missionaries were an important factor in the development of education in East Africa (Sifuna, 1988). Formal education in Kenya, like elsewhere in East Africa, was introduced by missionaries toward the end of the nineteenth century. Headteachers in those colonial days were like the heads of major early nineteenth-century schools in the United Kingdom who had to be both gentlemen and clergymen (Bernbaum, 1976, p. 11).

The chief responsibility of the Headteacher (invariably a male) used to be to promote Christianity through the school system. His teachers were expected to be faithful and committed Christians. Pupils were drawn from those African families which had been converted to Christianity. If the pupils came from a non-Christian background, they were expected to become Christians and commit their lives and service to the work of Christianity. Headteachers were, therefore, expected to ensure that the study of the Bible was the main concern of schools and the three Rs (arithmetic, reading and writing) were secondary.

However, the role of the Headteacher changed significantly in the middle of the twentieth century. He was expected to uphold the ethical code of the teaching profession (Mbiti, 1984, p. 50) and his Christian standing was no longer a criterion for selection into the teaching profession.

Headteachers were, and still are, placed in positions of considerable responsibility. They are in charge of communities of teachers and pupils who all look for guidance and direction from them. They need to know the community outside the schools well enough to be able to make the members of the community interested in what their children are doing.

The success of schools in Kenya in terms of provision of learning, teaching resources and facilities, depends largely on the Headteacher's public relations with the wider school community. All learning facilities and most of the resources are provided by communities voluntarily. While public secondary schools receive grants from the Government and charge fees from parents, primary schools by law do not charge fees and therefore depend on government grants and voluntary contributions from parents and community members. Secondary schools also raise development funds on voluntary bases because the grants do not generate enough money for maintenance of schools. Headteachers are in the centre of activities aimed at raising additional funds through the harambee spirit, as voluntary contributions are popularly known in Kenya. It is the duty of headteachers to ensure that these funds are well utilized and managed. Knowledge of financial estimation, budgeting and accounting is essential to headteachers.

Headteachers in Kenya are first and foremost the chief executives of their schools. They are charged with the great responsibility of fostering the right atmosphere for child growth and development. Education is a very valuable commodity to parents in particular and the Kenya society in general. Therefore, headteachers whose schools are not performing well, particularly in national examinations, find resistance and lack of cooperation from parents and community members. The school curriculum in Kenya is formulated centrally at the Kenya Institute of Education. Examination syllabuses are provided by the Kenya National Examination Council. Headteachers implement the curriculum and syllabuses handed to them by higher authorities.

Headteachers therefore supervise the academic activities of their teachers and students very closely to ensure that performance in examinations is excellent. However, as correctly pointed out by Konai Thaman (1987), school effectiveness is not just a question of student outcomes in terms of performance in standardized tests but, to many students, the ability of high school graduates to find paid employment after their studies (p. 5).

Development of work skills which is emphasized in the new education system referred to in Kenya as 8:4:4[1] is of great concern to headteachers of both primary and secondary schools. It was largely due to unemployment and lack of employable skills among primary school graduates that the primary education cycle was increased by one year to enable the pupils to develop work skills for self employment. Headteachers are therefore engaged in the implementation of a curriculum that emphasizes equally academic as well as practical subjects. The greatest challenges to headteachers are to find qualified teachers to handle practical subjects and to construct workshops with funds raised on a voluntary basis.

Professional Preparation of Headteachers in Kenya

Professionalization of administration is primarily a phenomenon of the twentieth century (Landers, 1977, p. 4) in the Western countries. Yet most observers of Anglophone African countries may be disappointed with the current neglect of administration training in the education sector (Lungu, 1988, p. 1). In Kenya, the twentieth century is coming to an end when efforts to train headteachers in educational administration are just beginning to materialize. The Kenya Education Staff Institute (KESI) established in 1984 has in-service programmes for headteachers as well as other administrators. The programme provides two-week courses for headteachers during school vacations. An important profession such as educational administration requires more than two weeks of training.

Kenyatta University is the only one among the four public universities that has masters and doctoral degree programmes in educational administration. However, since 1976 when the programmes were launched, a maximum of three students have been admitted to the masters programme every year because of lack of scholarships. Both undergraduate programmes at public universities and certificate programmes at teachers' colleges offer one course in educational administration. Therefore, most headteachers in Kenya, despite 'considerable responsibility' (Kanina, 1975, p. v), have had limited preparation for their jobs.

'It has been assumed in the past that a teacher with academic qualifications and the right personality could become a head, and that he can pick up the administrative side of his work as he went along' (Bernbaum, 1976, p. 9). This assumption is slowly changing in Kenya. The assumption was reasonably correct while the management function of the Headteacher was relatively straightforward and could be undertaken by a well educated man who had no special training for his role as a manager. However, this assumption is no longer valid for reasons listed in the *Times Educational Supplement* (12 February 1971, quoted in Bernbaum, 1976, p. 9):

(i) the increasing size of schools and their complexity of organization;
(ii) the increased expectations we have for big schools;
(iii) the fact that management techniques can be applied to many sorts of organizations other than business firms; and
(iv) the realization that a newly-appointed Head is moving from one kind of job to a different one.

Enrolment in Kenya schools has increased five-fold during the past two decades. Schools which had enrolments of 160 pupils in the 1960s had enrolments ranging from 800 to 1000 pupils in the 1980s. The Headteacher's role in setting the right environment for learning in these large schools cannot be overemphasized. Students have to be assisted to understand the importance of self-discipline, industry and time management to achieve the best out of the curriculum. Discipline in schools is of crucial importance since no learning can take place without proper discipline among students, teachers and administrators.

Headteachers' Role in Policy Implementation

It is generally recognized that major decisions require administrative support if they are to be translated into successful programmes (Simpkins, 1988, p. 6). Curriculum effectiveness stands or falls on the nature and the structure of educational administration. Headteachers in Kenya are in a position to know how the various educational policies affect pupils, teachers, parents and members of a wider school community.

Since 1963, when Kenya became a sovereign state, a number of policies initiated by successive governments involved headteachers considerably in the implementation phase. In 1964, the Government adopted recommendations of the Ominde Commission which required, among other things, integration of the education systems. During the colonial rule education was segregated along racial lines: there were schools for Africans, Asians and Europeans. Post-independence headteachers played a significant role in the integration exercise.

In 1974, Kenya adopted the resolution of the Organization of African Unity (OAU) which, in 1960, called on African states to provide universal primary education for all school-age children by the year 1980. Once again. headteachers, particularly those in primary schools, were directly involved in the implementation of the policy of universal and free primary education. As a result of that policy many primary schools expanded to double and even triple streams. Headteachers were to work closely and hard with parents and members of the wider school communities to provide learning facilities such as classrooms and desks to accommodate large numbers of pupils. While Kenya has not achieved complete universal primary education, about 90 per cent of its primary school-age children are now in schools. The role played by headteachers was significant.

The Mackay Commission of 1984 recommended, among other things, that the education system be restructured. Headteachers were directly involved in the restructuring of schools. For headteachers, the toughest assignment was restructuring the 8:4:4 curriculum.

The curriculum adopted aimed at providing an all-round education in the affective, cognitive and psychomotor domains. Academic, aesthetic and practical subjects were given equal emphasis. For primary school headteachers, home science and woodwork shops which did not exist were to be constructed and equipped with work-tables and tools. Funds for construction and equipment were to be raised on a voluntary basis. Stress signals, a response known to all educational leaders around the world, (Gmelch, 1988, p. 3) were evident among headteachers and teachers as the implementation of the 8:4:4 got into full gear.

Teachers were required to teach subjects they themselves had never studied either in school or in teachers' colleges. Headteachers were under pressure from teachers to provide facilities and equipment which neither the parents in some areas nor the Government had funds to purchase. However, headteachers and teachers as well were desparately trying to implement the 8:4:4 system despite the great difficulties.

Skills of an Effective Headteacher

The three basic types of skills which headteachers require are conceptual, human, and technical. A headteacher has to see his school as a whole, recognize how the functions and activities of teachers, students, parents and community members at large depend on one another; he has to visualize the relationship of his school to the Ministry of Education, the community around the school, the political, social and economic forces of the nation as a whole. To keep abreast of the activities of members of the school communities, headteachers are in constant meetings with teachers, prefects, parents, Board members, and ministry officials.

Headteachers also require abilities to work effectively with people as individuals and in groups to build cooperative effort within the schools and the outside communities. Human skills are therefore essential to effective leadership. Headteachers need to understand human behaviour and to be skilled in utilizing human abilities.

Technical skills imply an understanding of, and proficiency in, methods, processes, procedures, and techniques of school management. The 'Great Man' theory of leadership or the trait approach which dominated the study of leadership until the 1950s can no longer assure effective administration. Even Aristotle's belief, that at the hour of birth some are marked out for subjection and others for rule, does not hold water in the present-day administration of education in Kenya.

Issues Related to Headship in Kenyan Schools

The major issue currently facing educational institutions in Kenya is that of coping with population increase. Kenya's population is now the fastest growing in the world (over 4 per cent annually) which contributed to the country's inability to provide universal primary education as required by the OAU by the year 1980. However, many countries in the African region are far behind Kenya in efforts at providing universal primary education for various reasons, the major one being Government instability leading to coups and counter-coups. While Kenya has had stable Government since independence in 1963, the rise in population renders its efforts in the improvement of education inadequate.

Continued efforts have been made by the Ministry of Education to staff schools with qualified teachers. To do this the Ministry has within the last few years established four new primary teachers' colleges in addition to the previous seventeen; the intake in the colleges has tripled; and in-service programmes for the untrained teachers have been intensified. Despite all these efforts, the number of untrained teachers in the primary schools is still high.

In the secondary schools the training of teachers at the four national universities and the seven diploma colleges has intensified. As late as 1984, only one university and five diploma colleges were preparing secondary school teachers. The latest in the Ministry's efforts was the introduction of the Bachelor of Education (BEd) degree by distance teaching methods at the University of Nairobi.

The issue of unqualified teachers is of great concern to headteachers since headteachers spend a lot of time assisting untrained teachers. They also deal with disciplinary problems among students arising from poor teaching by some such teachers. Students, particularly those preparing for national examinations, do not tolerate poor teaching, since success in examinations, to students and their parents, is synonymous with success in life. There is, therefore, pressure on headteachers to provide teachers who can help students pass their examinations well. Given a chance, many teachers are usually willing to support headteachers in the task of management of the schools and implementation of programmes.

Another issue that is of concern to the Ministry and the headteachers is the quality of leadership in the schools. It is an issue that the current Minister for Education has addressed himself to on a number of occasions. Most of the administrators in the field of education first joined the educational administration profession as headteachers with little or no training at all in educational management. They then moved up the administrative ladder on the strength of experience.

The Ministry has, however, realized that it takes more than teacher education and experience on the job to make effective administrators. While there have been very successful headteachers without systematic training in educational management, the rate at which teachers are being recruited into administration is very fast and requires some basic training in the area of management. There have been many incidents of financial mismanagement and disciplinary problems in the schools which could have been avoided had the headteachers been properly trained.

Measures have been instituted by the Ministry as well as teacher education institutions to provide systematic training for educational administrators. As mentioned earlier in this chapter, KESI was established to provide in-service courses for school administrators. However, KESI has found that the task of in-servicing administrators in a country like Kenya with many educational institutions, is too big. What has hindered KESI is the fact that it can only in-service administrators when schools are on vacation. KESI has a small staff of about ten people and, therefore, depends on other training institutions for manpower and expertise. Headteachers thus have to wait for several years before they receive the two-week course mounted by KESI.

There is also an issue of availability of relevant literature in the field of educational administration. Because educational administration as a field of study is very new in Africa, there are few publications originating from the continent. Nigeria and Kenya seem to be making considerable efforts through local authors but their work is published by British firms and is, therefore, too expensive for local headteachers.

Women Headteachers

The women's dilemma in education started during the inception of formal education in Kenya, when most parents were reluctant to allow their daughters to go to school. Even today there are a few parents who remove their daughters from schools and have them marry at the tender age of 12 (*Daily Nation*, 1989, p. 17).

Despite difficulties, women have not only attended schools in large numbers but also have become a force to reckon with in the teaching and management of education. Some of the most successful schools in national examinations have women headteachers. St. Peter's Mumias Primary School, which is ironically a boys' school led by a woman headteacher, has been leading in national primary education examinations for several years. Among the secondary schools, Alliance, Precious Blood, Ngandu and Bunyore Girls have been famous for their performance in national examinations. These schools have been competing favourably with boys' schools headed by men.

The tradition of women being headteachers for girls' schools started during the colonial rule. Missionaries preferred single-sex schools. To some extent segregation by gender is slowly but surely passing away. More than 90 per cent of the public primary schools are mixed and a good number of them are under the leadership of women headteachers. Most of the day secondary schools are mixed too. However, most of the boarding secondary schools are single-sex schools. An attempt to integrate Kangaru Girls and Boys secondary schools, in Embu district, failed. It is hoped that more women will be appointed headteachers even for boys' boarding secondary schools. Women have been successful principals of teachers colleges such as Kisii, Highridge, Thogoto and Machakos, all of which are mixed and boarding, so there is no reason why they cannot become headteachers of boys' boarding secondary schools.

The Working Environment of Headteachers

Ozigi (1981, p. 74) said:

> As the head of the institution, you (headteacher) will have an office which may be either small and uncomfortable or big and well-furnished. Whether big or small, you should try to make the office look impressive, clean, tidy and well arranged. You should have

enough chairs in the office for visitors and staff members who come to see you.

Headteachers require good offices for offices are the nerve centres of schools. All the operations of the school start or end in the Headteacher's office. When officials of the Ministry of Education visit a school, they first want to go to the Headteacher's office before they engage in any other business in the school. Parents, who do not know anybody at the school, look for the Headteacher's office. Students, reporting to the school for the first time, go to the Headteacher's office. During students' stay at the school they visit the Headteacher's office many times. Teachers are frequent visitors to the Headteacher's office. Important meetings between school authorities such as the Board or School Committee members take place in the Headteacher's office, if it is large enough. Public officers, and even medical officers whenever they come to the school, go to the Headteacher's office. The office, however small it may be, should therefore command the respect it deserves.

When visitors walk into the Headteacher's office, chances are that they are met by the secretary, the clerk or messenger before they are ushered in to see the Headteacher. One's impression actually starts with the staff in the Headteachers's office. The way visitors are received by that staff is significant to the relationship between the school and the public. Even the behaviour of the students who may show the visitor the Headteacher's office counts in public relations. Headteachers, therefore, must insist that visitors are received cordially.

A good number of primary school headteachers in Kenya do not have good offices. There are several reasons why every school should have a good office for the headteacher. In addition to what has already been said, offices serve as the brain or memory of the school and important information concerning the school and its students is recorded and kept in offices. These records store information which may be required later.

A former student who returns to his/her school for a testimonial should have no cause for alarm if the school office has records to assist a new Headteacher preparing a testimonial for him/her. A new Headteacher who is having disciplinary problems with either some students or teachers should find useful information on any student or teacher that can assist in determining how to handle disciplinary problems. Development projects in Kenyan schools take a number of years to complete. Some projects such as the construction of tuition blocks may be started by one headteacher and be completed by another headteacher. Offices for headteachers need not only to be impressive, clean, tidy and well arranged but also to have well-kept records within easy reach of the Headteacher.

One of the major functions of the Headteacher in the school is to make decisions. Sound decisions are based on information available to the Headteacher. It is, therefore, essential for the Headteacher's office to have ample room to store information which can be retrieved easily to assist the Headteacher in making decisions.

A Headteacher's office requires communication facilities. In schools where there are no telephones, the working environment of the Headteacher becomes highly problematic since a Headteacher often needs to communicate with others or transmit information. There are many Headteachers in the Kenyan schools who cannot be effective because of lack of adequate communication facilities.

Conclusion

This chapter has discussed headteachers' roles in historical perspective and current trends. It is clear that headteachers in Kenya shoulder great responsibilities. However, their administrative knowledge is largely limited to that obtained from experience. Headteachers in Kenya require systematic training prior to assuming these important functions. The least that is required to benefit headteachers, particularly those without pre-service administrative training, is frequent attendance at in-service courses, seminars and workshops.

Note

1 Eight years of primary, four years of secondary, and four years of university education.

References

BERNBAUM, G. (1976) 'The role of the head' in PETERS, R.S. (Ed.) *The Role of the Head*, London, Routledge and Kegan Paul.

DAILY NATION No 8937, 19 August 1989.

GMELCH, W.H. (1988) 'Coping in a world of tension: The effective educator', *CCEA Studies in Educational Administration*, **48**.

KANINA, H.J. (1975) in *A Manual for Heads of Secondary Schools in Kenya*, Nairobi, Ministry of Education.

LANDERS, T. (1977) *Essentials of School Management*, Philadelphia, PA, W B Saunder & Company.

LUNGU, G.F. (1988) 'Attacking the elephant: Reforming educational administration in Zambia', *CCEA Studies in Educational Administration*, **48**.

MBITI, D.M. (1984) *Foundations of Schools Administration*, Nairobi, Oxford University Press.

OZIGI, O.A. (1981) *A Handbook on School Administration and Management*, Lagos, Macmillan Nigeria Publishers Ltd.

SIFUNA, D.N. (1988) *Contemporary Issues in Education*, Nairobi, Kenyatta University.

SIMPKINS, W.S. (1988) 'Policy projects and the administrator', *CCEA Studies in Educational Administration*, **49**.

THAMAN, K. (1987) 'Good schools (and bad) – Some issues in assessing school effectiveness in Pacific island contexts', *CCEA Studies in Educational Administration*, **44**.

11 The School Principal in Nigeria

Nicholas A. Nwagwu

History of Education and the Principalship in Nigeria

The development of Western-type education systems in Nigeria can be traced to the arrival of some Christian missionaries in Badagry near Lagos in 1842. They started a school the following year with the primary objective of converting the natives to the Christian faith and teaching them to be literate in the English language. This would make them useful assistants as clerks and interpreters to the missionaries and colonial administrators and traders. Some of the literate adults would also be used to teach other natives how to read and write English. Those who exhibited high intelligence and leadership qualities were appointed school heads and catechists. The Christian missionaries designed the curriculum and served as inspectors and supervisors of the schools they established. Keen competition among the various religious denominations, notably the Methodists, Anglicans, Catholics and Baptists, led to the fast expansion of education during the colonial era.

The guidelines and stipulations of the 1925 Education Memorandum and subsequent Education Code of 1926 forced the Church Missionary groups that had dominated the establishment, organization and administration of schools during the pre-independence era to consolidate and improve their performance. The importance of trained teachers was recognized, and teacher training colleges started to mushroom across the country. There was no special training programme for the preparation of school principals; rather, any experienced teacher could be selected by supervisors and inspectors for appointment as Principal. To be so elevated, the person must have demonstrated excellence in classroom teaching and management. One was also expected to have shown dynamism as a school and/or community leader. In addition the person should be a good, practising Christian whose exemplary life was transparent and worthy of emulation. His/her influence in church and community affairs was expected to help attract parents to send their children to the school and to support the school.

With national independence in 1960, the education system started to develop at such a fast pace that it became difficult to maintain standards already attained. The emphasis seemed to have changed from qualitative to quantitative growth. Young, unqualified and at times untrained teachers were given new schools to manage as principals. After the Nigeria-Biafra Civil War in 1970, most State Governments, especially in the South of the country, took over full control of the schools and abrogated the dual-control system by which the schools were jointly controlled and financed by the Government and the Missionary authorities. The immediate impact was the loss of valuable community support for the voluntary agency (missionary) schools, ineffective supervision of the schools, and elimination of the spirit of competition for high standards among schools belonging to the Government and different religious denominations. School principals found themselves at the crossroads as the Government could not give sustained financial and supervisory support to them nor could they get much material aid from the communities which previously taxed themselves to ensure they had good schools. This trend greatly affected the morale, efficiency and effectiveness of principals in Nigeria.

Appointment and Training of Principals

Nigeria operates the Federal system of Government, and the Constitution of the Federal Republic spells out clearly the legislative and administrative functions of each of the three tiers of Government in respect of the education system. Thus, education is on the Concurrent Legislative List and this enables the Federal Government to make education laws for the whole country while each of the twenty-one State Governments has powers to make education laws within its territory of jurisdiction. The third level of Government comprises the Local Government Councils which are charged with the control, management and supervision of primary education only. Principals of schools therefore operate within the laws made for education by both the Federal Government and the State Government in which the school is located. Primary school principals must in addition submit themselves to the laws made by their Local Government Councils for the organization and administration of their schools.

Though many systems and organizations in Nigeria, including the education system, are operated within the broad national principle of 'unity in diversity', there is much uniformity in the national education system. This is made possible by the existence of many federal bodies such as the National Council on Education (NCE) and the Joint Consultative Committee on Education popularly known as the JCC. The National Council on Education is made up of all the State Commissioners of Education and the Federal Minister of Education who serves as Chairman. This is the highest education policy-making body in the country. Its policies and directives are usually applied in each of the twenty-one states and the Federal Capital Territory (FCT) in Abuja with only minor modifications to suit local circumstances. The

Joint Consultative Committee (JCC) on Education is an umbrella which brings together all the professionals representing diverse interests in the field of education. The members represent the universities, colleges of education, Federal and State ministries of education, the Nigerian Union of Teachers (NUT), polytechnics and colleges of technology and other interest groups.

By nature of their composition and functions, the NCE and JCC perform complementary roles in the education system. The diverse professional interests in the JCC offer advice to the NCE which formulates national education policies. Thus, the JCC recommends to the NCE the qualifications and training that should be possessed by those aspiring to be appointed as principals of primary or secondary schools and their classification within the principalship cadre. If the NCE accepts the recommendations, these are passed on to each State Ministry of Education to implement within the framework of its resources and programmes. It is through such a process that university degree holders are accepted across the country as the appropriate persons to be appointed principals of secondary schools. In the more educationally advanced States of the Federation, the new emphasis is on holders of university degrees with teaching qualifications such as the BA or BSc degree plus a Diploma in Teaching Certificate, or the BEd degree which always incorporates courses in educational management. Those secondary school principals who hold only a university degree without a teaching diploma are often appointed because of their long and successful teaching experience and perhaps years of service as vice-principals.

In the case of primary school principals, they are expected to possess the Teachers Grade Two Certificate or the more advanced Teachers Grade One Certificate. An equivalent of the latter certificate came into being in the 1960s and became popularized in the 1970s. It is called the Associateship Certificate of Education (ACE). Initially, the ACE was designed as an in-service course for primary school heads and their assistants who were being groomed for the position of Principal. The programme was designed to improve their competence as school heads and the emphasis was on school administration and supervision. It was perhaps for this reason that the ACE college established in Bendel State early in the 1970s by the State Government in collaboration with the Institute of Education, University of Ibadan, was named 'The Headmasters' Institute'.

With the passage of time, the ACE institutions became centres for preparing classroom teachers for future roles as primary school principals. The JCC (Joint Consultative Committee on Education), however, insisted that only teachers with a minimum of five years' experience should be admitted to do the ACE course. In the 1980s, the ACE institutes were seen not merely as training centres for prospective and serving primary school heads but also as upgrading in-service centres for all primary school teachers. The course content was consequently modified to emphasize enrichment courses in various teaching subject disciplines and teaching methodology. Nevertheless, the Associateship Certificate of Education (ACE) has virtually replaced the

Teachers Grade One Certificate programmes and remains today the basic in-service training programme for the preparation of prospective primary school heads and the up-grading of serving headteachers.

It is to a large extent true that until the 1980s, the need to have all primary and secondary school principals trained specifically for their administrative functions was not generally accepted. Renowned Nigerian scholars and education specialists like Professors Babs Fafunwa and Ben Ukeje had right from the early 1960s argued that teaching experience alone, no matter how long or successful, was not sufficient preparation for the school principalship. They therefore launched a dynamic programme for the professional preparation of principals at the University of Nigeria, Nsukka, where they both served as Dean of the Faculty of Education. The present author was their student, and later joined them as Faculty staff, in the Faculty of Education. The University's pioneering role in professional teacher education is an historical reality in Nigeria, and the present-day training programmes for secondary school principals in Nigeria universities owe their origin to the innovative activities of these two scholars.

The training of secondary school principals in Nigeria has three patterns. The first and oldest is the one-year professional training given to holders of a first degree in different subject disciplines. This is the typical British approach. The graduates obtain the 'Diploma in Education' at the end of their post-first-degree one-year education course. All faculties and institutes of education of Nigerian universities offer the course. The second popular strategy for training to be a secondary school principal is to do a composite first degree course which concurrently incorporates education courses and subject discipline courses. The graduates receive the BEd, BA(Ed) or BSc(Ed) degree. This is typically the American approach, and the University of Nigeria, Nsukka, was the first to start the programme in the country in 1961. In both the first and second approaches, there are strong elements of courses in educational planning, administration and supervision in the curriculum. This is accepted as a good enough method for preparing future secondary school principals. The third approach is a Masters degree in Educational Planning and Administration.

The introduction of 'sandwich programmes' for serving teachers and principals by virtually all the universities in Nigeria has made it possible for Bachelors and Masters degrees in education to be obtained through in-service training courses taken during the long vacations. There is hardly a school Principal who has not taken advantage of the sandwich programmes to upgrade his or her professional qualifications. Primary school heads study for the Associateship Certificate in Education (ACE), then the Nigerian Certificate in Education (NCE). The more ambitious and intelligent ones proceed to take the BEd degree. For secondary school principals, the sandwich courses they take are normally for the Postgraduate Diploma in Education (DipEd), and the Masters degree in Educational Administration (MEd). There are thousands of practising school principals and prospective ones enrolled in the

Table 11.1 Schools and Enrolments in Nigeria 1912–1984

Year	Primary Pupils	Secondary Students	No Primary Schools	No Secondary Schools
1912	22,057	1086	N.A.	N.A.
1929	146,578	645	N.A.	N.A.
1937	165,762	3851	N.A.	N.A.
1947	670,000	9908	N.A.	N.A.
1957	2,410,000	45,000	N.A.	N.A.
1960	2,912,618	135,434		
1966	3,025,981	211,305		
1970	3,515,827	310,054		
1976	8,260,189	826,926	30,726	1660
1978	10,798,550	1,194,479	35,328	2249
1980	13,760,030	1,553,345	36,524	2769
• 1983	14,383,000	3,135,000	38,211	N.A.

Source: Adapted from Taiwo (1980) p. 228 and Federal Ministry of Education *Statistics of Education in Nigeria 1980–1984* (1985 Edition), Lagos, pp. 5–11.

• 1983 secondary school enrolments include students in technical/vocational schools. Figures for other years exclude them.

N.A. means 'Not Available'.

above sandwich courses in various universities and colleges of education across the country. Today, some State Governments are alarmed at the rate at which school principals are getting higher qualifications through the sandwich programmes. Their worry concerns the fast increasing salary bill at a time of serious economic crisis. However, the educationists are questioning the duration, quality and content of the sandwich courses. It is agreed by all that the courses should not be cheapened and that some parity needs to be maintained between diplomas and degrees earned by full-time students and those who pass through the sandwich programmes. The debate continues.

Progress and Trends of the Principalship

The image of the school Principal in Nigeria has dramatically changed in the last thirty years as a result of the various steps taken to professionalize the post. With improved qualifications for appointment into the principalship came higher salaries, more opportunities for upward mobility, and hence enhanced socioeconomic status in society. Table 11.1 reveals the phenomenal growth of the school system. Though primary school enrolment increased from 2.9 million to only 3.5 million in 1970, it jumped to 8.2 million in 1976, 10.8 million in 1978 and 13.8 million in 1980. The number of primary schools, and hence of primary school principals, increased from 30,726 in 1976 to 36,524 in 1980. Secondary school increases are even more impressive. Enrolments increased from only 135,434 at national independence in 1960 to 310,054 in 1970 and then rose to 1,553,345 in 1980. Similarly, the number of secondary schools, and therefore principals, escalated from 1660 in 1976 to 2769 in 1980, a period of only four years. It should be noted that the secondary school figures cited above do not include secondary technical and vocational schools which were mostly owned by private proprietors and individuals.

The major factors in the above development include the oil boom of the 1970s which brought much foreign exchange and economic prosperity from the sale of petroleum products; the introduction of universal, free primary education (UPE Scheme) in 1976; and the 'free education at all levels' scheme launched by five State Governments in the Federation in 1979. The States were Lagos, Oyo, Ondo, Ogun and Bendel. Both the UPE scheme and the 'free education at all levels' scheme have, since 1984, been discontinued due to the economic crisis the country has been witnessing with oil glut in the world market and grossly mismanaged national resources at home coupled with a badly planned and poorly managed education system. Nevertheless, the schools established in the economic boom years are there, each with its own principal. Between 1984 and 1986, some unviable schools, especially secondary institutions, were merged or closed down and some principals lost their positions. With political pressure and more candidates for secondary education, some of the closed down schools have been reopened.

It was unfortunate that the periods when the education system witnessed greatly accelerated, often unplanned, expansion also saw the appointment of many untrained, inexperienced teachers as school principals. This was most pronounced in the States where secondary education became suddenly free in 1979 and new schools mushroomed as each community went ahead to establish a secondary school in its locality to accommodate students from the area. Serious efforts have been made since then to upgrade the qualifications of the prematurely promoted principals through in-service courses, workshops and seminars. There is hardly a long vacation when workshops on educational administration are not organized for school principals by different State Ministries of Education, usually in collaboration with a faculty or institute of education of a nearby Federal or State university or college of education. The principalship has therefore gradually been recognized as a very important leadership position in the education system which requires some training and continuous upgrading.

Professional bodies like the Nigerian Union of Teachers (NUT), the Conference of Secondary School Principals, and the Association of Primary School Headteachers have played a great role in the in-service training of principals. They organize workshops and seminars on educational administration for their members, produce codes of ethics to guide the behaviour of principals, and serve as umbrellas that shelter the individual and collective interests of principals as they encounter various problems in their relationships with their employers. The collective bargaining power of the Conference of Principals of Secondary Schools and the Association of Primary School Headteachers is well respected by Federal and State Governments. Their strong and influential unions have been instrumental in shaping many educational policies in the country in addition to protecting and enhancing the conditions of service of principals.

The principalship in Nigeria would have developed into a stronger factor in Nigerian education if the primary and secondary school groups of principals had found a common ground for fruitful association. However, there are two separate groups often in conflict with each other. According to the Nigerian Union of Teachers (1974), the first Nigerian secondary school Principal was appointed in 1859. He was the Rev T B Macaulay who headed the new CMS Grammar School in Lagos. His successful headship of the school encouraged the European missionaries to appoint other Nigerians as principals. As early as 1926, the first Association of Headmasters of Ijebu Schools was founded. When the Nigerian Union of Teachers was formed in 1931 with Rev IO Ransoma-Kuti as the President, he made commendable efforts to ensure that primary school headteachers and secondary school principals united with classroom teachers and accepted one another as equal members of the Union. The common concern for joint action to express their views on educational matters and to fight for their rights, or to protest against measures they felt were inimical to their corporate interests, made it easy to bring them together under the NUT.

With the passage of time, however, things fell apart and the centre could not hold. The disparities in entry qualifications for the position of principals at the primary and secondary school levels and outstanding differences in their status and conditions of service created divisions between them. Though they still both belong to the NUT, each group pursues its own objectives using its own strategies. Indeed, there is mutual suspicion and mistrust between primary school principals and secondary school principals as each group struggles and lobbies the Government and the public to secure for its own members more attractive conditions of service.

Responsibilities and Constraints of Principalship

The functions of the school principal are many and varied. Lipham and Hoeh (1974) grouped the functions of the principal into five categories encompassing: (i) planning, designing and implementing the instructional programme; (ii) management of staff personnel; (iii) management of student personnel; (iv) providing and managing financial and physical resources; and (v) management of school-community relationships. These five broad task areas can be said to be common to all principals though with differences of amplification and execution arising from political and socioeconomic circumstances surrounding national education systems. Nigeria's highly centralized system of educational administration imposes a lot of uniformity on the responsibilities and functions of school principals.

Ogunu (in Nwagwu, 1988) examined the role of school principals in the implementation of Nigeria's new National Policy on Education. Though he produced a seventeen-item catalogue of responsibilities, the components can easily be incorporated in the five broad task areas examined above.

However, there are certain responsibilities of school principals in Nigeria that can be said to be unique. For example, they are charged with the task of collecting school fees and levies from students. In some States of the Federation, they also become a kind of tax collector in that, through their intervention, parents are made to pay their taxes and education rates. This is because the Principal is directed by Government not to admit into the school any student who does not produce a photocopy of the tax receipt of his father or guardian. In many communities, it is also the function of the Principal to liaise with community leaders to raise funds for school development. The people of the community provide free land, labour and materials for construction work in the school. Fund-raising ceremonies can be organized by the Parents-Teachers' Association or the community for development of facilities and buildings in the school. In some states in Northern Nigeria, the Principal also has the responsibility of preventing school drop-outs and reporting parents who withdraw their daughters from school in order to give them away in early marriage, for prosecution in courts by the Government.

Nigerian primary school principals are responsible for the registration and admission of pupils into their schools. However, at the secondary school level, principals have students allocated to their schools by the State Ministry of Education. Those running Federal Secondary Schools which are controlled by the Federal Ministry of Education receive their students from all the twenty-one states of the Federation under the 'quota system' which is meant to ensure 'Federal Character'. These schools are also called 'Unity Schools' because they were established, two in each state and the Federal Capital Territory at Abuja, to ensure that a favourable social and learning climate is provided for children from different tribal, religious and geographical backgrounds to live and learn together as brothers and sisters. At the school and community level, principals enjoy a lot of respect and authority, and every teacher aspires to occupy the position before retiring from service.

But the school Principal in Nigeria also experiences a lot of constraints and frustrations in the job. Notable causes of this state of affairs include the perennial shortage of infrastructure, facilities, equipment and instructional materials. Funds are hard to come by and many schools depend on the goodwill and generosity of parents and community leaders to survive. Many principals also do not have the teachers they need to ensure effective teaching and impressive outcomes or results in public examinations which serve as popular yardsticks for judging a 'good school' and hence an effective principal. Indeed, principals do not often have any say in the recruitment of teachers sent to teach in their schools. The teachers are recruited by the Ministry of Education and 'posted' to the schools. Principals therefore receive teachers whose competence, character and loyalty they cannot vouch for since they did not participate in their interview and employment. In some cases, principals have to run their schools with inadequate numbers of teachers and some untrained teachers.

There is also the constraint of too much centralization and attempts at uniformity in the education system. This hampers innovativeness and initiative from principals. Moreover, there are regular complaints of interference in the work of principals by Ministry of Education officials. Too much control by Ministry officials also makes student management difficult as some principals cannot promptly discipline erring students. They also often have to go to the Ministry of Education to collect much of what they need to administer their schools, from registers to footballs and science/workshop equipment. In many cases, schools do not own vehicles nor do the principals own their own cars, yet they have to make frequent visits to the 'Ministry' which may be located scores of kilometres away. Principals who often serve as paymasters have been known to lose teachers' salaries to armed robbers as they travelled from the Ministry of Education to the bank and back to the school with cash. However, in spite of the numerous constraints, many principals enjoy job satisfaction and exert themselves to operate effective schools.

Current Issues and Future Prospects

Perhaps the most central controversial issues today related to the school principalship in Nigeria are how to prepare principals for their task, how to foster their professionalization, how to classify them to eliminate unnecessary dichotomies and conflicts, how to deploy trained principals, and the conditions of service of principals. Each of these will be examined with pointers to the future prospects of the principalship.

Preparation of Principals

For some time to come, primary and secondary school principals will have to be educated separately for their assignments. This assertion stems from the fact that the two groups have a wide gap between them in terms of educational backgrounds, job orientations and environments. As already indicated, almost all secondary school principals have university first, second or even third degrees whereas most primary school heads have qualifications below the bachelors degree. However, a much debated issue is whether or not to introduce a full first degree programme in educational administration as a direct method of preparing prospective principals. The Faculty of Education, University of Ibadan, has a BEd degree in Educational Management. Other universities criticize the programme for being ambitious and unrealistic.

It is argued that all secondary school teachers should take educational planning and administration as one of the core professional courses for their BEd degree in conjunction with a 'teaching subject'. In this way, the graduate will have a subject discipline to teach in school as he or she gains experience and matures to occupy positions like Head of Department, then Vice-Principal, and eventually gets promoted to the rank of Principal. The present author belongs to this school of thought (Nwagwu, 1976). The logic is persuasive because people are not normally appointed to the principalship immediately after graduating from a university, unless they had gained much experience as primary school principals before they entered the university to obtain the BEd degree.

Professionalization of the Principalship

The second issue is whether or not holders of degrees and other qualifications in single subject disciplines but without professional education courses and diplomas should be appointed as principals. Some argue that where such people have good qualifications and classroom teaching experience, they could be appointed as principals. However, most Nigerian educationists are opposed to the practice. They insist that the individual should go to a faculty or institute of education of a university for at least an academic session to obtain qualifications in professional education, preferably in educational management. Alternatively, a series of short in-service workshops and courses in education could suffice. The argument is that professionalism can never be achieved in teaching, let alone the principalship, if it is not ensured that those aspiring to serve in leadership positions in schools do possess professional education diplomas. The practice in other respected professions is usually quoted, and the argument is strong. The principalship should not be an all-comers affair. If shortage of qualified personnel made the practice necessary and tolerable in the past, there seems to be no justification for it not to continue in present-day Nigeria. There is optimism that the principalship will become completely professionalized by the year 2000.

Classification of Principals

Primary heads are classified as Headmaster Special Grade, Headmaster Grade I, Grade II and Grade III while secondary heads are classified as Principal Special Grade, Principal Grade I, Grade II and Grade III. There is currently some confusion over the classification of school principals in Nigeria. To start with, primary school principals are classified differently, and so are the secondary school principals, even when they possess the same qualifications. The confusion stems from unclear criteria used for the classification of principals and vice-principals. Years of experience rather than educational qualifications and assessed performance effectiveness seem to be over-weighted in the appointment, promotion and categorization of principals. Nwagwu (1987) opines that appointments and promotions based on religious, ethnic or geographical quota systems, which in turn emphasize years of experience to the neglect or deemphasis of merit, were patent acts of discrimination which were both demoralizing and against provisions of the Nigerian Constitution. It is believed that qualifications and demonstrated leadership qualities should take precedence over experience and quota systems in the appointment and promotion of principals. However, the prospects for adopting this ideal practice seem to lie far in the future within the Nigerian context.

Deployment of Principals

There is evidence to show that the best principals in the system are posted to the best schools, often located in the cities and urban areas. Most of the poorly educated and untrained principals are to be found in small rural schools as if there is a conspiracy to keep such schools perpetually underdeveloped. To worsen matters, most of these schools are poorly equipped and staffed with small enrolments. The practice of deploying and classifying principals according to the size of the schools in which they operate is counter-productive. Thus, the very large schools are classified as Grade A schools and therefore automatically attract Principals Special Grade and Grade One Principals. Luckily, this method is being abandoned to give way to a more rational approach which deploys dynamic and effective principals to weak schools in order to develop and improve the schools. Such principals should suffer no disabilities or disadvantages merely because they are deployed to small or rural schools.

Conditions of Service of Principals

Teachers in secondary schools in Nigeria have historically enjoyed, and still do, better conditions of service than primary school teachers. The same applies to secondary school principals compared to their primary counterparts. Today education is seen not just as a human right but also as an investment in human beings. Nwagwu (1978) points out that the primary school headship is the most numerous and widespread of all posts in educational administration. He posits that any nation that ignores the welfare and job satisfaction of its primary principals runs the risk of organizing schools in which both its teachers and students will be frustrated and unproductive. It is unfortunate that Nigerian Governments and peoples have consistently underrated the importance of primary school principals, yet they blame them for most of the failures of the education system. Principals of both primary and secondary schools need to be encouraged through welfare schemes, fringe benefits and enhanced salaries in order to provide dynamic, dedicated and purposeful leadership for their schools.

Conclusion

Education policies, decisions and programmes require educated, professionally trained and devoted school principals for their effective implementation. Leadership in education can only be provided by persons who derive satisfaction from their jobs through attractive conditions of service which provide a healthy climate for progress, growth and optimal productivity. In the view of Lulsegged (1986) 'management in education is a science as well as an art and a discipline'. The principalship has stopped being a job for any 'educated' person, and needs professional training in educational administration and supervision. The fast expansion of education in Nigeria, as in many African countries, must not be an excuse for down-grading the principalship through the appointment of unqualified or professionally unsuitable persons into the post. Quantitative growth and qualitative improvement of the education system are not mutually exclusive concepts and pursuits. What is needed is careful planning of the education system and implementation of policies through innovative and realistic strategies and programmes which recognize the central importance of the school principal.

References

British Colonial Office (1925) *Memorandum on Education Policy in British Tropical Africa* (Cmd 2374), London, HMSO.

Federal Republic of Nigeria (1985) *Statistics of Education in Nigeria, 1980–1984* (1985 Edition), Lagos, Federal Ministry of Education.

Lipham, J.M. and J.A. Hoeh, Jr. (1974) *The Principalship: Foundations and Functions*, New York, Harper and Row.

Lulsegged, A.N. (1986) 'Training needs in educational planning and administration in the third world countries' in Ukeje, B.O., Ocho, L.O. and Fagbamiye, E.O. (Eds) *Issues and Concerns in Educational Administration*, Lagos, Macmillan Nigeria Publishers, pp. 355–64.

Nwagwu, N.A. (Ed) (1976) *Universal Primary Education: Issues, Prospects and Problems*, Benin City, Ethiope Publishing Corporation.

Nwagwu, N.A. (1978) *Primary School Administration*, Lagos, Macmillan Nigeria Publishers Ltd.

Nwagwu, N.A. (1987) *Education and the Law in Nigeria: The Rights of Teachers and Students*, Owerri, KayBeeCee Publications Ltd.

Ogunu, M. (1988) 'The role of school administrators in the implementation of the new national policy on education' in Nwagwu, N.A. *et al.* (Eds) *Education for Self-Reliance and National Development*, Owerri, Nigerian Association for Educational Administration and Planning (NAEAP).

Smyke, R.J. and Storer, D.C. (1974) *Nigerian Union of Teachers: An Official History*, Ibadan, Oxford University Press.

Taiwo, C.O. (1980) *The Nigerian Education System: Past, Present and Future*, Lagos, Thomas Nelson (Nig.) Ltd.

Part B

The School Superintendent/ Education Officer

12 The School Superintendent in Canada

Robin H. Farquhar

Education in Canada is constitutionally the responsibility of the provinces, and there is no national Ministry or Office of Education. The ten Canadian provinces, spread across a huge expanse of land whose sparse population is concentrated along the American border, are generally considered to fall into five main geographic regions, and each province operates its own distinctive system of elementary and secondary education: British Columbia (the Western-most province), the Prairie Provinces (Alberta, Saskatchewan and Manitoba), Ontario (the largest, central province), Quebec (the province with French as its principal language), and the Atlantic Provinces (Newfoundland and the Maritime Provinces of Prince Edward Island, Nova Scotia and New Brunswick). The Canadian provinces, in turn, have delegated considerable responsibility for education to locally elected boards of school trustees, which typically employ school superintendents to manage their school systems. The role of school Superintendent has undergone substantial evolution in recent decades, with significant variation among regions, and the purposes of this chapter are to illuminate certain aspects of Canadian distinctiveness by examining the role, to highlight some of the key features of its evolution, and to speculate briefly on its future development. (Canada's Northern region, comprising the Yukon and Northwest Territories, is not included herein because there are only two locally employed school superintendents in that entire geographic area.)

Characteristics of Canada Reflected in the Superintendency's Development

The evolution of the role of Canadian school Superintendent has been influenced by the country's history and geography, its political and social nature, and its attitude toward itself. Historically, Canada was established through the efforts of individuals from other countries interacting with the original peoples, one another, and the environment. They were seeking land, wealth, adventure, and religious freedom. The country was colonized by two founding nations, England and France, with the former eventually conquering but granting certain guarantees of linguistic and cultural protection to the latter; and it was settled in a gradual flow of migrants from East to West and of immigrants first from Western Europe and the US and subsequently from virtually all corners of the world. The educational systems which Canadian superintendents now administer evolved in ways that reflect this historical development of the country. The supervised, inspected, centrally guided system of education that emerged in Ontario was typical of Britain at the time; this influence was apparent also in America's New England and, to some extent, in the Atlantic provinces (especially New Brunswick) and British Columbia as well. The additional Acadian (French-speaking minority) heritage of New Brunswick is reflected in its parallel and distinct English and French provincial school systems. Quebec imported and maintained for nearly three centuries a church-administered system from France, supplemented after the 1759 conquest by English clerics. Subsequent immigrations from other countries (including those in central Europe) and migration from Eastern Canada and the United States resulted in a richer mix of influences and patterns for the establishment and administration of school systems on the Prairies, with the main organizational model in this region being imported from Ontario (reflecting that province's dominant position throughout anglophone Canada).

Canada's geography also had an impact, two dramatic examples being the Cabot Strait and the Rocky Mountains. The former separates Newfoundland from the other Atlantic provinces, and the multi-religious educational systems for which Newfoundland superintendents are responsible differ markedly from those in the three Maritime provinces. Similarly, the British Columbia Superintendent works under conditions that are quite different from those in the remainder of Western Canada lying east of the Rockies. And Canada's geographic proximity to the United States has had a substantial impact on the role as well; a significant number of Canadian school superintendents (and university professors with whom they work) pursued their educational administration graduate programmes in the US, many of them undertake in-service training experiences there, several have chosen (consciously or unconsciously) American role models, and the organizational structure of today's educational systems in Canada more closely resembles that of the United States than those of any other countries (notwithstanding the relatively stronger role played by Canadian provinces than by American states in educational governance).

The political structure of Canada, with educational authority delegated to the widespread and diverse provinces, accounts for such factors as the greater strength of provincial than national superintendents' associations, their low mobility among provinces, and the regional jealousies and chauvinism that limit the profession's ability to shape national goals and standards in Canadian education. Religious, linguistic and cultural features of the country also impact upon the role. The original schools in virtually all provinces were established by religious orders, and there remain four distinct denominational school systems in Newfoundland as well as separate provincial systems of publicly-funded schools for Roman Catholics in Alberta, Saskatchewan and Ontario. School boards in Quebec are differentiated by both religion and language, and New Brunswick (as noted previously) has two unilingual provincial systems of education (English and French). Moreover, ancestral, heritage and native language schools and programmes are developing rapidly, especially in the larger cities, as Canada strives to foster its distinctive multiculturalism. Many school superintendents thus face interreligious, interlinguistic, and interracial conflicts and discrimination that are insoluble through education alone, hence requiring them to work closely with leaders of other community services (for example, health, housing and welfare), the legal profession, business and industry. The role has also been shaped by Canada's demographic and economic development — notably urbanization, which has necessitated the closing of schools and consolidation of districts in rural areas along with the accommodation of difficult adjustment and relocation problems in metropolitan centres, creating new challenges for school superintendents in both locations.

Canada's attitude toward itself is characterized by modesty, and this too is reflected in the school superintendency. Canadians do not fight wars of their own, they view themselves collectively as facilitators of harmony, they do not produce or recognize heroes, they dislike concentrations of power, they are unsure of their national identity, they do not aspire to dominate on the world scene, they want to be universally liked, and they evince a basic humility. Canada's school superintendents, portraying this collective self-concept, tend not to be highly visible, outspoken power-brokers but rather go about their work by leading gently and sensitively, often behind the scenes, reflecting a strong Protestant ethic. They are typical Canadians — human but not heroic, diligent but not dramatic, respectable but not revered.

Major Developments in the Evolution of the Role

The contextual influence of the country's nature on the development of the school superintendency has been supplemented by responses to certain tensions that have contributed more directly to the professional evolution of this role. There are six such tensions that deserve particular attention here.

The first is centralization vs decentralization. The delegation of certain responsibilities for educational governance from provincial governments to local boards occurred gradually and at varying rates across the country. It resulted from such factors as population growth and the tendency of people to cluster in communities, the consolidation of school districts for both economic efficiency and educational effectiveness, the popularization of a management philosophy espousing the devolution of policy formulation to a level as close as possible to the point of implementation responsibility, and the concomitant increase in competence of local trustees and superintendents. Yet, the authority of boards to employ their own superintendents varies: it is mandated by provincial legislation in Saskatchewan but subject to certain provincial constraints in Alberta; the appointment and dismissal of superintendents require Ministerial approval in Ontario; and the Atlantic provinces, among the earliest to establish schools, were among the latest in authorizing locally employed superintendents (the Maritime provinces, unlike their counterparts to the West, continue to concentrate the financing of education at the provincial level, and New Brunswick retains a higher degree of central control than do any of the other provinces). In Quebec, the conditions affecting superintendents' work are highly centralized in the Ministry of Education and British Columbia also remains relatively bureaucratized at the provincial level, with the result that superintendents in both these provinces seem somewhat more technocratically oriented than their counterparts elsewhere across the country; consequently, the tension between centralization and decentralization in them continues to be extreme and the relative stability achieved in other provinces remains apparently remote. This tension is uncomfortably threatening, frustrating and confusing to those in the superintendency and it impacts on the relative status of the role and its development as a consciously distinctive profession; where decentralization has progressed furthest, ambitious and able professionals aspire to a major local superintendency rather than to the deputy ministership, whereas the opposite seems true in the more centralized provinces. Overall, however, the tension between centralization and decentralization has been reduced in most regions by a notable shift in the latter direction which, in turn, has contributed to the increased professionalization of the Canadian school superintendency.

A second important tension in the role's evolution involves dual vs unitary structures. In the early phases of decentralization, responsibility for managing school districts was split between secretary-treasurers who administered financial affairs and school superintendents who administered educational programmes. The trend in confronting tensions which naturally arise from this situation has been away from the dual structure toward a unitary one in which the Superintendent of education has become the Chief Executive Officer of the board, but again this evolution has not been uniform across the country. While city school superintendents are virtually all chief executive officers, the incidence of unitary structures varies in non-urban areas. Moreover, superintendents are chief executive officers in Ontario and all the Atlantic provinces but almost half of the school districts in British Columbia still retain the dual system of management; on the Prairies, the unitary structure is provincially mandated in Saskatchewan, permissive in Manitoba, and variable in Alberta which retains a county system of government for rural areas wherein the educational and municipal jurisdictions are coterminous. Indeed, while this tension is in general being resolved in the direction of a unitary structure, it is still reflected in the continuing debate over whether or not chief business officers in school districts should be eligible for elevation to the superintendency.

A third tension relates to the role model of public servant vs corporate executive. The movements toward decentralization of educational authority to local boards and toward the unitary structure of school district management involve a fundamental shift in the professional orientation of school superintendents, from that of a provincial civil servant to that of a local CEO. This shift entailed a change in loyalty, a growth in loneliness, and an assumption of accountability; the Superintendent moved from being one of a group of individuals all identically accountable to a senior officer at the provincial level on whose expertise one could depend, toward being the only officer accountable to a board of lay people at the local level who had to be 'oriented' before they were capable of exercising their authority responsibly. Instead of following orders, the Superintendent became expected to issue them, to become concerned with doing right things and not only with doing things right. The obvious tension generated by this dramatic change in orientation is, however, diminishing with the gradual retirement of the cohort that had to make the adjustment.

Another identity-related tension is that of professional educator vs political manager. School districts have become larger with consolidation due to population concentration, trustees have become stronger with decentralization, knowledge and technology have become more complex and dominant, citizens have become more opinionated and demanding, social and economic problems have become more difficult and severe, and life in general has become more complicated. Consequently, the content and process of education have become so sophisticated and demanding that no single person can be expert or strong enough personally to direct the entire enterprise; hence, superintendents must delegate most of what constitutes instructional leadership. Moreover, environmental forces (such as socioeconomic crises, competing pressure groups, and media scrutiny) have gained such power that they require the direct energy and attention of the Superintendent since no one else has the position or information needed to encounter them. The result of these two factors is that the superintendent's ability and opportunity to lead as a professional educator have declined and the need and expectation for him or her to manage the politics of educational administration have increased. Thus, the tendency is for this conflict to be resolved in the direction of the political manager's role and away from that of the professional educator.

A fifth tension impinging upon the Canadian superintendency is that of external regulation vs self-determination. In most 'true' professions, the practitioners themselves establish educational requirements, administer licensing to practise, and determine entry to, and expulsion from, employability. For the school Superintendent, however, these powers are distributed among government agencies, professional associations, employing boards, and universities — and the pattern of distribution varies among provinces in Canada. External regulation is strongest in Ontario, the only province in which all educational supervisory officers are required to hold a certificate (based on oral and written examinations administered provincially) although the superintendents themselves remain sceptical of the value and validity of this procedure. Provincial regulation is least imposing in Manitoba, Nova Scotia, and Prince Edward Island where there are no legislative requirements for employment as a school superintendent, and most other provinces specify the amounts of university education and of teaching and administrative experience that are required for initial appointment as a Superintendent (although none mandates in-service training once such a position has been obtained). The preponderance of provincially regulated qualifications for the school superintendency in Canada, although clearly less imposing than in the United States, seems inconsistent with the trend toward decentralization mentioned previously. While the latter suggests a movement toward eventual self-determination, this evolution is severely retarded by the maintenance of external regulation at the provincial level in most parts of the country — hence, a tension which shows no clear signs of approaching resolution in the near future.

Finally, the Canadian school superintendency encounters tension in the balance of power with teachers and trustees. As noted previously, decentralization has strengthened the role of trustees, who have become at times competitive partners with administrators in the management of education. Thus, superintendents (virtually all of whom began their careers as teachers) have had to associate themselves more closely with trustees than with the teaching force. Other factors contributing to this trend are the responsibility of superintendents to trustees as their employers, the growing politicization of educational governance and industrialization of teachers' federations, the concentration of superintendents on the guidance and implementation of policy for which trustees, rather than teachers, are the supreme authority, and the increased bureaucracy of school districts that removes superintendents from much direct contact with teachers through delegation of instructional supervision, labour relations, and human resource management to subsidiary officials. The tension created by this shifting alliance at the individual level is exacerbated by the fact that, collectively, provincial teachers' and trustees' associations tend to be more powerful than provincial associations of school superintendents, with the possible exception of the one in Saskatchewan (which has the strength of establishment under its own Provincial Act). At the national level too, superintendents collectively enjoy less power than teachers and trustees. These differentials are not surprising, given the comparative recency of the superintendency's emergence as a role evolving toward consciously distinct professionalism, but the fact that the superintendent must continue to 'play catch-up' for some time to come inescapably adds tension to the evolution of this role.

Prospects for the Future

Notwithstanding the variegated nature of Canada as a country, and the consequent diversity of responses to tensions impinging upon the school superintendency, the role is gradually evolving, inevitably and inexorably, toward a distinctive and increasingly self-conscious profession nationwide. Certain features of its future development can be anticipated, and others can at least be aspired to.

As Canada's economy continues to shift from dependence on goods to reliance on services, from an agricultural and manufacturing base to a knowledge and information base, and from exploitation of physical resources to capitalization on human talents, one can reasonably expect an increase in the perceived importance of education and hence in the status of the school superintendent. This growing recognition will be fostered by superintendents themselves as they become more committed to and skilful at 'marketing' their systems. Just as Canada in general is, perhaps reluctantly, beginning to admit its production of a few 'superstars', so also may the school superintendency produce a few individuals recognized as 'great men' or 'great women' in the international firmament of education. This in turn should result in the according of more trust and respect to the role of Superintendent and that should accelerate its progress along the path of professionalization.

There are, however, a few clouds on this otherwise bright horizon. One concern is the veritable sameness of school superintendents across the country — typically white, middle-aged men with several years of teaching and administrative experience and some graduate study in educational administration (usually a master's degree). Like most Western industrialized nations, Canada's leadership tends to have been dominated by Caucasian males (many good ones) and this is certainly true of the school superintendency where, as in the United States, fewer than 3 per cent are women (even though at least a quarter of elementary principals are female) and the number of visible minority members who are superintendents is so negligible as to be indiscernible. This is patently inequitable and wasteful of human talent, and efforts to correct it are gradually emerging; but the initiative one might expect in the management of school districts is not yet apparent. It is difficult to preach the elimination of racism and sexism convincingly without practising it with visible success.

Other problems must be resolved as well if the potential for advancement of the superintendency is to be realized. Several studies claim that Canadian school superintendents have little if any time for thinking, planning, and studying (which bodes ill for the progress of this profession); one wonders if perhaps superintendents are too willing to allow external forces to determine how they spend their time, rather than taking conscious control of their work calendars themselves — perhaps reflecting a predisposition toward a self-image as pressed functionaries rather than thoughtful professionals. A somewhat related concern is that there is virtually no formal training available in

Canada specifically for the role of school Superintendent (although there is for the Principal) and the establishment of a national centre for this purpose needs to be seriously considered, perhaps along the lines of those that exist in the United States and elsewhere. This aspiration may be unrealistic, however, given the current provincial balkanization of Canadian education. It would be desirable for more influence in education to be applied at the national level, as is already the case with Canadian universities. It must be made easier for Canadians to move from one province to another and among regions without the confusion and risk of damage they currently confront in the education of their children. Constitutional constraints notwithstanding, ways must be found to permeate interprovincial boundaries and seek a more national perspective on the leadership of school districts in Canada. It is possible that the professionalization of the superintendency, if it continues to evolve, may in itself contribute to such a development. Two welcome corollaries might be the increased mobility of superintendents among provinces and a strengthened educational presence for Canada in international circles.

In conclusion, it has been argued here that Canada is a distinctive nation, its arrangements for the provision of educational services have developed in unique ways that reflect the particular distinguishing features of the country, and the role of the school superintendent is evolving in a characteristic manner. Despite the importance of trustees and community leaders, teachers and principals, parents and students, politicians and civil servants, it is the school Superintendent who is the leading professional educator in this country. The role must be understood, its incumbents' professional development has to be nurtured, and their work needs to be recognized, appreciated and fostered. They have come a long way professionally, but they have further to go. They must earn, through strong advocacy and demonstrated competence, the right to govern the development of their own profession. It is not yet clear that they have either the will or the ability to do so, but if they do not then the lost opportunity for dramatic educational leadership will be detrimental to the advancement of Canada as a whole. Recent trends, as outlined in this chapter, justify a cautiously optimistic outlook.

Acknowledgements

This chapter is based on material published in *The Canadian School Superintendent*, edited by J.W. Boich, R.H. Farquhar, and K.A. Leithwood (1989) Toronto, OISE Press. Reproduced by permission of the publisher.

13 The State Director of Education in Malaysia

Tunku Ismail Jewa

Malaysia as a country is made up of Peninsular Malaysia, which is situated on mainland South-east Asia, and the states of Sabah and Sarawak on the island of Borneo. The two regions with a total land area of 330,433 km² and an estimated population of seventeen million in 1989 are separated from each other by 740 km of the South China Sea. Politically, the country is a federation of thirteen states and two federal territories and has a Parliamentary system of Government.

The Malaysian Constitution provides that education is the responsibility of the Federal Government and thus the control and management of education falls to the Ministry of Education. The administration of education generally can be divided into four distinct hierarchical levels and the institutions representing these levels are the Ministry of Education at the federal level, the Education Department at the state level, the District Education Office at the district level, and the schools at the school level. However, in the states of Sabah and Sarawak, due to their large geographical regions, an Education Office is also established in each administrative unit of the state known as a Division.

At the federal level the Ministry of Education is headed by an elected Minister who is responsible for the country's education policy and at the state level the Director of Education is the Chief Executive of the State Education Department and is responsible for executing and implementing the educational programmes, projects and activities in the state. The Director is also responsible for the proper management of the District Education Office, which is actually an extension of the State Education Department and all the schools in the state. The size of the state in which each Director has to serve varies from 795 km² to 123,985 km².

Historical Development of State-level Administration

The administration of education at the state level is closely associated with the political development of the country and this, in turn, has influenced the role and tasks of the Director of Education. During the course of educational development in the country the Director of Education had been given different designations such as Inspector of Schools, Advisor on Education, Superintendent of Education and Chief Education Officer; but essentially the person is the Chief Executive of the Education Department in the state or territory. In the discussion which follows the administration of education at the state level during the Pre-Second World War Period (1900–40), the Japanese Occupation Period (1941–45), Pre-Independence Period (1946–56), and Post-Independence Period (from 1957) are examined.

Pre-Second World War Period (1900–40)

In 1900 the states in Peninsular Malaysia were made up of three different political units known as the Straits Settlements, the Federated Malay States and the Unfederated Malay States. British influence on them varied; for example, in the Straits Settlements the British had complete control while in the Federated Malay States the British colonial Government had partial control and in the Unfederated Malay States the British had no say in the state administration. However, by 1914 all the states in Peninsular Malaysia had secured British protection by treaty agreements. The administration of education in Peninsular Malaysia during this period was influenced by the British colonial policy of 'divide and rule'. This was convenient as the country had a multiethnic population composed of the Malays and other indigenous people, and the immigrant races who were mainly Chinese and Indians. As the result of this policy, education in the country was available in separate school systems serving different purposes using either the Malay language, Chinese, Tamil or English as the main medium of instruction.

Education for the Malays was provided by the Government up to the elementary level only and the main purpose of schooling was to teach Malay boys and girls reading, writing and arithmetic. Some vocational skills were also taught to enable pupils to become better farmers and fishermen. However, the British colonial Government did not take the responsibility of providing education for the Chinese and Indians, who were regarded as immigrants. Vernacular Chinese education became the responsibility of the Chinese community and employers in the rubber estates were responsible for building Tamil schools for the children of their employees as required by the Federated Malay States Ordinance of 1923. Education in English schools was available for all races in urban areas due to early efforts by Christian missionaries and the curriculum in these schools was patterned after the grammar school curriculum in Britain, with the view of producing junior administrative officers to support the British administration.

During this period the administration of education in the Straits Settlements and the Federated Malay States was centralized. An expatriate administrative officer was appointed as Director of Education to administer education in the states and was assisted by an Assistant Director of Education for Malay Schools, Chief Inspector of English Schools, Assistant Director for Chinese Education and Inspector of Tamil Schools. It can be seen that the main concern in educational administration at that time was to ensure that there was proper instruction in the various language-media schools and that attendance by pupils was satisfactory.

The administration of education in the Federated Malay States, on the other hand, was the responsibility of either the State Councils or Education Boards of the state governments concerned. The Director of Education of the Straits Settlements and the Federated Malay States also acted as the Advisor on Education in the Federated Malay States. At the state level a Superintendent of Education was appointed to manage the State Education Department and to organize and establish new schools according to the direction of the state governments.

During this period the administration of Sabah and Sarawak were still the responsibilities of the British Borneo Company and Rajah Brooke, respectively, although the two states were British protectorates since 1888 and so educational development there was based on the philosophies of the British Borneo Company and the Brooke family. Both states established education departments to manage schools and in the case of Sarawak the Department was headed by a Director while that in Sabah was managed by inspectors of schools.

There was little change in the organization and administration of education in the Straits Settlements, Federated Malay States and Unfederated Malay States during this period until the outbreak of the Second World War when the Japanese invaded the country on 8 December 1941.

Administration of Education During the Japanese Period (1941–45)

During the Second World War, the states forming the present Federation of Malaysia were occupied by the Japanese. During the Japanese military occupation of the country in 1941–45, Japanese education policy was that Malay and Tamil schools were to continue as before but with the addition that the Japanese language must be taught in the schools. The Japanese military administration established Japanese language schools to replace Chinese and English schools. During this period also, secondary education was discontinued and in its place several technical and vocational schools were established.

The administration of education during the Japanese occupation of Malaysia was centrally controlled by the Japanese military government and, therefore, administration of education at the state level ceased to exist. However, in 1943 four northern Malay states in Peninsular Malaysia (Kedah, Perlis, Kelantan and Terengganu) were given to Thailand for annexation as they were considered former Thai territories. Thus, the Thai Government was responsible for the civil administration of those states. During the short period of Thai administration the Thai authorities managed to set up an Education Department in each state with a Superintendent of Education to manage the schools. However, the war had damaged many school buildings and facilities and due to the shortage of staff and other resources the Superintendents found themselves ineffectual. Moreover, the Japanese remained the real masters of the country until the war ended in 1945.

Pre-Independence Period (1946–56)

When the Japanese occupation of Malaysia ended in August 1945, the country was placed under British Military Administration until the establishment of the Malayan Union in 1946. The Malayan Union was opposed by the Malays in the country and finally it was replaced by the Federation of Malaya in 1948. During this period a unitary central government was established with legislative powers. Thus, with the establishment of a strong central Government, Peninsular Malaysia was no more divided into Straits Settlements, Federated Malay States and Unfederated Malay States.

Post-war educational reconstruction in Peninsular Malaysia was chiefly aimed at unifying the Malays, Chinese and Indians to form one common nationality. This was important if the country was to achieve self-government. During this period the administration and financing of education became more centralized. The State Education Department in each state was headed by a Superintendent of Education. The tasks of the Superintendent of Education in the state became more varied than before the war as they now included the implementation of educational policy in the state, registration of teachers and pupils, examinations, finance, scholarships, staffing, in-service training, and other matters related to school administration.

In 1946 the states of Sabah and Sarawak became British Crown Colonies and the increased resources available enabled them to tackle their own post-war educational problems. The Directors of Education at the State Education Departments of Sabah and Sarawak continued to be responsible for the administration of education in their states.

Post-Independence Period (after 1957)

The Federation of Malaya achieved independence in 1957 and for the first time in the history of the country there was a definite national education policy. The ultimate objective of the policy was to establish a national system of education for all using the Malay language as the main medium of instruction. In 1963, when the Federation of Malaysia was established incorporating all the states of Peninsular Malaysia and the states of Sabah and Sarawak, this policy was later extended to East Malaysia.

During this period a Ministry of Education with an elected Minister of

Education was established to be completely responsible for all levels and aspects of education in the country in accordance with the Education Ordinance, 1957 and later the Education Act, 1961, which provided for the appointment of a Chief Education Officer in each state to be responsible for the administration of education at the state level. Thus, the designation of the Chief Executive of the State Education Department was changed from Superintendent of Education to Chief Education Officer during this time. This change reflected the new appointment to the service and also the nature of work now delegated to the State Education Department. After independence the post of Chief Education Officer was Malayanized and so local senior officers from the Malayan Education Service had to be appointed to the position and not expatriate officers from the administrative service as before.

The volume of work in the State Education Department had also increased with the implementation of the national education policy and was no longer limited to the supervision of schools, pupils, teachers and the curriculum. The main functions of the State Education Department now included construction and extension of schools, maintenance of schools, proper distribution of pupils, deployment of teachers, supervision of schools, disbursement of development funds, service matters, in-service training of teachers, examinations, and registration of pupils, teachers, schools, PTAs and School Board members. Today, the responsibilities of the State Education Departments have increased further with the reorganization of the Ministry of Education after the implementation of the Aziz Report on Teaching Services and, since 1973, the Chief Education Officer has been redesignated Director of Education.

The State Education Office can be considered as the agent for the Ministry of Education and the Director of Education its operating arm. The Director of Education has to work closely with twelve professional divisions in the Ministry of Education, which include Educational Planning and Research, Schools, Teacher Education, Curriculum Development Centre, Examination Syndicate, Federal Inspectorate of Schools, Technical and Vocational Education, Educational Media Service, Islamic Religious Education, Schools and Teachers Registration, Textbook Bureau and the National Institute of Educational Management. Thus, the structure and organization of the State Education Department administration are aimed at achieving efficiency in the implementation and execution of educational programmes, projects and activities planned by the Ministry of Education.

According to the Educational Planning and Research Division of the Ministry the administrative functions of the State Education Department at present include organizing and coordinating the administration of schools in the state with respect to staff and personnel establishment, finance and physical development; supervising education programmes in the state, especially those concerning curriculum, educational television and radio, textbook loan scheme, school libraries, co-curricular activities, guidance and counselling, language teaching, supplementary feeding scheme, the Malaysian School

Sports Council and other co-curricular programmes and activities; formulating and implementing state education development plans; and advising the Ministry, where necessary, on steps to be taken for the smooth implementation of the National Education Policy. The organizational structure of the state Education Department is displayed in figure 13.1.

New Roles and Challenges

Before Malaysia achieved independence in 1957 the legislative and executive authority for education rested with the State and Settlement Governments. However, after 1957 education became the responsibility of the Federal Government and a Ministry of Education was established to control and manage education in the country according to the Education Act, 1961. The Ministry was organized as a vast bureaucracy to do the job and the State Education Departments became part of the hierarchy in the bureaucratic organization.

In Malaysia today there are thirteen State Education Departments and one Federal Territory Education Department. The Education Departments are headed by thirteen male directors and one female director showing the trend that in the administration of education at the senior level male officers are still preferred although there are more women than men in the Malaysian Education Service.

The appointments of Directors of Education are still closely linked to the terms and conditions of the country's Civil Service. This means, among other things, that an officer can be transferred to a more senior post in the Ministry of Education or to another State Education Department with a higher salary grade. Thus, professional competency and efficiency have become secondary to seniority in terms of promotion. This sometimes may jeopardize the administration of education at the state level.

Although the Ministry of Education appears to be highly centralized in the administration of education, there is a certain amount of decentralization in practice especially in the implementation of education programmes at the state level. The Ministry of Education is mainly concerned with education policies but the success of such policies will depend on how efficiently the State Education Departments can implement them. As the state education chief, the State Director of Education is responsible to the Ministry of Education, as well as to the State Government through the State Executive Council, for any action taken relating to education. Sometimes decisions on school projects, educational programmes, posting of teachers, enrolment of pupils, etc. have to be changed by the Director because of political pressure and this dilemma will definitely pose a great challenge to the person.

The State Education Departments have become more complex in their organization with more funds to manage and more projects and programmes to implement. This will no doubt increase the responsibilities of the directors as their duties have become multifarious. The trend now is to delegate

Figure 13.1 The State Education Department

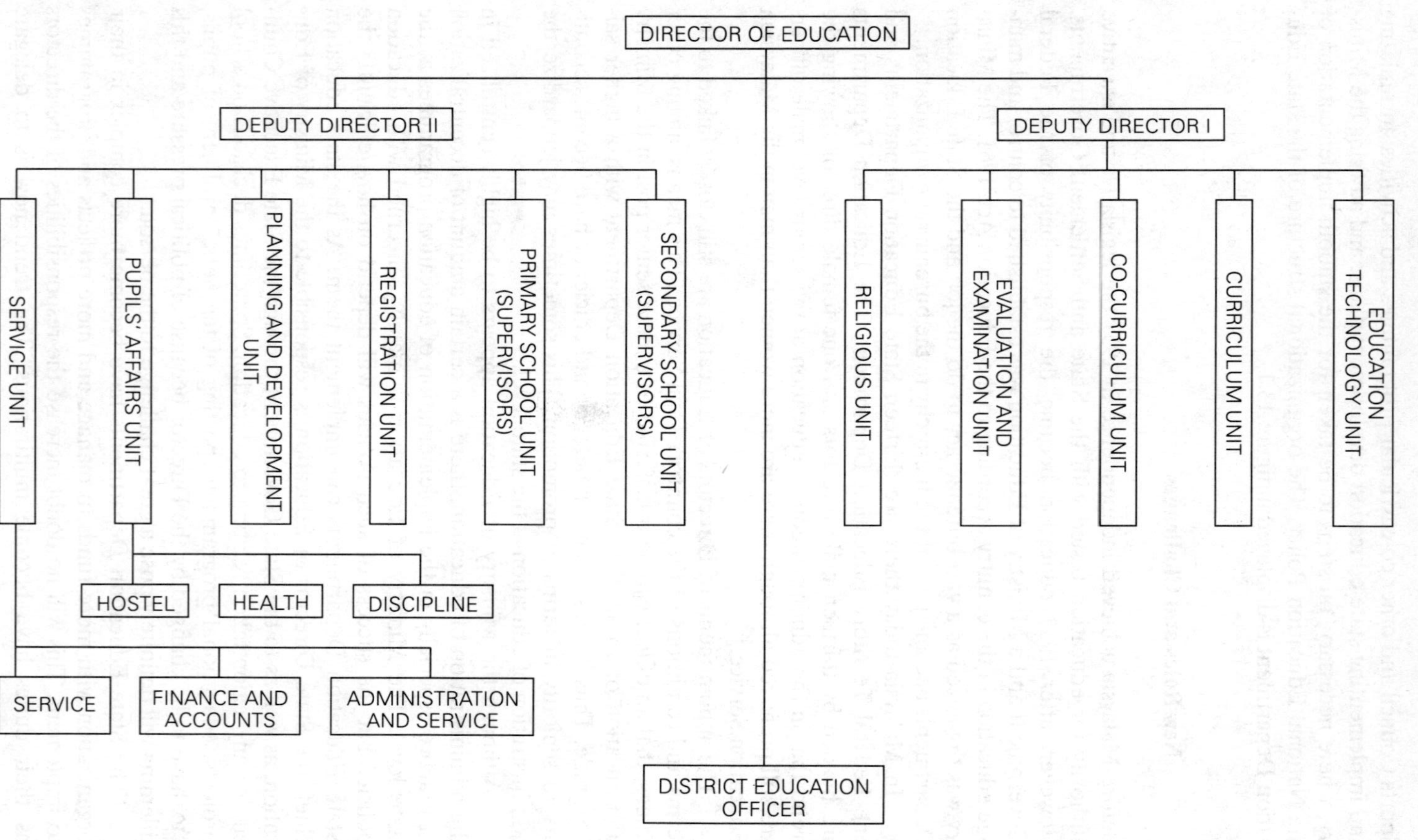

Source: The Educational Planning and Research Division, Ministry of Education, Malaysia.

specialized duties to specialist officers in the Education Departments and the District Education Offices. District level administration will become more important as the implementation of new curriculum, professional supervision of teachers and school supervision are given special attention.

Normally, in the administration of the State Education Department the State Director of Education has a dual role to play, as both the chief professional officer and the chief administrator. This can be rather demanding on the person as most Directors of Education have not had professional training in educational administration or other specialized areas of education after obtaining a first degree and basic teacher training. Few of them have higher degrees. However, with more postgraduate scholarships available from the Ministry future Directors of Education may receive specialized training relevant to their job.

Most Directors of Education handle more funds than their respective State Governments and need to be accountable. They also need to make important decisions regarding the interpretation of policies, implementation of educational programmes and projects, deployment of staff, building of new schools, purchase of land, staff training, etc. under the country's five-year development plan. The State Education Department therefore cannot expect to function as the clearing agent for the Ministry or be directed all the time by it. The Director of Education has now to function as an efficient and effective manager in order to make important decisions at the state level. Gone are the days when the Director could function as an overseer, professional officer or department director. The role is thus evolving towards that of a professional educational administrator.

References

Abdul Aziz Bin Mohd Zain, T.S. (1971) (Chairman) *Revised Report of the Royal Commission on the Teaching Services, West Malaysia*, Kuala Lumpur, Jabatan Cetak Kerajaan.

Abdul Rahman Bin Haji Talib (1960) (Chairman) *Report of the Education Review Committee*, Kuala Lumpur, Jabatan Cetak Kerajaan.

Abdul Razak Bin Hussain (1956) (Chairman) *Report of the Education Committee*, Kuala Lumpur, Government Printer.

Andaya, B.W. and Andaya, L.Y. (1988) *A History of Malaysia*, Hong Kong, Macmillan Education Ltd.

Chang, M.P. (1973) *Educational Development in Plural Society*, Singapore, Academia Publications.

Mahathir Bin Mohamad (1979) (Chairman) *Laporan Jawatankuasa Mengkaji Perlaksanaan Dasar Pelajaran*, Kuala Lumpur, Kementerian Pelajaran Malaysia.

Wong, H.K. and Ee, T.H. (1971) *Education in Malaysia*, Kuala Lumpur, Heinemann Educational Books (Asia) Ltd.

Wong, H.K. and Gwee, Y.H. (1972) *Perspectives: The Development of Education in Malaysia and Singapore*, Kuala Lumpur, Heinemann Educational Books (Asia) Ltd.

14 The Education Officer in New Zealand

Kenneth A. Rae

Ka pu te ruha; ka hao te rangitahi — the old net is cast aside; the new net goes fishing — whakatauki Maori

Introduction

On 1 October 1989 in New Zealand educational administration a new organization commenced operations — the Education Review Office — staffed by a newly-created class of education officers, Education Reviewers. The inspector of schools, known to pupils and teachers of primary and secondary schools of the nation in a variety of roles since 1877, has departed from the educational scene. To write in New Zealand in the early 1990s of the education officer/reviewer/inspector is to attempt an analysis in the midst of radical and system-wide change outlined in chapter 3, before the changes have been fully effected in practice at school level.

New Zealand has had, since the Education Act of 1877, a national system of primary education. From 1903 a national secondary pattern was provided for and universal entry into secondary schools achieved in 1945, after major curriculum reform which introduced the current 'core curriculum' and the raising of the school leaving age to 15. Significant amendments of the Education Act occurred in 1914 and 1964. A further major amendment was required in 1989, and from the Department of Education emerged a reshaped Ministry of Education, the new Education Review Office as a separate Government department, and a range of supplementary agencies or quangos. Restructuring at tertiary level required legislative action again in 1990.

The main islands of Aotearoa/New Zealand, Te Ika a Maui (The Fish of Maui) and Te Wai Pounamu (The Water of Greenstone) are together about the size of Britain or Japan. They were settled by a navigator people from Polynesia at least 1000 years ago. At the time of Captain Cook's voyages of exploration 220 years ago the Maori people of these islands probably numbered about 100,000 (Harker and McConnochie, 1985, page 10). The second wave of migration from Great Britain, and to a minor extent other parts of Europe, followed the whalers and sealers of the early nineteenth century, and proceeded apace subsequent to the signing of the Treaty of Waitangi in 1840 between a representative of Queen Victoria and a number of chiefs of the Maori tribes. Later in that year New Zealand was proclaimed a British colony by Governor Hobson – by consent in the north, by discovery in the south.

The population is not evenly distributed between the two main islands. Pastoral farming of sheep and the discovery of gold in the south during the last century, and the effects of land wars between colonial government and Maori in the north, meant that a majority lived in the South Island in 1900. Today just 26 per cent of the population of 3.3 million, a declining proportion, live there and 800,000, or just under 25 per cent of the total population, live in metropolitan Auckland, the largest city, in the north (Department of Statistics, 1987, page 110). The total population reached 2,000,000 in 1952 and 3,000,000 in 1973. A falling birthrate and patterns of external migration suggest it will not reach 4,000,000 until 2011. The Maori population, once predominantly a rural population, is today 403,000 or 12.5 per cent of the total. This is an increasing proportion, with a resurgence from a level of 40,000 at the turn of the century (Department of Education, 1982, page 12). The application 150 years later in an urbanized situation of the Treaty of Waitangi was a focus of debate on New Zealand's social structure and its education system in 1990, a year of commemoration and of a national election.

The Drive for Educational Change

After the election of 1987 returned New Zealand's fourth Labour Government for a second term, the education portfolio was taken by the Prime Minister, the Right Honorable David Lange. He had chosen to campaign in 1987 on the need to effect changes in the subsequent three years in the areas of social administration – health, education and social welfare – which would match the changes in economic management, fiscal policy and monetary policy achieved by his government in the face of financial crisis in its initial three-year term. (In August 1989 suddenly he announced his resignation from the Cabinet.) The emphasis on 'efficiency' in the first term was, however, to be supplemented in the second by an emphasis on 'equity'. The implicit tensions and their impact on education are discussed in the final sections of this chapter.

In July 1987 the Task Force to Review Education Administration, to be chaired by Mr Brian Picot, a prominent businessman and member also of the Council of the University of Auckland, was given the following terms of reference by the Government:

> To examine:
> — the functions of the Head Office of the Department of Education with a view to focusing them more sharply and delegating responsibilities as far as is practical;
> — the work of polytechnic and community college councils, teachers college councils, secondary school boards and school committees with a view to increasing their powers and responsibilities;
> — the department's role in relation to other educational services;
> — changes in the territorial organisation of public education with reference to the future roles of education boards, other education authorities, and the regional offices of the Department of Education;
> — any other aspects that warrant review. (Task Force Report, 1988, page 1).

The task force was charged also with ensuring that proposed structures were flexible and responsive to community needs and government objectives, that it identified costs and benefits of its recommendations and that it recommended on transitional arrangements. The review signalled a shift of the new minister away from the Curriculum Review pursued over three years by his predecessor with input of 30,000 public submissions. The terms of reference focus on administration as distinct from curriculum, and have posed considerable difficulty for those who believe educational administration is about administration of a curriculum, about its appropriateness, and about evaluation of change in the learners. The terms of reference reflected advice to the Government on education from its 'control departments', the Treasury and the State Services Commission.

The task force reported its findings as 'Administering for Excellence'. The recommendations reflected its terms of reference. Not surprisingly, but in contradiction of OECD reviewers of only five years earlier who had commented on the degree of satisfaction in New Zealand with the education system (OECD, 1983, page 10), it found that substantial changes were required, that present structures were 'creaking and cumbersome' and, without overall plan or design, the result of 'increments and accretion'. It concluded:

> The time has come for quite radical change, particularly to reduce the number of decision points between the central provision of policy funding and service, and the education delivered by the schools or institutions. (p. 36)

The changes to be noted in the proposed new structures were:

> — the establishing throughout the land of single-school boards elected by parents with powers of governance and the appointment

of staff, a structure long known in secondary education but a bold initiative in the primary sector, the more so given the size of a majority of primary schools;

— the bulk funding of the boards, with responsibility on them to adopt a budget on the recommendation of the Principal, who, as a member of the board in the role of manager, enters into a new relationship with the staff;

— the passing to the board of responsibility within nationally negotiated industrial awards for setting up a personnel policy which conforms to the 'good employer' and 'equal opportunity' criteria of state sector industrial relations legislation;

— the charging of each board with responsibility for maintenance and minor capital works;

— the complete removal therefore of property supervision, personnel, finance, and professional guidance roles of education boards and regional offices of the department and their removal from the scene;

— at the centre a fined-down ministry, and clear separation of policy makers from deliverers of 'services';

— the knitting together of centre and periphery, to meet concerns for national comparability and equity for disadvantaged groups, by the device of the charter, a schedule of agreed school objectives within national guidelines, seen by the task force as a 'lynch pin';

— the achievement of quality assurance by an independent review and audit agency, charged with measuring the educational and managerial achievements of schools against their charter objectives by school visits every two years; and

— two safety nets to allow discussion and negotiation without fallout — at district level the Community Education Forums able to make representations to the Ministry and at national level a Parents Advocacy Council able to report to the Minister on the one hand or advise parents on issues such as home schooling on the other.[1]

Amended in some details in the light of the public response invited over the next six weeks, the task force proposals were incorporated in a policy document prepared by Government officials, signed by the Minister in August 1988, and published as *Tomorrow's Schools* (Lange, 1988).

Through early 1989, after installation of a change agent Director-General recruited from the restructured Ministry of Forestry on an eighteen-month contract, working parties completed their follow-up to the policy statements of *Tomorrow's Schools*. Attention then focused in turn on the election of boards of trustees, accomplished with the help of massive television publicity in April; development of charter material, especially the national guidelines component, delivered to the new boards in May; and creation of the appropriate block-funding formulae for an operating grant and a salaries grant, the former delivered in preliminary form to boards in June. The grant included loadings for equity concerns — to support work with Maori pupils and in support of Maori language, and to support schools with pupils disadvantaged by socio-economic factors. Because of difficulties of implementation, bulk funding of salaries was put on hold for at least one year.

At the centre, in May 1989 a combined briefing by the Implementation Unit of the Department of Education and by the State Services Commission revealed to education employees and board members the new structures of the national network — a reshaped Ministry of Education (with a significant district presence); a new Education Review and Audit Agency (with ministerial approval renamed and reshaped by its new Chief Executive after one month as the Education Review Office); two new quangos, the Special Education Service and the Early Childhood Development Unit; and in outline the Teachers Registration Board and the Parents Advocacy Council.

Administering for Excellence and *Tomorrow's Schools* had been paralleled in the early childhood field by *Education to be More* and *Before Five*. In the tertiary and allied fields the *Report of the Working Party on Post-Compulsory Education and Training* was to be followed by *Learning for Life I* and later *Learning for Life II*. Changes in the early childhood field were built into the structures to operate from 1 October 1989. Decisions by the Government and legislation were scheduled for 1990 in the tertiary field of PSET (Post-School Education and Training), although the initial appointments in advance of legislation have been made to a National Education Qualifications Authority while the University Grants Committee is set down for dissolution.

The New Model of Educational Reviews of Effectiveness

Administering for Excellence in May 1988 proposed (page 60) that a Review and Audit Agency would make judgments on both local and national concerns, the Ministry as well as the boards, as it was responsible for:

- the review and audit of every institution's performance in terms of its charter; and
- the provision of independent comment on the quality of policy advice, and on how well policies are implemented at national level.

At the school level the review was to have as its purpose (page 60) 'helping the institution assess its own progress towards achieving its objectives' (a catalyst role) and providing 'a public audit of performance in the public interest' (an audit role).

Reviews in the proposals of the task force (page 61) would be undertaken at two-year intervals by 'a multidisciplinary team' consisting of one or more 'curriculum specialists', a coopted principal, a community representative and a financial/property/management support officer. Preliminary data-gathering would be followed by a visit to produce a report on strengths and weaknesses, which would make recommendations for improvement. The review was capable of being a 'cooperative attempt to improve the quality of education being provided ... an impartial and informed assessment ... able to be incorporated in the institution's staff development programme'. This report in preliminary form would be left with the school to allow comment and/or changes in school practice. After a second visit one term later the final report would be made public and referred to the Minister. One outcome for the Board of Trustees of the school could be a requirement to ensure change — failing which there could be dismissal by the Minister and replacement by a commissioner. For the review team, there was a prohibition against further advice and guidance outside of the report, to ensure autonomy in their audit function. In the subsequent negotiations of the officials groups, stress fell increasingly on the audit role, but the emphasis has shifted back in the Education Review Office subsequently created.

Negotiations had to incorporate the later reports on educational restructuring. The parallel report on early childhood education recommended annual 'developmental' visits for such institutions and services, to be provided by the Office; the other report, on post-school education and training, recommended audit of the performance of tertiary institutions with regard only to the equity and equal employment objectives of the charters which they are from 1990 required to draw up. School visits are being fitted, in the light of these requirements, to a three-year cycle — which matches the term of office of the boards of trustees but is a target the former inspectorates found difficult to achieve.

The Office has come into existence with a central office, four regional managers and eleven district teams. Personnel are grouped for each review visit according to the planning of the district manager from among the total district corps of available reviewers. One reviewer in each district has been recruited for expertise in financial management, one for expertise in property management, and one to report on development in institutions of policies of equal employment opportunities. One officer has been appointed in each region to coordinate oversight of issues of Maori education and to knit together those officers identifying as Maori or supportive of Maori interests.

The reshaping of the department to a 'Ministry of Education' has seen the shedding of some functions to other agencies — the advisory services to teachers colleges and special education support and early childhood support to new quangos, the Special Education Service and the Early Childhood Development Unit respectively. These agencies, like the Ministry, are subject to comment from the Education Review Office on their efficiency and effectiveness in their impact on schools.

Gianotti, the Chief Executive, was formerly Secretary to the Picot Committee, after a career in education spanning primary teaching to District Senior Inspector of Primary Schools. He has stated clearly his belief (1989) that the Office can fill its role of guarantor of educational standards only if it wins confidence by recruiting reviewers of proven experience in management — i.e. officers drawn from traditional inspectorate sources of principalships in the larger primary schools and from senior head of department and above in secondary schools. Guiding principles for reviews developed by managers of the Education Review Office have reinforced the shift from processes of external audit to internal appraisal and review. Improved education for learners is posited as the central goal and a review is to be consultative and to build on the institution's own review processes — to encourage all places of learning to develop mechanisms of self-evaluation.[2] Snook (1989) has observed that 'the Review and Audit Agency has been reclaimed by the profession'.

Advice to the New Zealand Government from Outside Education

The changes in educational administration being put in place in New Zealand have been shaped by a range of pressures from within the structures of the New Zealand state which are responding to political and economic crisis. They derive especially from thrusts by the 'control departments'. These pressures were apparent in the lead-up to the creation of the task force, were reflected in the report, and continued to be felt in the negotiations at officials level to prepare the policy document *Tomorrow's Schools* after the 1988 period of public comment. The appointments of educationists as chief executives of both the Ministry of Education and the Education Review Office suggest some movement back from earlier control coming in from beyond 'the education family'. Both the Treasury and the State Services Commission continue as significant actors in the new patterns of educational administration, however, alongside the Ministry of Education and the Education Review Office.

The Treasury Critique

The Treasury in 1987 published a critique of education policy and administration as 'Government Management: Brief to the Incoming Government, 1987, vol II. Education Issues'. The Treasury's principal concern was development of policy — and costs — in education by accretion, without prioritization and without trimming of programmes considered to have served their time. The Treasury was offended also by absence, as in the Curriculum Review 1984–87, of any calculation by the Department of Education of economic costs and benefits. Their published critique also suggested possible decline of educational standards, noted an absence of responsiveness to government policy and to economic change, and alleged the 'capture' of the service by its providers, who for no economic benefit discernible to the Treasury had inflated Vote-Education, in their own interest. It expressed concern also at the persistence of inequity, and so inefficiency, in the differential achievement of disadvantaged populations. It affirmed present costs were not sustainable and the role of the state in education required redefinition.

The most extensive analysis of these Treasury views as an example of policy proposals arising from a 'New Right' philosophy is that of Lauder, Middleton, Boston and Wylie (1988) published in successive numbers of the *New Zealand Journal of Education Studies*. They cite extensive research from New Zealand and overseas that indicates inequality of educational opportunity arises rather from the inequalities of the society in which the education takes place. They cite also evidence refuting claims of declining standards. The most extensive analysis of the processes creating educational and social inequality in New Zealand is probably that of Nash (1986, page 136). He has drawn on Bourdieu and Boudon to distinguish 'primary' and 'secondary' effects as children from class-located families make crucial choices in the cultural processes of education and schooling and in their movement to work, or further study, or to unemployment. The Treasury analysis is inadequate by comparison.

The Treasury, through its sponsorship of public sector accounting legislation and the new requirements on annual reporting formats, continues in 1990 to influence management practices at school level, and has placed demands on the boards as for authorities controlling major 'State Owned Enterprises' and on principals as on their CEOs.

The State Services Commission Agenda

The Commission, the other control department, has responsibility for effective personnel and management policies throughout the state sector. The commissioners had by 1987 a long-standing concern about the management style of the Department of Education and its habit of extended consultation with the associations of teachers and of employing boards. The Commission was dismayed in particular from 1986 that the recommendations of the first project of Parliament's new Education and Science Select Committee, a bipartisan report on *The Quality of Teaching* with an emphasis on an audit function to promote 'efficiency' in schools, had not been taken up by the Department.

The State Services Commission believed that a new management ethos in education was needed at the levels of both the department and the schools — and that the absence of clear objectives and management planning could no longer be tolerated. They combined with the Treasury in 1987 in advising Government on the terms of reference for the 'task force to investigate educational administration'. The terms were clear signals for a diminished department with a more closely specified set of functions. Their combination is the subject of several papers by Macpherson (1989), a researcher from Australia on secondment to SSC in the early part of 1988. His analysis of the New Zealand restructuring accords increased significance to the commission vis-a-vis the Treasury, locating their work on education within a network of task forces reporting to the Deputy Prime Minister as Chairman of the Cabinet's Social Equity Committee.

The Commission in 1990 in terms of state sector legislation maintains a significant role to school level, as the lead actor for the new School Trustees Association in negotiation of personnel policy, no longer a responsibility of the Ministry of Education, and as writer of the draft principal's contract.

The Education Perspective

Mainstream education thinking in New Zealand on effective schools has emphasized the recruitment of a qualified and trained teaching force, and has charged the principal to work in a collegial manner with the staff to develop school schemes of work appropriate to the strengths of the professional team and to the needs of the student population and the community. The major theoretical thrust has been that of 'school development' (for example, Stewart and Prebble, 1985) which was disseminated particularly in 1978–84 in-service courses on educational management, sponsored by the Department to create a network of resource persons in all districts. Education was, however, at a disadvantage at system level in 1988 as the task force reported.

Following the retirement of Renwick as Director-General an interregnum occurred with no permanent appointment made. In the time of public response after the task force report, 'the education family' continued at a disadvantage concerning a proposal put to communities as a laudable matter of community choice and the confounding of bureaucracy. The recommended abolition of education boards and major sections of the Department meant that comment by educational administrators could be dismissed as self-interested views. This may be linked back to the perspective developed in the earlier Treasury critique of education as a self-serving profession.

However, a majority of the task force members, when appointed in July 1987, were educationists, administrators lay or professional. Although constrained by the terms of reference, they found room in their report for an emphasis on review complementary to audit, and for a degree of cooperation in the relationship proposed between the authority and schools. Recruitment to the newly-announced Education Review Office, as proposed in 1989 by its Chief Executive who had been their Secretary, and the developing review methodologies are confirmation of that thrust.

Discussion

The dominant energizing 'myth' (Beeby, 1986; Renwick, 1985) of New Zealand education for forty years was that of 'equality of opportunity'. By the 1980s, under the sponsorship of Renwick as Director-General, increasingly the discourse was of 'equity' as measured by educational outcomes. From the first report of the National Advisory Committee on Maori Education, 'He Huarahi' (1972), it was evident that such equity of outcomes had not been achieved through a generation of rapidly expanding educational provision. The social debate has broadened discussion of equity issues since to incorporate women and girls, learners with special abilities, and New Zealand's other ethnic minorities. In line with the Government's strategy for its second term and in the lead-up to 1990, the new structures of educational administration were frequently praised by Prime Minister Lange because they 'empowered' the trustees of boards of the 2700 schools of the nation in the common search for equity. This final section of the chapter suggests a turning point in the debate on equity and the tensions that will persist for those charged with supervision of education in New Zealand. Whether the tensions will be dynamic or satisfying will depend on management decisions taken at both national and local levels. They will test the judgment in particular of education reviewers appraising school managements in the performance of charter responsibilities negotiated with or imposed by the ministry.

Equity Issues

For the new structures government policy statements of 1988–89 proposed achievement of equity as a criterion – but linked to effectiveness, efficiency and economy, so giving at least two strikes to those whose concern for change was in the direction of closer financial management. Financial flows were to be 'targeted', and the laying of equity responsibilities on boards of trustees in the model charter objectives was accompanied by the setting up of an Education Review and Audit Agency to measure outcomes. In the May 1989 recruitment handout to staff moving to the new structures, however, 'equity' was defined as 'distribution of resources to promote equality *of opportunities*, even if this means unequal distribution' (my emphasis). This appears a move back from the goal of equity of outcomes, as proposed in past years by Renwick.

Equity as a matter of informed educational choice and of mere logistics of targeted resource flows is, however, an inadequate concept. It requires deeper analysis in the light of the concepts of 'habitus', and of schooling as 'cultural reproduction', derived from Bourdieu. Such perspectives have been advanced in a critique of New Zealand Maori education policies by Harker and McConnochie (1985), and more extensively applied by Codd, Harker and Nash (1985, pp. 10–12) in establishing 'strategies of family reproduction' in a class-society as the driving force behind persisting educational and social inequality within New Zealand's system of State-sponsored education. Both Lauder *et al.* (1988) and Snook (1989) have even gone so far as to doubt the genuineness of those in the control departments in their propounding of the principle of 'equity' in tandem with 'efficiency'.

Equity is a matter of values, efficiency a matter of technique; equity a matter of ends, efficiency a matter of means. They are of different orders of consideration, and their achievements are not of necessity linked. Snook (1989) concluded:

> A free market economic system as advocated by the Treasury cannot deliver equity; at every step of the way it operates against equity. The invocation of the term 'equity' is a blatant appeal to local concerns and is in no way a genuine feature of the reforms. To be cynical 'equity' is the dogma used to sell freemarket policies to New Zealand. (p. 10)

Objectives and Community-Based Charters

The new structures propose clarity of objectives as the path to clarity of evaluation of educational outcomes. Education, however, is about growth and change. More fundamentally, educational objectives spring from values, about which there will be contestation and debate. It is to be expected, therefore, that ambiguity and tension concerning objectives will persist, especially in issues thrown up by the evolving policy of the government concerning the Treaty of Waitangi and a bicultural New Zealand, and imposed by model objectives on boards in some cases reluctant to accept this lead.

Tension will also persist between the centre and the periphery, especially if the centre views education as mere service delivery and the periphery sees schools as learning communities. There will be tension between accountability of the Minister in Parliament to questions on a centrally-funded system, and a different accountability of each board and school to its community. In these communities social inequalities have been increased in recent years as a consequence of policies of economic restructuring. Changing patterns of incomes and heightened levels of unemployment, especially youth unemployment, have struck communities differentially across New Zealand, initially hitting the regions rather than the cities. The stress has focused also on the Maori and Pacific Island communities in particular.

The charter as 'lynch pin', as outcome of three-way negotiation between Minister, board of trustees and community, has been flawed in the process of the initial implementation. Debate over delayed funding of schools raised doubts in late 1989 for many boards on the nature of the agreement they were being asked to reach. The drive to produce guidelines early in 1989 produced not performance objectives but blanket demands on schools, in some cases achievements beyond the ability of the state with all its resources in the past to provide (for example, management training and development for principals, staff and trustees — and access to education in Maori for all students whose parents so desire). As a management tool and a basis for review, a charter composed of the present compulsory components is not an adequate starting point. The charter and the guidelines require further development, preferably out of negotiation in a partnership relationship with schools as learning communities, and out of consideration of ethics and values as well as of administrative techniques. The Education Review Office will be required to comment on such issues.

Support for Schools

Support services in times of change are vital to sustain the teachers and especially the principals. The changes occurring in New Zealand have been based on the thesis, however, of reallocation of existing resources. So resources that could have been devoted to consultancy in school development and community consultation, or a network of district superintendences of schools, or alternative models of development and supervision, have not become available because of policy decisions in favour of close monitoring of an accountability laid directly on the local school, its trustees and the principal.

Tensions will persist because of the pressures of the timescale imposed on the total change in educational administration. There is New Zealand evidence especially from Ramsay (1984, p. 224) that schools in touch with their communities do meet their students' needs more effectively. Schools, however, need time to establish ongoing and self-sustaining procedures of consultation. The current changes in New Zealand were a process of cultural interruption in 'the education family', marked by break-neck speed and observed symptoms of 'future shock' among teachers and administrators. (CRRISP, 1989, page 37).

Education Service Centres, free-standing client-driven supporters of schools in the Picot design, had a difficult and belated birthing, fraught with political charge and counter-charge. They are unique to New Zealand in their provision of support for schools in all areas except the core business of curriculum. They may in fact develop in this area, and so come into competition with the colleges of education, to whom are currently assigned the Advisory Services of the former Department.

The Crowded Playing Field

The Picot Report in 1988 presented administrative structures elegant in their simplicity, on first approach. The reality for schools in 1990 was not simplified relationships but multiplying relationships. Former communication pathways disappeared on 1 October 1989. Communication pathways within, as well as between, the organizations at the centre have yet to be fully established. Building networks across the education family became a priority in 1990. Sallis (1988) from England is quite clear that partnership between the professionals and the governors is vital to the restored health of a state education system under conditions of devolved responsibility. Such a perception could be the motivation for the State Services Commission to maintain a participation that is impacting at the level of personnel relationships in the individual school as it continues its educational agenda promoting a narrowly technical concept of efficiency.

From the perspective of the players, the 1990 playing field did not appear very level. It certainly appeared crowded. The problem was that the Ministry was charged with marking the field for the precision plays of netball in its directive charter requirements, the review office prefers the fluid and close associations of rugby in its proposed cooperative reviews, and the commission is likely to determine that the game for this month is not hockey but hurling as it assumes the role of employers' advocate in the annual rounds of award negotiations.

The State and State-Schooling

At a deeper level, tensions discussed above will be confounding to the extent that concepts of 'community' and 'the state' remain untheorized. The substantial normative overlay of the concept of community has already been referred to in passing. The 'reform' of educational administration was presented in 1988 as desirable because it returned 'power' to the community from the bureaucracy. The locus of 'control' on the other hand was yet to be established by practice, as schools presented charters locally developed for approval by the new Ministry for the first time in 1990.

A powerful analysis from within New Zealand of contesting theories of the state was advanced by Wilkes (1982), who in the context of issues of community development critiqued the pluralist state of the Weberian tradition driven by the purpose of serving 'the common good' as an 'instrument of reason.' Drawing on Habermas he posed by way of contrast the structuralist analysis of the role of the state in a developed capitalist economy like New Zealand, engaged of necessity in functions of class production and class reproduction, resultant ambiguities providing contestable locations for those seeking social reform. Such a perspective has been lacking from the educationist side in the New Zealand debate on state-sponsored education of recent years.

Conclusion

In an address to school principals in early 1989, Prime Minister Lange stated the Government's goals for education:

> By international standards we have good schools. But the quality of our education system must be improved for the sake of our students and our country. We must make education more responsive to changes in our society. We must make our allocation of resources more equitable.

> For our young people to make their way in the modern world, and for New Zealand to be competitive in international markets we need better schools, schools in which our young people are happy, are stretched and learn well. Standards must be met. Basic skills must be learned. Scholarship must be valued and rewarded at all levels.
>
> The Government wants to see every young person leave school with a sense of achievement, a sense of self-esteem, and a sense of purpose. These are the government's goals for education.

Within national guidelines and nationally-determined resource allocations, the responsibility for managing to achieve such goals has been devolved to principals and trustees at school level, embodied in the objectives of the charters of their schools. The officers of the Education Review Office are charged to be guarantors — to Government, to parents, to students — of quality education in each school and comparability of outcomes among schools.

The quality of the officers and their development of perceptions beyond the technical (of schooling as cultural process in a wider sociological perspective), and the quality of the relationships they establish with the leaders of the schools based on such understandings, will determine their Office's effectiveness, its efficiency and economy — and whether or not equity is to be served. Government decisions in the spring of 1990, to downsize the Office, are also likely to have an impact on its performance.

> Nau te rourou, naku te rourou
> Ka ora ai te manuhiri.
> With your food basket, and with mine,
> the guests will be well fed.

Notes

1 The 'Executive Summary' of the Task Force to Review Education Administration (pages xi–xii) read as follows:

> Individual learning institutions will be the basic unit of education administration. This is where there will be the strongest direct interest in the educational outcomes and the best information about local circumstances. People in the institutions should make as many of the decisions that affect the institution as possible — only when it could be inappropriate should decisions be made elsewhere.
>
> The running of learning institutions should be a partnership between the teaching staff (the professionals) and the community. The mechanism for creating such a partnership will be a board of trustees.
>
> Each institution requires clear and explicit objectives, drawn up locally within national objectives. These objectives would reflect both national requirements and local needs, and would be set out in a charter.

The charter is the 'lynchpin' of the structure and would act as a contract between the community and the institution, and the institution and the state.

Each institution would be held accountable, for meeting the objectives set out in its charter, by an independent Review and Audit Agency. This agency will report directly to the Minister and would also comment on the performance of other elements of the administrative structure.

In a structure in which responsibility is placed mainly at institutions which are free to choose their own services, there is no longer a need for education boards in their present form. There will, however, be an increasing demand for education services and so there are considerable opportunities for education boards to turn themselves into education service centres which supply a range of competitive services to all sectors from early childhood to tertiary. Institutions will also be free to cooperate within their own groupings and to buy any services they want, where they want.

Community education forums will be established to promote debate on educational issues and to provide an opportunity to raise ideas and concerns. Forums will assist the local resolution of problems, as well as channelling information into the policy making process.

A Ministry of Education will provide policy advice to the Minister, through an Education Policy Council, and will implement national policies approved by the Minister. To avoid confusion of roles and to keep policy free of self-interest, the Ministry will have no part in the provision of education services. The Ministry will be managed by one Chief Executive and will have three units. These are for policy formation, for policy implementation, and for property services. We decided against three separate structures in order to avoid confused accountability and lack of coordination. The internal structure of the Ministry will be a matter for the Chief Executive.

To promote openness and to bring a wider perspective into policy advice, an Education Policy Council is proposed. The Council will consist of the four most senior officials of the ministry and four outside appointees. Two of these will be appointed by the Minister and two by an electoral college. The Education Policy Council will ensure that policy advice retains the confidence of parents, teachers and the wider community.

Providers of education are likely to remain better funded and organized than consumers. To redress the balance by helping parents to promote their views and to become better informed about how the system works, a Parent Advocacy Council will be established. The Parent Advocacy Council will also assist parents who are seeking programmes which are within the national objectives, but which no local school is willing to provide. When no school can be persuaded to offer the programme, and when at least twenty-one children are involved, the Parent Advocacy Council will negotiate with the Ministry to set up an alternative institution. This institution will have state funding, perhaps as a 'school within a school'.

The Education Policy Council was not adopted by the government. The restructured Ministry currently has eleven divisions.

2 An interim statement on principles for reviews of schools, developed by managers of the Education Review Office in November 1989, read as follows:

> A review will lead to improved education for all learners (students and staff) in the institution.
>
> A review will be a forward looking, empowering experience, building positively on the strengths of the institution.
>
> A review must be centred on the institution's charter objectives and reflect the context, the nature of the school and its community. A review must be culturally appropriate and sensitive to community expectations.
>
> A review will engage teachers, trustees and community and be concerned with change in practices leading to the institution improving its effectiveness in its use of resources from Vote-Education.
>
> A review will be consultative, and within the time available, involve negotiation of assessment criteria with the institution and cooperative planning between the institution, the community, and the Education Review Office.
>
> The review team will aim to reach agreement with the board and principal on the purpose of the review before the review starts and use a process that is transparent to the institution.
>
> A review will focus on the institution's own review processes and mechanisms to encourage the school to develop such self evaluation.
>
> A review report must present a realistic, substantiated and balanced perspective/ description/analysis of the institution's performance.
>
> A report should be written in such a way that it will be appropriate for all audiences, especially the community and general public.
>
> A report should be useful, helpful, honest with no gloss and convey clear messages. Good communication should be paramount.
>
> A review must be based on agreed explicit district methodologies developed within nationally agreed principles.
>
> Review teams should be led in the first instance by people with sector credibility and include reviewers from a range of disciplines.
>
> Reviews should be carried out effectively and efficiently.
>
> Note — These principles are seen as capable of further development.

References

ALCORN, N. (1988) 'Towards policy guidelines of educational management training in New Zealand' in WYLIE, C. (Ed) *Proceedings of the First Research into Educational Policy Conference*, Wellington, New Zealand Council for Educational Research.

APPLE, M.W. (Ed) (1982) *Cultural and Economic Reproduction in Education*, London, Routledge and Kegan Paul.

BALLARD, R. and DUNCAN, P. (1989) '*Role of the Principal and Trustees in Tomorrow's Schools*' based on a paper presented to annual conference of Secondary Principals Association of New Zealand (mimeo), Wellington, Department of Education.

Barrington, J.M. and Beaglehole, T.H. (1974) *Maori Schools in a Changing Society*, Wellington, New Zealand Council for Educational Research.

Caldwell, B.J. and Spinks, J.J. (1988) *The Self Managing School*, London, Falmer Press.

Codd, J., Harker, R. and Nash, R. (1985) *Political Issues in New Zealand Education*, Palmerston North, Dunmore.

Curriculum Review Research in Schools Project (1989) *The Initial Impact of the Curriculum Review Exploratory Project*, CRRISP Occasional Paper No 3 and *Effecting Change in Schools: Some Implications of the Initial Phase of the Curriculum Review Exploratory Project*, CRRISP Occasional Paper No 4, Hamilton, University of Waikato.

Currie, G. *et al.* (1962) *Report of the Commission on Education in New Zealand*, Wellington, Government Printer.

Dakin, J.C. (1973) *Education in New Zealand*, Newton Abbot, David and Charles.

Department of Education (1982) *Education Policies in New Zealand Report prepared for the OECD Examiners by the Department of Education in March 1982*, Wellington, Government Printer.

Department of Education (1987) *Submission to the Royal Commission on Social Policy from Department of Education*, Wellington, Department of Education.

Department of Education (1989) *The Reform of Education Administration in New Zealand; Information for Employees* (mimeo), Wellington, Department of Education.

Department of Statistics (1987) *New Zealand Pocket Digest of Statistics*, Wellington, Government Printer.

Education and Science Select Committee (1986) *Report on the Inquiry into the Quality of Teaching*, Wellington, Government Printer.

Gianotti, M. (1989) *Education Review Office* (mimeo), Wellington, Department of Education.

Harker, R.K. and McConnochie, K.R. (1985) *Education as Cultural Artefact: Studies in Maori and Aboriginal Education*, Palmerston North, Dunmore.

Kawharu, I.H. (Ed) (1989) *Waitangi Maori and Pakeha Perspectives of the Treaty of Waitangi*, Auckland, OUP.

Lange, D. (1988) *Tomorrows Schools: The Reform of Education Administration in New Zealand*, Wellington, Government Printer.

Lange, D. (1989) *New Directions for Schools*, speech to Auckland University Principals Centre Seminar (mimeo), unpublished speech notes.

Lauder, H., Middleton, S., Boston, J. and Wylie, C. (1988) 'The third wave: Critique of the New Zealand Treasury's report on education', *NZJEA*, **23**, 1 and 2.

McKenzie, D. (1988) 'Responses to Picot: Education after the Picot Report', *NZJEA*, **3**.

Macpherson, R.J.S. (1989) 'Why politicians intervened in the administration of education in New Zealand', *Unicorn*, **15**, 1.

Matthews, K. (1987) 'The long and winding road: The role of the nineteenth century school inspector: A case study' in Openshaw, R. and McKenzie, D. (Eds) *Reinterpreting the Educational Past: Essays in the History of New Zealand Education*, Wellington, New Zealand Council for Educational Research.

Nash, R. (1983) *Schools Can't Make Jobs*, Palmerston North, Dunmore.

Nash, R. (1986) 'Education and social inequality: The theories of Bourdieu and Boudon with reference to class and ethnic difference in New Zealand', *New Zealand Sociology*, **2**.

OECD (1983) *Review of National Policies of Education, New Zealand*, Paris, OECD.

ORANGE, C. (1987) *The Treaty of Waitangi*, Wellington, Allen and Unwin and Port Nicholson Press.

RAE, K.A. (1988) 'Rural education in New Zealand: A case study in provision and policy making', *NZJEA*, **3**.

RAE, K.A. (1989) 'New principles and models for reviewing New Zealand education: A critique' in *NZJEA*, **4**.

RAMSAY, P.D.K. (Ed) (1984) *Family School and Community Perspectives in the Sociology of New Zealand Education*, Sydney, George Allen and Unwin.

RAMSAY, R., SEDDON, D., GREENFELL, J. and FORD, I. (1987) 'The characteristics of successful schools', *Set*, **1**.

RENWICK, W.L. (1985) 'Forty years on in New Zealand: A new net goes fishing', *NZJEA*, **2**.

RENWICK, W.L. (1986) *Moving Targets: Six Essays on Educational Policy with an Introduction by C. E. Beeby*, Wellington, New Zealand Council for Educational Research.

SALLIS, J. (1988) *Schools, Parents and Governors: A New Approach to Accountability*, London, Routledge and Kegan Paul.

SHUKER, R. (1987) *The One Best System? A Revisionist History of State Schooling in New Zealand*, Palmerston North, Dunmore.

SNOOK, I. (1989) 'Education reform in New Zealand: What is going on?', paper presented to the conference of the New Zealand Association for Research in Education, Wellington (mimeo).

STEWART, D. and PREBBLE, T. (1985) *Making It Happen: A School Development Process*, Palmerston North, Dunmore.

TASK FORCE TO REVIEW EDUCATIONAL ADMINISTRATION (1988) *Administering for Excellence, Effective Administration in Education*, Wellington, The Task Force.

THE TREASURY (1987) *Government Management: Brief to the Incoming Government, Vol II, Education Issues*, Wellington, The Treasury.

WILKES, C. (1982) 'Development as practice: The instrument of reason' in SHIRLEY, I. (Ed) *Development Tracks the Theory and Practice of Community Development*, Palmerston North, Dunmore.

15 School Supervision in the West Indies: Focus on Trinidad and Tobago

Claudia Harvey and Gwendoline Williams

Introduction

The Commonwealth countries of the West Indies share a similar geography and history. The region stretches between the mainland territories of Belize in the North and Guyana in the South and also includes Jamaica, the Windward and Leeward Islands, Barbados and Trinidad and Tobago. All are producers of primary tropical products, although there have been various attempts to diversify their economies to expand the manufacturing and service sectors. All these territories were colonized by Britain and, at different points, other colonial powers such as the Spanish, French and Dutch, from the fifteenth right up to the twentieth century. In all the territories, formal educational provisions by the state closely mirror various historical developments. Such provisions were started in the post-1838 period with the emancipation of the slaves and the coming of East Indian indentureship.

In all the territories, educational governance emanated from Britain and change was frequently sparked by institutional crisis, followed by the intervention of royal commissions or other special investigating bodies. Problem resolution usually took account of the peculiar economic, political and social circumstances in both the colonial and post-colonial periods, thereby creating differences in the ways in which the various education systems evolved and functioned. For example, the system of supervision in a country like St. Kitts is simple in structure, with education officers performing a complex of different specialist tasks. The larger territories of Jamaica and Trinidad and Tobago have more complex systems. In the former, expansion and functioning of the supervisory system has been hampered by economic constraints while the latter, fuelled by an oil boom, experienced rapid expansion in both educational provisions and the system of educational management.

In view of the differences in educational supervision in the member countries, it became necessary in planning this chapter to undertake a country-by-country appraisal of the system. This exercise revealed the dearth of documented analyses of this vital aspect of educational management. Reporting on the management systems in all the territories would require extensive study of original documents produced by historical and field research. Consequently, a case study of supervision as part of educational management in Trinidad and Tobago was done on an exploratory basis so that the insights gained could trigger off field research in the various territories.

This chapter reports on the research done and provides:

(i) a brief historical background of the various administrative roles as those relate to the supervisory functions of the education management system in Trinidad and Tobago;
(ii) an examination of each role by analyzing official job descriptions and specifications; and
(iii) an assessment of role performance by analyzing the monthly work programmes and performance records of administrative supervisors as well as interview data collected from the present Director of School Supervision. (The interviews also provide a senior management perspective on both intent and performance of the various roles.)

From the data sources outlined above, emergent issues pertaining to school supervision in Trinidad and Tobago are identified and analyzed. These findings serve as an example of educational supervision in the Commonwealth Caribbean. It is situation-specific, but further country-by-country research may reveal cross-country similarities and differences in educational supervision in the Caribbean.

As a final verification check, current practitioners in the field were asked to read the first draft of the report. Their comments have been considered in preparing the final version.

Description and Analysis of Supervisory Roles

From Inspector to Supervisor at the Primary Level

Most of the Commonwealth Caribbean territories, by the 1950s, acquired Departments or Boards of Education headed by expatriate Directors of Education. It is with the coming of independence in the 1960s and 1970s, however, that the most dramatic changes in education took place. Education was seen as the key to self-realization for individuals as well as a lever for economic growth, social cohesion and cultural identity. With the expansion of educational provisions, there were comparable changes in educational administration.

The changes were quite marked in the Republic of Trinidad and Tobago, the twin island country closest to Guyana in the Caribbean chain. The expansion of education was fuelled both by the policy objectives which were shared by the other territories and by an oil boom from the mid-1970s which provided the necessary funds to facilitate the change.

The old inspectorate was replaced by school supervisors. Perhaps the most remarkable change was the increased number of specialized administrative and professional posts. The various specializations — curriculum, technical-vocational education, pre-school, guidance, special education – came on stream at different times during the period 1962–1989. The organizational structure as it obtained in 1989 is illustrated in figure 15.1.

Prior to the 1950s, the primary school inspector was a regular member of the public service and did not have to be a member of the teaching profession. Subsequently, inspectors were required to be experienced headteachers. These were categorized as senior inspectors, North and South; district inspectors; and lady inspectors for needlework and infant methods. This phase of the inspectorate was replaced by the present supervisory system in which there are two levels of supervisors. Senior supervisors or school supervisors II are responsible for one of eight geographical divisions and supervisors I are responsible for districts within divisions. Districts usually comprise sixteen to twenty schools, and divisions vary from thirty-five to eighty-four schools.

Interviews with the Director of School Supervision indicated that the major difference between the inspector and the school supervisor centred around the degree of emphasis placed on regulating curriculum and instruction. The inspector examined students orally and in writing. Teachers were assessed according to the attendance and performance of their students and were remunerated based on 'payment by result'. This placed the inspector at the heart of the curriculum and instructional development process.

In the period since independence, the school supervisor at the primary level has had a far more multifaceted role. The Director of School Supervision noted:

> The inspector was more thorough. He focused on work and the curriculum, even though he had to get to the school on horseback or in coastal boats ... The school supervisor now is into so many other activities associated with education: reading and spelling tests; literacy; quizzes; banking; credit unions; the Lions Club; AIDS education ... (Interview Schedule, 2 August 1989)

Examples of work given in the official job specification of the school supervisor I support this statement by the Director of School Supervision. Such examples include:

- inspects schools to ensure that the education programme and policy are being efficiently carried out;

Figure 15.1 *Organizational Chart of the Technical Units of the Ministry of Education Showing Positions of School Supervisors (1989)*

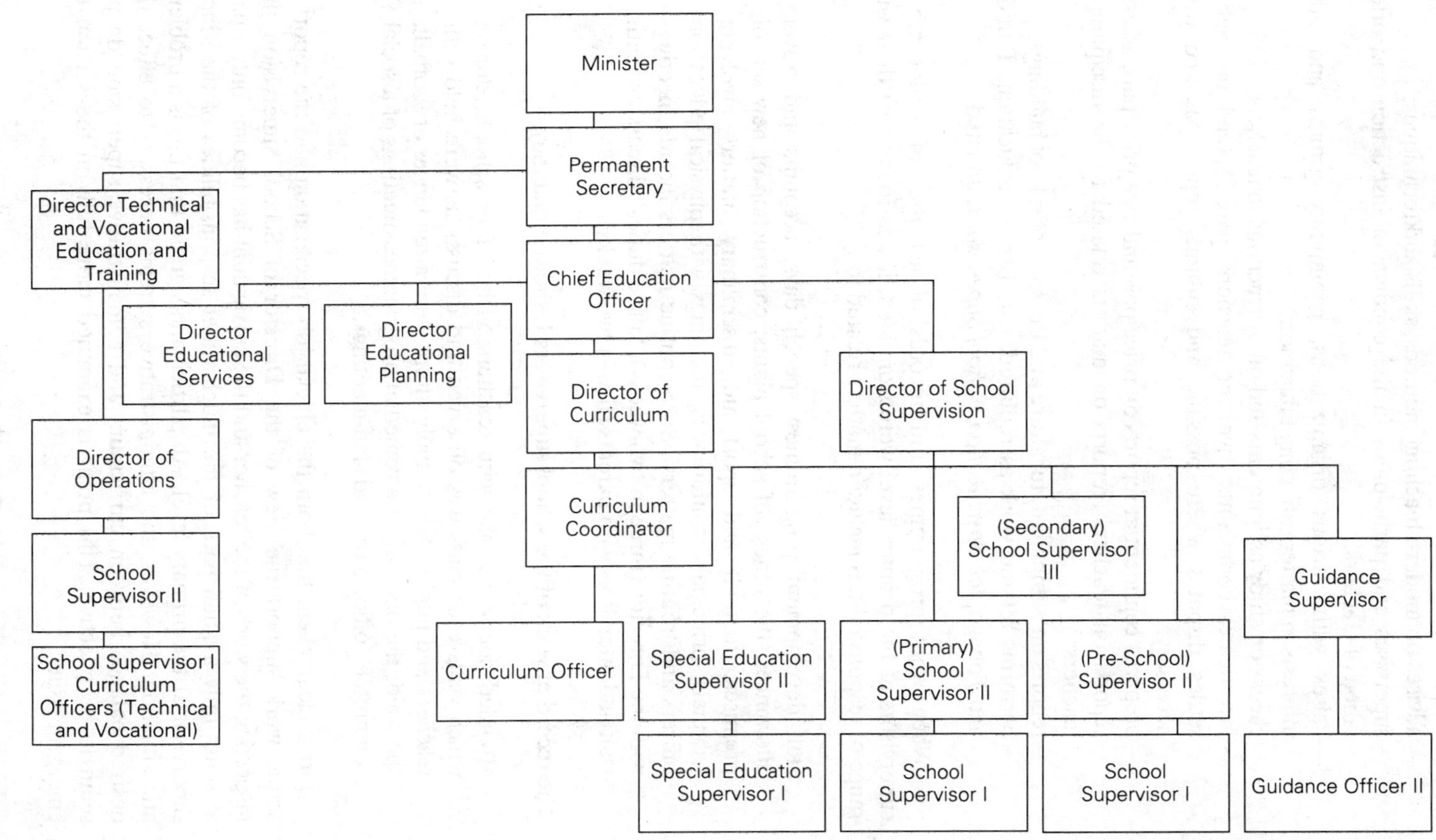

— advises on modern teaching methods, skills and techniques;
— supervises and participates in the conduct of instruction and orientation of teachers;
— liaises with various organizations, community groups and other interests in matters affecting education;
— checks on study assignments and on instructions to teachers;
— investigates complaints involving teachers, parents, and the public, settles disputes where possible and submits reports as and when necessary;
— prepares confidential reports on principals and vice principals, assesses reports on teachers, reports on matters related to the discipline of teachers;
— reports on equipment, furniture and the state of school buildings;
— performs related work as required. (Ministry of Education, Trinidad and Tobago, *Job Specification, School Supervisor I*, undated)

When work programmes and records of activities of senior school supervisors at the primary level were examined, it was found that their wide range of responsibilities included matters related to:

> staff development programmes; speech days; accounts and travel allowances; the fitness of school plants; construction of new school premises; football and sport aid; disciplinary matters involving tribunals; principals' conferences; meetings with physical education officers and 'routine matters'. Such routine matters include meetings with the Director (three in two weeks); 'office duties'; discussions with staff and interviews with parents (five in two weeks).

The record of work of the school supervisors I, showed that they:

> attended courses; spoke with teachers; visited four schools, during which visits each class was observed and discussions were held with teachers and pupils. Additionally, there were attendances at football; sport aid; the opening of a remedial programme; meetings of a social committee; 'office days' and staff meetings.

It is clear, then, that both the official job specification and the report of actual work support the view of the Director of School Supervision that inspecting the work of the teacher and the curriculum has become only a part, at times only a small part, of the much wider responsibilities of the school supervisor at the primary level. All participants agreed that this is a problematic situation. However, the administrative systems necessary to effect the desired balance between curriculum and administrative supervision do not seem to be effective. This point is examined more fully in the section on emergent issues.

The Secondary School Supervisor

The school supervisor III for secondary schools was introduced in 1970. Secondary schools had been viewed as part of the academic tradition and, previously, principals and teachers were frequently expatriates. Not having been promoted from the 'ranks of the masses' as were primary school teachers and headmasters, secondary school staffs were subject to far less central control. The main means of assessing their effectiveness had been by way of the external and scholarship examinations.

With the expansion of the secondary school sector and the role it was earmarked to play in producing skilled human resources and a committed leadership, stricter Government control was established over those schools. Consequently, supervisors were appointed to be intermediaries between the Directorate of the Ministry of Education and secondary school principals. By 1984, there were five school supervisors, each of whom was responsible for sixteen to twenty schools and could be assigned to any set of schools in Trinidad. Subsequently, the five supervisors were made responsible for schools in specified districts in Trinidad.

A sixth supervisor is assigned to Tobago, the only educational district separated by water from the head office of the Ministry of Education. Consequently, the administrative arrangement in Tobago is somewhat different. The supervisory function is more integrated, with two school supervisors I of the primary sector reporting to the school supervisor III, who is also responsible for the four public secondary schools in Tobago.

The establishment of the House of Assembly in 1980 has led to stronger local government in Tobago. The school supervisor III reports to the Secretary for Education of the Assembly, while all other supervisors report to the Director of School Supervision. This causes some role strain because, in terms of educational policy, curriculum and school management, the school supervisor III, Tobago must be guided by policies from the Ministry of Education, even though he reports to the Secretary for Education of the Assembly. This gives the supervisor both more scope for decision-making, since he is the main technocrat responsible for education on the island, *and* constrains him, since he has responsibility to a dual authority.

Because secondary supervisors were allocated schools in concentrated geographical areas, their roles are similar to district superintendents in some North American settings. To date, except in Tobago, the primary and secondary sectors are separate administrative entities, even though both sets of supervisors report to the Director of School Supervision.

Secondary school supervisors are required to have the following knowledge and skills:

— extensive knowledge of modern educational theories, methods and practices;

— extensive knowledge and appreciation of the programme of the secondary schools and teachers' colleges;
— considerable knowledge of education administration;
— ability to undertake research and investigate educational problems;
— ability to inspect work in secondary schools and teachers' colleges;
— ability to foster and maintain good relationships between the secondary schools and the Ministry of Education. (Ministry of Education, Trinidad and Tobago, *Job Specification of the School Supervisor III*, undated)

Further, they are required to:

> assist in research with a view to raising academic standards; advise on all matters related to the organization and administration of schools; supervise the programme required by the curriculum and advise on the formulation and revision of the curriculum; investigate problems; prepare confidential reports on principals; report on school building, equipment and furniture; assist in the promotion of training courses for teachers and perform related work as required. (Ministry of Education, Trinidad and Tobago, *Job Specification of the School Supervisor III*, undated)

The reported composite activities of two secondary school supervisors for one month showed the pattern of response to the myriad demands made on their time. The activities listed and the number of times each was engaged in are presented below:

— business management committee meeting[1]
— school supervisors meeting[2]
— routine matters at the office[9]
— staff development seminars including stress management seminar[1]
— seminar on AIDS, principals conference[5]
— anniversary, graduation and prize-giving[5]
— attending to school staffing matters including giving approval to attend part-time courses[7]
— suspension of students[2]
— meeting with guidance officers[1]
— meeting with maintenance area superintendent[1]
— routine school visits[4]
— disciplinary matters including Civil Service tribunal[4]
— accompanying the Minister on official visits[2]
— site visit re: physical expansion[2]

The description, as illustrated both in the job specification and the reported activities, indicates that the supervisor is indeed responsible for various aspects of administration — the most focused being the supervision of school

Table 15.1 Sample of Activities of Secondary School Supervisors by Nature of Activity and Number of Times Mentioned

	Number of Times Matters Mentioned in Report by Supervisors A, B and C		
	A	B	C
Number of schools visited	7	8	10
Nature of matters handled: (sum of all schools)			
Personnel (including teacher discipline)	6	11	10
Programme (including curriculum, time-tabling and student related matters)	6	3	7
Student related matters (especially discipline)	0	1	1
Plant (including construction, repairs, maintenance and security)	6	7	7
Other (including matters related to finance, cafeteria and transport)	0	5	3

personnel, plant and programmes. Such supervision of schools would be expected to be undertaken during 'routine visits'. An analysis of the reporting forms on such visits for three supervisors for one month each is illustrated in Table 15.1

The analysis suggests that, on visiting secondary schools, supervisors do attend in a fairly balanced manner to issues related to the core areas of personnel, programmes and plant. The difficulty arises, however, in the competing areas which limit the frequency with which they can visit schools. Chief among these competing areas are extra-curricular activities like assisting with sports and business management activities of schools, and participating in ceremonial activities like anniversaries, graduations, valedictory functions and accompanying the Minister on visits to schools and educational functions.

One teacher-researcher, commenting on the role of the supervisor, noted:

> During her eleven years of teaching at secondary school, the writer's encounter with school supervisors, both administrative and curriculum, has been limited to brief exchanges at social gatherings, to her direct visits to the supervisor to collect circularised information, and to supervisors' short attendances at school functions, such as sports meetings and graduation exercises. (Nagee, 1985, p. i)

Consequently, as with the primary school supervisor, it seems that the secondary school supervisor's stated role is not always effected in practice. Factors affecting and issues arising from this situation are discussed in greater detail in a subsequent section.

Along with the administrative supervisors already described, there are other officers, some of them within the Division of School Supervision and others located in other divisions, who also perform supervisory functions.

Specialist Supervisors

The expansion of the school system brought with it a need for an expanded supervisory function. This was instituted in the areas of pre-school, special education, school guidance, technical-vocational education and curriculum.

Pre-school supervisors also report to the Director of School Supervision and are responsible for government and government-assisted pre-school centres. The pre-school unit was established in 1970 within the supervision division, and consists of one senior and two other supervisors. Most pre-schools are community-based and the supervisors determine suitability for establishment, monitor existing centres and train the relevant early childhood educators. The work of pre-school supervisors also includes responsibility largely for personnel, programme and plant.

The special education unit was established in 1981 as part of the supervision division and consists of one senior and one other supervisor. The latter also functions as a curriculum officer in special education. Prior to 1988, all special schools were controlled by voluntary agencies with the assistance of government grants. In 1988, the first government special school was established. The thrust towards mainstreaming of special children into regular schools wherever possible, and diagnosing and catering to their needs in these schools, as well as the training of teachers and facilitating the work of special schools, all fall within the jurisdiction of this unit. Much of the activity of this unit involves work with 'regular' educators to sensitize and/or train them as necessary to work with special children. The special education supervisors must therefore work closely with all other supervisors.

The guidance unit was established in 1969 as part of the Division of School Supervision with special responsibility for the pastoral needs of students. There is one guidance supervisor who heads the unit. She is assisted by four senior district guidance officers who supervise forty guidance officers, who are attached to secondary schools. There is usually one guidance officer per school but, in a few cases, one supervisor may work with more than one school. There are two officers attached to primary schools.

In the division of technical-vocational education and training, there are officers responsible for the design of this specialist curriculum and supervisors responsible for monitoring the implementation of programmes. Such supervisors function at both the primary and secondary levels. Their areas of responsibility include agriculture, metal and woodwork, home economics and business studies.

Curriculum officers were once also part of the supervisory division. However, with the expansion of the system, a separate curriculum division was formed. Curriculum officers have special responsibility for the design, implementation and evaluation of the aesthetic and academic curricula at the primary and secondary levels. Their areas of responsibility include language and literary studies, mathematics, science, social studies, music, art and craft, physical education and family life education.

Emergent Issues in School Supervision

The expansion of the supervisory system in Trinidad and Tobago has given rise to several issues. These include role ambiguity and overload, the generalist versus specialist dilemma, issues related to career tracking and to coordination among different elements of the system. A discussion of these issues follow.

Role Ambiguity and Overload

The administrative supervisors at the pre-primary, primary and secondary levels are expected to be responsible for programme, personnel, plant and 'related duties'. In practice, a situation of dissonance is created for the supervisor who is constantly made aware of the duality of roles: the need to emphasize curriculum and instruction as well as those tasks that are essentially administrative in nature. The issue is one of role ambiguity brought about in the main by the elaborated role and function of the supervisor as the education system expanded. This situation is exacerbated because the various tasks have not been prioritized to effect an adequate balance between the curricular and administrative aspects of the supervisory function.

A related issue is that of time management in the face of the multiplicity of tasks, frequently resulting in 'overstretching' the resources of supervisors so that they often feel unable to address what is seen as their core task of quality control of programmes.

Generalist Versus Specialist

The qualifications required to become a supervisor at any of the three levels do not necessarily equip officers to be specialists in the various curriculum areas. At the primary level, teachers, and subsequently principals, are usually generalists and in theory, on becoming supervisors, should be able to monitor the entire programme. However, precisely because they are generalists, those primary school supervisors who are unable to keep abreast of curriculum developments frequently claim insufficient subject matter content to play an important role in curricular matters in schools. Indeed, it is sometimes claimed that teachers are more familiar with developments in subject areas than are some of the supervisors who, consequently, frequently emphasize administrative, regulatory functions rather than perform professional leadership roles as seem to be preferred by teachers. This problem is being addressed by recruiting supervisors from the ranks of former primary school teachers who became subject matter specialists and were promoted to secondary schools as well as by providing expanded training in curriculum for practising and prospective supervisors.

At the secondary level, supervisors may be perceived to have greater subject matter competence but *only* in one or two subject areas — the areas in which they were specialist teachers before they were promoted to the ranks of principals and subsequently supervisors. At this level, then, the complaint is that they cannot effectively supervise the entire secondary school programme because of the specialist nature of the various programmes and their training in only one specialization. To solve this problem, reference is frequently made to the specialist curriculum officers, whose job description focuses on instructional leadership. However, their numbers (usually two per subject area) are too few to service all primary and secondary schools.

Indications for future development seem to point in the direction of augmenting the ranks of the curriculum officers by the addition of more field staff. This has been done in the areas of mathematics and reading, where specially trained senior teachers, referred to as 'facilitators', work with curriculum officers in diffusing and monitoring curriculum innovations and improvements.

Two other trends may support these developments in specialist curriculum supervision. Primary schools are themselves moving towards semi-specialization among teachers, so that there can be both better articulation of subject matter at upper primary levels with that at the secondary level and better links between curriculum officers and teachers. Simultaneously, there is a new emphasis on training principals at both levels in instructional supervision. Such training would assist them in the use of existing in-school resources and peer support and so decrease the expectation that such leadership would be provided from external sources.

Recruitment/Promotion/Career Tracking

A related issue arising from the generalist/specialist debate is that of the relationship between primary and secondary supervisors and the career path available to them.

Currently, following a 'normal' career path, a primary school teacher can become a senior teacher, vice principal, principal, school supervisor I, and lastly a school supervisor II. Unless there is a switch of streams, there can be no aspiration to go to the level of Director of School Supervision and beyond.

For the graduate secondary school teacher, such an aspiration can exist within stream, despite the high level of competition, which may be an inhibiting factor.

This issue is related to the recruitment and promotion policy in the entire education system. Without examining the whole, one can delineate some of the implications for supervisors. If parallel but unequal systems exist, then the primary school level is likely to be considered not as worthy as the secondary, with subsequent impact on professional performance at the former and the tendency for the professionally mobile to seek to switch streams. Moreover, the separation of the streams hinders the articulation of curriculum between the primary and secondary systems except, again, through a third force — the curriculum unit. This issue is currently being examined to allow for recruitment from a wider cross-section of practitioners and easier transfer between levels.

Coordination Across Specialist Units

Yet another issue is coordination of efforts across specialist units. Historically, the expansion of the system revealed a variety of needs which led to the emergence of several specialist units, all related to different aspects of supervision — administrative, curriculum, guidance, technical-vocational and special education. Yet, each specialization has as its *raison d'être*, meeting the needs of the student and, organizationally, of the school. Frequently, however, great difficulty can be experienced in articulating and coordinating the delivery of the various services. Consequently, members of the school community often complain of an inability effectively to receive the services offered. Technically, it is the administrative supervisor (school supervisor I, II or III), working with the principal, who should monitor and regulate the flow of information and services, but the foregoing discussion indicates reasons why such regulation is difficult for the supervisor.

Articulation Within Administrative Supervision

Articulation within the supervisory function itself is another issue which needs to be addressed. Because of the multiplicity of tasks as outlined in the job specification quoted earlier, supervisors may select those tasks most compatible with their own styles/competence and focus on those. Thus, one district may focus on curriculum programmes, another on guidance and counselling, a third on sports. This poses the risk of an unbalanced programme for students.

The need for articulation across supervisory functions and within supervisory functions is currently being addressed. The Ministry of Education is in the process of articulating and prioritizing its goals in the interest of efficient and effective service delivery at least cost. One aspect of this exercise is to provide combined services at the divisional level. The intent is that each division would have at least one officer specially trained and responsible for one of the following areas: general administration, curriculum, guidance, physical facilities and educational technology. This should address both the issue of a wide dissemination of services to, and that of the integration of services within, districts. Any such change, however, would also have simultaneously to enable the various specialists to interact and support each other, lest professional isolation occur. Thus, the needs of both decentralization and professional development would have to be met. It would be necessary, also, to streamline systems in the areas of communication and the management of information to ensure that the functions of the different geographical and professional divisions of the system are effectively coordinated.

Conclusion

Supervision provides quality control in the delivery of services within the education system. As the delivery systems change and expand, the supervisory function is expected to be responsive to the change process. Yet, because quality control is often seen as mainly regulatory, school supervision can be viewed as conservative and as hindering change rather than fostering it.

In the West Indian context, the colonial school inspector was frequently perceived by social analysts as a bastion of the transmission of colonial culture — freezing personnel and pupils into authoritarian modes of obedience and control. Expansion of the system and the thrusts towards indigenization and development led to a greater focus on more specialized roles and a greater degree of professionalism among supervisors. However, the specialization among supervisors from professional units (curriculum, guidance, technical-vocational, special education), on the one hand, and the multiplicity of roles of the administrative supervisor, on the other, have led at least one senior administrator to look back nostalgically to the critical role played by the inspector in monitoring the implementation of programmes and assessing the effectiveness of learning.

In Trinidad and Tobago, the range of responsibilities to be undertaken by the respective levels of supervisors reflect competing demands for quality control in the core areas of curriculum and instruction as well as in routine administration and public relations. The exploratory research findings reported in this chapter reveal the irony that supervision of curriculum and instruction was increasingly deemphasized even as the demand for it intensified in a period of curriculum renewal. This was in part a result of the myriad administrative responsibilities which resulted from the expansion of the system and which make an almost inhuman demand on the time of supervisors who experience severe role strain in trying to effect a more meaningful balance between the curricular and adminstrative management functions.

In the face of these difficulties, educational managers in Trinidad and Tobago are examining the issues and instituting changes in policies and practice related to recruitment and placement, continuous professional development, decentralization, management of information and the strengthening of in-school supervision. These measures are being undertaken in an attempt to ensure more effective programme delivery and pastoral care to the eventual clients of all educational programmes — the students.

Acknowledgements

The authors gratefully acknowledge the expert advice and assistance of Mr Ralph Attong, Mrs Sylvia Baptiste, Mr Bronson Merritt and Mrs Mennen Walker-Briggs, all formerly or currently of the Division of School Supervision, Ministry of Education, Trinidad and Tobago.

References

GORDON, S.C. (1963) *A Century of West Indian Education*, London, Longmans, Green Company Limited.

GOVERNMENT OF TRINIDAD AND TOBAGO (1974) *Draft Plan for Educational Development 1968–83*, Trinidad and Tobago, Government Printery.

KING, R.H. (Ed) (1987) *Education in the Caribbean: Historical perspectives*, Mona, Jamaica, Faculty of Education, University of the West Indies.

MINISTRY OF EDUCATION (n.d.) *Job Specifications*, School Supervisor I, School Supervisor II, School Supervisor III, Curriculum Officers, Trinidad and Tobago.

MINISTRY OF EDUCATION, DIVISION OF SCHOOL SUPERVISION (1987 and 1988) *Work Programmes and Records of Activities of School Supervisors I, II and III*, Manuscripts, Port of Spain, Trinidad and Tobago.

NAGEE, J.A. (1985) 'The supervisor, primus inter pares: Some perspectives on school supervision in the secondary school of Trinidad and Tobago', dissertation, In-Service Diploma in Education Programme, St. Augustine, University of the West Indies.

REPUBLIC OF TRINIDAD AND TOBAGO, MINISTRY OF EDUCATION (1985) *Education Plan 1985–1990*, Port of Spain, Trinidad and Tobago.

Comment

Robin H. Farquhar

The chapters in this section contain a great deal of information about the historical background, current status and projected future of the school principalship and superintendency and, either explicitly or implicitly, about the development of selected countries in the Commonwealth. While it would not be useful to repeat that information here, it may be worthwhile to attempt a brief interpretive summary. In retrospect, what has been learned from these discussions of key administrative roles in the educational systems of nine different parts of the Commonwealth?

First, it is evident that education is characterized by tremendous change in almost all of the countries considered (with the possible exception of Canada) as they enter the final decade of this century. Virtual reform is taking place both in the structures and processes of education and in concomitant administrative training, reflecting the escalating priority accorded to schooling for purposes of national economic, social and technological development. One relatively common element of this change is a clear trend towards decentralization of responsibility to the local level and towards increased lay involvement in educational decision-making; this is apparent, for example, in the delegation of authority from state to local levels in Australia and Canada, the fund-raising efforts and community-liaison activities of school principals in Kenya and Nigeria, the nationally-driven decentralization to the level of individual schools that one finds in England and Wales to an extent probably unequalled elsewhere in the Commonwealth and the very substantial decentralization in New Zealand from the national Government to local community boards at the individual school level where a great deal of authority has been vested since the 1989 reform period there.

A perhaps countervailing characteristic of the changes underway is an evidently increased concern by national governments with respect to accountability and effectiveness as measured by examination results (with the apparent exception, again, of Canada). Examples of this thrust from national governments are obvious in Australia, in Kenya's use of national examinations and attention to the employability of school leavers, in the British Government's insistence on techniques of management and planning and on efforts to render schools more competitive through entrepreneurial and market-oriented approaches and in New Zealand's retention at the national level of responsibility for reviewing effectiveness.

A second feature common to these chapters is the extent to which the stimulation and pace of educational change are being influenced by cultural, economic and political forces rather than by developments from within the field of education itself. The influence of cultural factors can be seen, for example, in the significant impact on principals' performance of the general social ethos in India and particularly its structure of castes and tribes, in the original influence of Christian missionaries on the introduction of education in almost all the countries considered, in the importance of tribal and religious differences to the provision of education in Nigeria, in the significance to Canadian education of historical patterns of immigration as well as religious and linguistic variations, in Malaysia's efforts to establish Malay as the main medium of instruction in its schools and in the very comprehensive recognition of Maori needs in New Zealand.

The influence of economic factors is evident, for example, in the rapid growth of Nigeria's education enterprise (including the introduction of universal free primary education) brought on by the economic expansion due to the oil boom in the 1970s (as occurred in Trinidad and Tobago as well) and the stalling of this development when the oil glut in the world market led to economic crisis in the 1980s. This influence is also apparent in the fact that the requirements of economic development are the primary stimuli for most of the educational reforms that are discussed (New Zealand is a good example) and in the frustrations of educators in countries where the technological infrastructures (equipment, materials, training opportunities, etc) required to implement the desired reforms are unavailable because of insufficient economic capacity in several countries of the 'new Commonwealth'.

The impact of political conditions on the direction and pace of educational change is illustrated by the lack of country-wide coherence in Canada and India where the provinces or states have a great deal of constitutional power in education, by the perhaps confusing variety of educational laws in Nigeria where all three levels of government have some authority, and by the impact on Malaysian education of the Japanese occupation during World War II.

Finally, it can be observed that, emanating largely from the above phenomena, a great deal of flux and ferment in the key administrative roles is common to the state of education in virtually all of the countries treated in this section. Much uncertainty and confusion are evident as the desired pace of change exceeds the capabilities of educators to keep up in terms of organizational infrastructure, financial capability and training provisions; this is evident in concerns about principals' ability to cope with the new national pressures of accountability in Australia, in the weak provisions for training educational administrators lamented by several of the authors (for example,

Sapra, Bolam, Olembo and Maneno), in the virtual disappearance of the school superintendent-type role from the New Zealand educational scene and in the continuingly confounding separation of the primary and secondary sectors of education in such countries as Nigeria and Trinidad.

Notwithstanding these encumbrances, however, one may discern a general Commonwealth-wide trend toward the increased professionalization of these key administrative roles; this is facilitated, in most of the countries covered, by such trends as those towards decentralization, towards a corporate executive and away from a public servant orientation, towards a political manager and away from a 'super teacher' model, towards an increase in training programmes focused specifically on educational administration, towards greater self-determination and away from external regulation and towards active participation in educational administration professional organizations at the regional, national and Commonwealth levels (notably CCEA). Consequently, despite the numerous issues and problems acknowledged by the authors, the reader is left with some feeling of optimism about the prospects for the emergence of leadership from educational administrators in the key roles examined in this section of the book; several of the chapters conclude with explicit comments on this optimism, and the only frequently mentioned 'downside' (a significant Commonwealth-wide failure) is the continuing and ubiquitous underrepresentation of women in the profession of educational administration — the correction of which probably represents the greatest challenge now facing the leaders of education in the Commonwealth. Its implications for selection and training will be considered in the opening chapter of the final section of the book.

The above comments, selective and subjective as they are, indicate that the authors of chapters in this section have succeeded in revealing some important features about their respective countries, their rich variety and common thrusts, by examining the evolution and conditions of key administrative roles in the educational systems chosen for study. The general purposes established for this section of the book have thus been achieved.

Section 4

Resources for Educational Advance

Introduction

Meredydd G. Hughes

Resources are almost invariably in short supply. If school principals and system level administrators, faced with complex issues of practice, are to be involved creatively in the implementation of purposeful change, the use of resources is a key consideration. To achieve educational advance the resources available have to be deployed wisely and effectively, i.e. they need to be well managed. This applies, for instance, to the formidable array of material requirements — buildings, books, equipment and expendable items — which are involved. It applies also to the *human* resources of teachers, administrators and support staff. In particular, those involved in planning and managing educational development should themselves be regarded as vitally important resources for achieving educational advance. This was a point recently strongly affirmed at the 1990 International Congress in Mexico City (UNESCO, 1990).

We may note that it is not only within the educational community itself that the need for high quality educational leadership is internationally recognized. One may cite, for example, a wide-ranging World Bank policy paper (World Bank, 1985), which expresses concern about 'the heavy demands on educational administration and management' made by 'the unprecedented expansion of education systems during the past twenty-five years' (p. 53). Its assessment of the consequence, though expressed in the restrained style of official documents, is unambiguous and disturbing:

> Despite efforts to cope with these demands, the development of national managerial, administrative and analytic capacities lags behind the growth in size and complexity of the educational enterprise. Some programs of educational development suffer because of poor management. (*ibid*)

The policy paper proceeds to make detailed recommendations for improving management, planning and research capacities. These are broadly in accord with the activities described and the ideas developed in the three chapters in this final section of the book.

The section begins with a comprehensive review of the selection, education and professional development of educational administrators. Examples are provided of good practice and encouraging new developments in different parts of the world and attention is drawn to an increasing awareness of gender inequality as an issue to be addressed.

A major objective of many programmes of professional education and training, whether the approach is mainly didactic or activity-based, is to illuminate administrative practice, and hence to improve it. There is thus a challenge to devlop a relevant and coherent underpinning of theory and research. The next chapter takes up this theme and examines a number of alternative perspectives which seek to bridge the gap which often appears to separate theory and practice. The application of the perspectives in different situations is considered, using mainly the CCEA literature, and the claim that theory and research can be regarded as catalysts of change is critically examined.

The matters discussed in the first two chapters of the section have been consistently recognised over two decades as major concerns of the Commonwealth Council for Educational Administration and its affiliated national associations. The third chapter therefore appropriately consists of John Weeks' panoramic view of the CCEA in action, closely linked with the Commonwealth Secretariat and the Commonwealth Foundation. These are all organizations which, in different ways, may be regarded as powerful resources for educational advance through their promotion of common understanding and mutual help. The emphasis again is on *human* resources, CCEA and the Commonwealth being seen as living organizations for development.

Such a conclusion fittingly brings our book to a close, giving promise of renewal and growth and of further joint endeavours across the world to advance education in ways most appropriate to the needs of the twenty-first century.

References

UNESCO (1990) *Planning and Management of Educational Development: Final Report*, Documents of the International Congress in Mexico City, Paris, UNESCO.

World Bank (1985) *Education Sector Policy Paper*, Washington DC, World Bank.

16 The Selection, Preparation and Professional Development of Educational Administrators

Colin Moyle and Bernadette Taylor

Introduction

The main body of this chapter consists of two simple but interrelated components: the selection of educational administrators and the preparation and training of those administrators. The term educational administrator will serve to cover personnel, at all levels within the educational system, who assume responsibilities beyond the purely pedagogical. Their selection and preparation are believed to be of crucial importance if institutional change is to occur.

The literature about professional development frequently does not distinguish between preparatory and in-service programmes. It is possible to conceive of 'preparatory in-service programmes', for example, a Deputy Principal seeks training for further promotion. Thus training programmes are viewed as a continuum which does not differentiate between the two except for areas of content and emphasis, and possibly the balance between the modes of training provided.

Programmes themselves frequently include participants who are representative of the continuum. Indications of this can be gained from such words in the prospectus as 'the programme is designed for principals and those aspiring to be principals of schools'. Such programmes provide ample opportunities for all participants to benefit: the neophytes from the experiences of those already confronting the challenge of a leadership position; and the experienced from the neophytes who are searching for simple, practical tools to enable them to act with reasonable confidence and competence when their administrative appointment becomes effective.

With regard to training programmes in general, Murphy and Hallinger (1987) note the emergence of

> a new movement in administrative training characterized by alternative content and delivery systems for training, and emphasis on more varied instructional methodologies, and different assumptions regarding the role of administrators as teachers and learners. (p. xiii)

Brief descriptions of this 'new movement' will appear as appropriate in the text of the chapter.

Educational administrators work at many levels in an educational system, from pre-school to tertiary level. However, two broad categories may be discerned, namely, administrators at the institutional level, and system level administrators. The selection processes for administrative positions at these two levels vary widely both within and between countries, as do the attitudes and actions concerning the preparation and training of these personnel.

It is clear that around the world the increased awareness of the need for professional development programmes for principals is linked with an awareness of the need for restructuring the economy. This will demand a highly responsive education system, a reality widely accepted throughout OECD countries. Administrators must meet these needs without sacrificing the liberal arts or the fostering of lateral and creative thinking. Those in administrative positions will need the ability to manage change and to work effectively with their colleagues in strategic planning type activities that ensure the schools are able to meet the needs of their societies and the individuals within those societies. All research points to the critical role of principals as the key leading planners and change agents.

Previous chapters have shown that in some parts of the world school administrators and their communities are being given greater responsibility for the management of their schools and this too highlights the changing role of the school administrator. The New Zealand Government, for instance, has recently decentralized the administration of education to each individual school which is expected to set its own priorities and manage itself although all this is to take place within centrally determined policies, priorities and frameworks for accountability. Such a dramatic change in approach was preceded, it may be noted, by a massive professional development programme.

The highly responsive school and the associated requirement for self-management within centrally determined policies, priorities and frameworks for accountability, imply an extension of what has already been undertaken in other places so far as local selection of principals and other leaders are concerned. This could be extended and phased to include local selection of teachers. A controversial issue will be the extent to which contracts for school staff should in fact be made with school councils or their counterparts. There are many implications for policies on the preparation and selection of principals and other leaders, not the least of which is the importance that gender equity be addressed.

Some of the conclusions drawn as a result of the introduction of a more decentralized system in New South Wales, Australia, were that:

- the school, not the system, is the key organizational element providing teaching and learning;
- schools will best meet their needs if they are enabled to manage themselves in line with general guidelines. (Scott, 1989, pp. 5–6)

This is apparently a worldwide phenomenon. At present, policy initiatives which will lead to decentralization are being explored in many countries. However the development of these policies may well be impossible if local administrators are not prepared for the structural and role changes which follow in the wake of policy implementation. The necessary corollary to these policy initiatives therefore is appropriate preparation programmes for school and system administrators.

The development of principals will also have valuable professional development effects for other members of staff and the school community. Individuals who engage in leadership and management roles within the school have the responsibility to enhance their own capacities. Individuals, including principals, will also need formal and informal professional development activities mandated, and mainly provided by employing authorities to ensure that they carry out new roles effectively. The commitment to this approach should assist in ensuring that a wider range of teachers participate both in leadership roles and in other professional development activities.

Individuals and the system will benefit if the particular roles and capacities which contribute to effective educational leadership and management at various levels are clear. For this reason, a profile of these roles and competencies should be developed, taking into account research work already completed in other areas. Such a profile should enable individuals to plan the development of their careers. It should also contribute directly to the achievement of system priorities by identifying those capacities and experiences which enhance educational leadership and management. It will have the further effect of improving local selection for principalship when this occurs by offering broad criteria to selection committees.

This view of professional development should influence all activities and forms of provision proposed within the action areas. These should be developed to provide a comprehensive programme of professional development for principals and aspiring principals which meets the needs of schools as well as each individual in these areas:

- as a member and leader of a school team
- as a leader within a school community
- as a manager in the system
- as a member of a peer group

Selection of Educational Administrators

As the chapters of section 3 make evident, selection processes for educational administrators vary enormously throughout educational systems. The most common method has been self-selection usually involving seniority, some form of evaluation, and a desire on the part of the individual to seek an administrative post, or promotion. Some higher level posts requiring well-defined specific skills, for example, in the area of financial administration, or curriculum development, are more carefully filled. Generally, however, selection has been heavily biased towards seniority, as noted by Sapra (chapter 9) in the Indian context, but this is showing distinct signs of change.

In some developing countries much closer attention is currently being paid to the selection processes of administrators while in others where there is an explosive demand due to rapid expansion there is frequently no established set of criteria for selection, which frequently is not based upon administrative experience. The distinct possibility therefore arises that where change and effective administration are highly desirable, 'unqualified administrators might undercut reform initiatives' (Blank, 1987).

The relatively recent push for decentralization of administrative authority in developed countries, for example, United Kingdom (Judge, 1989) and New South Wales, Australia (Scott, 1989), is being echoed in developing countries as more efficient and responsive educational systems are required.

Accounts of recent developments in two countries are instructive both for comparative purposes and the potential they have to inform about selection procedures. The first (case study 1), describes radical changes to procedures in Victoria, Australia, that had been in use for decades. The second (case study 2), written by Kabini F. Sanga, Chief Education Officer of the Solomon Islands, gives a graphic picture of how a developing country attempts to select and train its school principals.

Preparation and Training of Educational Administrators

An appreciation of the desirability of formal preparation for educational administrators has been slow in developing, but 'Right now, training educational administrators seems to be an area of intensifying interest, at least in quite a few different parts of the world ... (and) is equally visible in industrialized countries as in the Third World' (Rodwell and Hurst, 1986, p. 117). Some higher education institutions have a training record dating back to the 1950s, for example, the University of New England, Australia, and the University of Alberta, Canada, while elsewhere the emphasis is not only new but diverse, for example, the Institute of Education, Singapore, and the Open University, UK (as demonstrated by case study 6 later in the chapter). An important development was the emergence of professional associations with a specific focus on educational administration, such as the CCEA and its

CASE STUDY 1
The Selection of Principal Class Personnel
VICTORIA, AUSTRALIA

In 1983, after years of promotion by assessment for suitability and seniority, a dramatic change in the promotion process took place — School Councils became involved in the selection of Principals. In schools with a Principal Class vacancy Councils now draw up a job description and advertise for a suitable applicant. The Council then sets up a Selection Panel consisting of the Council President, Council Representatives, Teacher Representatives, Union Representative, Ministerial Representative and, where the vacancy is for a Deputy/Vice Principal, the Principal of the school. The task of this Panel is to shortlist then interview applicants, decide on the relative merits of the applicants in priority order, and submit its recommendations to Council. Council then accepts or rejects these recommendations and forwards its decision to the Appointments Board.

This change has had a dramatic effect on the promotion process because it has meant that any teacher who is suitably qualified, and is registered by the appropriate Teacher Registration Board is now eligible to apply. Seniority no longer is the final deciding factor, nor is merit as adjudged by assessment. The Education Department, or Ministry of Education as it is now known, no longer decides on the eligibility of applicants to obtain the position — this is decided by a panel of lay people and professionals. The Ministry has only one representative on this panel.

affiliated national associations. Some existing professional associations also provided a forum for educational administration, an early example being the Canadian Educational Association, which established its Banff Centre for Short Courses in the 1950s.

The relative tardiness of the acceptance of educational administration as a specific field of study could be attributed to several factors among which are the priority attached to teacher training; the former roles of administrators which had the incumbents subservient to prescribed regulations and supervisory practices; the lack of appreciation of the emerging complexity of an administrator's role as necessary changes (including devolution and decentralization of responsibilities) began to occur; and the negative attitude towards the relationship between theory and practice, possibly related to the pioneering activities of institutions in North America where the work 'was often heavily oriented to research and theory building' (Miklos, 1983, p. 164).

The recent accelerated interest in educational administration indicates that most of these constraints have been overcome. However the theory—practice dichotomy, more fully considered in the following chapter, continues

CASE STUDY 2
Meeting The Administrative Needs of Schools
SOUTH PACIFIC (The Solomon Islands)

The Solomons, being a young, small, isolated but scattered group of islands that make up a nation, faces similar constraints as other developing countries.

Our school Principals are selected and appointment is made of the 'best' candidate who may not necessarily satisfy the required qualifications as advertised for. But this is normal.

Government policies on localisation often mean that Solomon Islanders only may apply for Principalship. It is therefore, very usual to have a young, inexperienced and less qualified National Principal with a number of experienced, older and more 'qualified' expatriates. You will be aware that there are some good reasons for such policies.

As there is still a general shortage of trained personnel, our Principals do not stay very long in their positions. Most are sent overseas for either formal training or higher qualifications. Many enter national politics and become Parliamentarians instead. A few are taken out to do administrative jobs at the Ministry, and a few are sacked for one reason or another.

Being a Secondary Principal in the Solomons requires much more than just being the administrative head of a school. Because our schools are mostly boarding and coeducational, Principals often play the roles of Community Chief, Government Agent, Community Advisor, Pastor and a 'big man'. We do not have female Principals as yet!

The responsibility of developing principals or potential principals professionally has never been an issue to question. No one had the resources to talk or do anything about it. One's own staff development used to be one's own responsibility.

Numerous factors such as; lack of funds, lack of trained personnel, geographical constraints, high turnover of principals, etc., are some of the reasons for the situation described above.

I am organizing a Principals' Conference mainly aimed at staff development. The Principals are very enthusiastic about the conference. One of my major problems has been in trying to identify enthusiastic, educational or other professional managers who could lead sessions on professional development topics. We just don't have them around.

to plague those whose vision can see the fundamental interrelationship between the two. Miklos (1983) contends that there are alternative strategies for the solution of this perceived problem which include, 'improving instructional methods and materials, making field experiences more significant in the training of administrators, and focusing preparation more specifically on the skills that are central to effective practice'. Daresh (1988, p. 182) provides us with a salutary reminder that administrative life is such that no-one can ever be totally prepared for it. He contends that the best that might occur during a preservice programme 'is for a person to be provided with some basic skills, attitudes, and values that will guide that person's continued learning throughout his or her future career'.

The formal preparation of all personnel for their administrative tasks can be informed by similar principles, with specific emphasis being given to the practical applications required by their future role.

Reference must also be made to priorities or requirements of such regulatory bodies as legislatures. An example of the latter resulted from changes mandated recently by the Government in the United Kingdom whereby heads of schools required new skills in the areas of public relationship and communication skills, and financial and resource management skills (Glatter, 1988).

In response to such challenges new Management Training Programmes have been developed such as the ones described in the following case study by John Moore, a Regional Staff Trainer in Scotland (Case Study 3). The varied activities and approaches reported give rise to a more general issue: What do educational administrators really need to know both in preparation for, and in implementing their role?

A frequent criticism of preparatory programmes offered, usually in award-bearing programmes at tertiary institutions, is that the relationship between what is learnt, and the actual requirements of positions to be assumed by students, is tenuous. Opinions vary about what educational administrators need to know. Cooper and Boyd (1987) identify four sources of criticism about current tertiary level preparatory programmes in developing countries (p. 15).

These could be instructive for other countries beginning to implement, or contemplating models adapted from extant programmes. They are:

- (i) that what programmes teach is not what candidates need to do their jobs;
- (ii) that the research base on which training is based is inadequate to guide practice;
- (iii) that administrators cannot strike a useful balance between general learning (applicable to all administrative posts) and specialized training (for jobs as Curriculum Specialists, Budget Finance Director, etc); and
- (iv) that the courses themselves are taught in boring, unapplied and unchallenging ways.

CASE STUDY 3

Management Training for Headteachers in Dumfries and Galloway

SCOTLAND

Dumfries and Galloway is one of the smallest regions in Scotland. With a largely rural population of about 140,000, it has 116 primary and sixteen secondary schools. About half of the region's primary schools have three or less teachers (including the headteacher), and only a quarter have eight or more staff. A few, larger, primary schools have Deputy Headteachers.

In most of the secondary schools there will be one or more Assistant Headteachers (AHT), and a Deputy Headteacher (DHT). With the Headteacher, they are normally referred to as the Senior Management Team. The roles of AHT typically include responsibility for curriculum, student welfare and faculty leadership.

There has been a great deal of change in education in Scotland in recent years. Many headteachers were appointed at a time when their primary function was to keep the education system running efficiently. There is a growing awareness that effective communication in a changing social environment demands a different form of management. This is being turned into reality, although slowly, and at times painfully.

Until four years ago, management development for senior management of schools was largely an 'ad hoc' matter. Courses run by the Scottish Centre for Secondary School Administration (based in Edinburgh, 100 miles away from the centre of the region) were the main source of management training until then. Other development for senior management included industrial secondment, and study for MEd degrees.

With the introduction of a Government-funded programme of In-Service Training for Teachers (TRIST), a more systematic approach began. Unfortunately, this programme excluded the primary sector, an imbalance we are still trying to redress.

Since the primary sector was excluded, the Primary Advisors, in association with a College of Education, developed a comprehensive management development programme for headteachers. The programme included five days of residential course work, and involved each participant in developing one aspect of school policy during a full year. It has been superseded by a self-pacing open-learning package commissioned by the region. It is hoped that a combination of structured self-study and workshop activities will be pursued in the primary sector in the future.

During 1986, a transition was made from external training sources to the development of 'designer programmes' at all levels in Secondary school management. These began with three-and-a-half day residential programmes, aimed at a range of management levels, and covering situational leadership and problem solving areas. Industrial action by teachers in

Scotland coincided with the TRIST initiative, thus restricting the range of activity which could be carried out. In the end, it proved to be a blessing in disguise, as the management development programme was not embargoed and was able to proceed quickly.

The early emphasis was on short courses, to raise the awareness of senior management to the issues and skills of leadership in a changing education service. This has been supplemented with short workshops on specific topics carried out in pupil-free days or 'add-on' in-service time.

In the primary sector, with the imminent introduction of Career Review for all teaching staff, there is growing interest from groups of headteachers in developing their own skills. This is being achieved both by short courses, and by consultancy work in school, either with the Headteacher alone or with groups of teachers. Most primary headteachers have now had their first Career Review interview (with an Advisor), and are beginning to implement targets in a more systematic way.

With the imminent introduction of School Boards (similar to School Councils), the Scottish Education Department has sponsored a comprehensive management development programme. This is based on a mixture of self-study and workshop methods, and incorporates video productions in its material. This will be in use in the near future.

Up to now, the topics covered in training for senior management have included the skills associated with personnel management (including leadership and teambuilding) and effective communication (in particular — negotiation, interviewing and running effective meetings). It will in the future include training in financial management, monitoring school effectiveness, marketing and the law.

There is a growing awareness of the need for peer support amongst senior managers, and this is being encouraged. A more structured approach to this form of development is likely to be considered in the near future. With the introduction of Career Review, the principle of a supportive management culture has been established. More work is needed to make sure that the grape does not wither on the vine.

Those developing preparation programmes must reflect on and address these criticisms thus ensuring that such programmes will not only have an enhanced reputation, but will provide their graduates with a confidence and a momentum which should be reflected in general improvement in performance throughout an educational system.

An advice paper from the State Board of Education to the Ministry of Education in Victoria, Australia, (1989) probed this issue:

> The focus of development activities for school principals will be on the enhancement of educational leadership and resource manage-

ment capacities. The ability of the principal to provide educational leadership and manage the school is critical to the effectiveness of the school. It also contributes to the development of the capacities of other members of staff and the school community. Professional development should assist in making principals aware of a range of leadership styles and in developing their ability to adopt different approaches in different situations. It should focus on those skills and capacities which enable principals to fulfil the requirements of the General Statement of the Role of the Principal in Ministry of Education Schools. The statement endorses a significant leadership role for the principal within a commitment to partnerships and to a collaborative approach to the running of the school. This means that principals need to develop skills which enable them to act as effective team leaders, to delegate responsibility and to foster cooperative and democratic modes of decision-making. Development programs for principals and aspiring principals should provide a balance of theory and practice and should relate theoretical and practical components; should include a focus on on-the-job experiences; should include learning and support based on teams and managed by those teams; and should provide for a wide range of experiences. The Institute of Educational Administration[1] should play a major role in the delivery of such programs. Attempts should be made to minimise the time required to be spent out of school, whilst maximising the tasks that are undertaken within schools by teams of people.

The paper defines the three main areas of professional development required. The first, *Preparation for Principalship* suggested 'that a profile of roles and competencies which contribute to effective educational leadership and management should be identified to:

- enable individuals to plan and develop their careers;
- contribute directly to the achievement of system priorities by identifying those capacities and experiences which enhance leadership, management and an understanding of broader educational issues;
- improve local selection for principalship by offering broad criteria to selection committees.'

It is further suggested that such a profile could be supported by:

(i) short courses for potential principal applicants to help them prepare for principal selection;
(ii) the establishment of means by which individuals can be assisted in evaluating their own capacities and experience and take action to improve them;

(iii) the provision of access for all teachers to a range of positions which would provide leadership experience and enhance the competencies identified.

This fostering of such access through the delegation of appropriate tasks to staff members is seen as an important part of the principal's role.

The report further recommends that: specific strategies to provide increased opportunities for women to gain administrative experience are required. These may include:

- requesting administrative committees in primary schools and Local Administrative Committees[2] in secondary schools to be mindful of the particular need to provide women with administrative experience when allocating duties;
- developing guidelines for administrative committees to ensure that account is taken of the full range of experience of applicants for higher duties;
- requiring schools to provide information to a central EEO co-ordinator on the gender breakdown of all responsibility positions including Higher Duties Allowances distributed each year.

Strategies such as these are included in the second Action Plan for Women in the Teaching Services. Beyond this, the Office of Schools Administration should advise selection panels in schools, school support centres, regions and branches seriously to consider the appointment of eligible women applicants to positions which arise, including acting positions, in order to redress current imbalances. Such an approach could be supported by:

- in-service selection panels on equal employment principles;
- providing professional development to prepare women candidates for the selection process;
- compiling a central register of women who are prepared to act in positions of responsibility for which they are eligible;
- adopting specific targets to apply to all responsibility positions.

It is also recommended that the Office of Schools Administration should report annually on the impact of these strategies in increasing the number of women principals.

A responsibility, all too seldom undertaken, of those who currently hold administrative posts is that of preparing future administrators through processes of tutoring, delegation, mentoring and other informal on-the-job training techniques. For example, a Deputy/Vice Principal of a school should be 'taken under the wing' of the Principal.

Brian Caldwell, the former Dean of Education at the University of Tasmania, reported in a communication to the writers that:

All newly appointed leaders in TAFE in Tasmania are required to undertake a management development programme with a mentoring arrangement built in. Each newly-appointed leader is assigned a mentor. Leaders and their mentors undertake two days of training with regular monitoring. Appraisal to date is very positive. Similarly at lower levels of a school's hierarchy, e.g. Department Head, prospective future senior administrators should be identified and inducted into the processes of school administration.

The educational system in which prospective and/or current administrators work must bear the major responsibility for the training needs of its personnel. Most systems have concentrated heavily on teacher training. However, there is increasing evidence of encouragement being given for institutions to provide, and for personnel to attend formal programmes, while the system itself generates induction and other ad hoc one-off programmes for its personnel. Concerning formal programmes, Olembo (1986) reports that graduate programmes in educational administration are offered in the Commonwealth Caribbean and Africa.

'Many of the universities seem to imitate the universities in the United Kingdom, Canada, United States and Australia' (*ibid*, p. 108) with regard to admission requirements, however, 'the scholarships available limit the intake to a very insignificant number ... but the graduates are deployed in key positions' (p. 105). The programmes lead to certificates, diplomas and undergraduate degrees, but very few of the institutions organize their programmes so that weekends and long vacations are utilized.

Information available from the University of Malta, as described in the following case study, provides a helpful model for administrator preparation by programmes conducted in the evening.

CASE STUDY 4
Preparation Programme — Formal
MALTA

The Faculty of Education at the University of Malta offers an evening programme of two years duration which leads to a Diploma in Educational Administration and Management. Participants in the programme have to be serving teachers, working either in the Department of Education, or with private schools. The intention of the course is to provide the Maltese education system with personnel capable of taking over the running of schools when vacancies occur.

The course is structured so that a balance is retained between the administrative side of education and the latest developments in educational theory and practice. Specifically the programme 'aims to acquaint participants with theories and research in the behavioural sciences that are related to the study of organizations. Within the framework of current developments in educational theory and practice it also aims to provide participants with opportunities to analyse situations and formulate strategies for administrative and management problems in education' (Farrugia, 1987).

The course comprises thirty units. It is taught from January to June and from October to December, fifteen units per year of fifteen hours per unit. Enrolment is limited to thirty persons who must possess a locally recognized teaching qualification together with five years teaching experience, or equivalent qualifications.

The course content is balanced as follows:

A	*Theoretical Perspectives for the Study of Educational Administration.*	*10 units*
B	*The Planning and Management of Educational Institutions.*	*10 units*
C	*Current Issues in Educational Theory and Practice.*	*5 units*
D	*Long Essay/Project.*	*5 units*

The Diploma is awarded to those who successfully complete the course and the final examination. A rigorous set of rules guides and controls the evaluation process.

A perusal of the titles of the units reveals that a judicious blend of theoretical and practical perspectives is presented during the two years on such matters as leadership, managerial behaviour, managerial control, economics and school management, school ideologies, planning and decision-making, educational innovation and curriculum development, motivation, performance evaluation, computers, office management, group dynamics, time management, stress, managing change, assessment and evaluation, special education implementation of goals in the Maltese educational system.

Regarding induction training programmes, Sapra (1984) reports, for example, that the recruitment of India's inspecting officers is achieved either by promoting suitably qualified, competent and senior persons from within schools, or by direct recruitment. Both categories undertake some training in the principles of educational administration in the various states. It is envisaged that a National Staff College of Educational Administration will provide training programmes for personnel from and above the level of District Education Officers, and that staff training institutions will be established for lower ranks in all states in collaboration with well-developed University Departments of Education.

However, a major constraint on adequate training in most Third World countries is the shortage of appropriate training materials for use in both the formal and informal training of educational administrators. Rodwell and Hurst (1986) note the importance of stimulating 'institutional development processes and the adoption of more diverse training methodologies by Third World trainers' (p. 116).

In supporting the importance of training for administrators, Rodwell and Hurst observe that in Third World countries 'efforts to reform education have made relatively little progress, ... that it is the implementation of these reforms that is the weak link in the chain ... (and) if education is managed at the middle and lower levels by people who have had no training, then ... they are not particularly effective, efficient or responsive to change' (*ibid*, p. 118).

It is concerns like this that have led to the establishment of training centres such as the one in Pakistan described in case study 5.

Crucial to the success of any training programme is the capacity of the trainers to develop and present relevant materials in a manner appropriate to the level of development and relative independence of the learners, and to the cultural context in which the learning is taking place.

If trainers supplement or base the material being developed upon administrative theories derived from another country, they must constantly think about and adapt these theories which to some extent at least will reflect the cultural boundaries of that country. Formerly training programmes in developing countries were often provided directly, and unmodified by personnel from donor agencies. Now the strong tendency is towards testing of programmes by local administrators and trainers who are also more involved in the preparation of suitable training materials (Weeks, 1988). All trainers must be well-trained, knowledgeable in subject content and competent in adult learning techniques.

Their challenge is to embrace what has been termed non-traditional approaches to training based upon the increased understanding of how adults learn. The essence of this method of training is that the trainer 'acts as a facilitator who creates a mechanism for mutual learning and designs a pattern of learning experiences with suitable techniques and materials' (Rodwell and Hurst, 1986, p. 198). The participatory techniques involved in these approaches provide an experience of reality during which the participants discover and practise for themselves by dealing with problems derived from the here and now of administrative activity. Thus more attention is given to doing, exploring and thinking about problems in educational institutions facilitated in accordance with the four assumptions of androgogy: 'adults are self-directed, have a reservoir of experiences to draw on, learn what is necessary to perform their evolving social roles, and are problem centred in their orientation to learning .... Teaching approaches believed to be effective with adults include discussion/discovery methods, observational learning and modelling, and self-regulation' (Pitner, 1987, pp. 31–9).

Non-traditional approaches can also include training sessions at times not

CASE STUDY 5

The Academy for Educational Planning and Management

PAKISTAN

Pakistan has a population of 106 million people with 72 per cent of the people living in rural areas. The official literacy rate is 26 per cent. Universalization of primary education has the highest priority in the education sector, but teacher shortages, especially in rural schools, is a strongly inhibiting factor.

Despite the enormity of the problems to be overcome there has been a sizeable expansion in the educational opportunities in Pakistan during recent decades. At all levels of education, primary, secondary and university growth in student enrolment, number of Institutions and teachers has increased almost tenfold from 1947/48 to 1987/88. The highest priority in the education sector has been given to the universalization of primary education.

A commensurate expansion in the management structure of education has not taken place because of the non-availability of qualified educational planners and administrators. In addition, until 1983 there was no institution in the country to provide in-service education to educational managers. The establishment of an Academy for Educational Planning and Management (AEPAM) was first mooted in the 1970s as a means of strengthening the country's capacity in the planning and management of the education system at local, provincial and federal levels.

AEPAM was formally established in 1982 and became functional in February 1983 as an autonomous organization of the Ministry of Education. A Board of Governors under the chairmanship of the Federal Education Secretary has been set up to administer the affairs of the Academy. The aims and objectives assigned to the Academy are:

- *(i) to identify, develop and evaluate various projects based on modern planning and management techniques;*
- *(ii) to collect and consolidate educational statistics and information;*
- *(iii) to develop training modules for the grass roots planners and administrators;*
- *(iv) to provide in-service training to the planners and administrators so as to enhance their capabilities;*
- *(v) to impart pre-service training to those educationists who are being considered for appointment as educational administrators and planners at various levels;*
- *(vi) to conduct specialized training programmes in the area of computers and data processing for educational planners and administrators;*

(vii) to develop liaison with the trainees for monitoring their performance and providing feedback for the improvement of the training programmes;

(viii) to contract and carry out action-oriented research studies in order to facilitate the effective implementation of the Action Plan;

(ix) to organize conferences, seminars and workshops on important themes of educational planning and management; and

(x) to provide expert advisory services to the provincial education departments and other institutions in the country, if required.

The Academy is housed in its own two-storied building for the various functions of staff. It has a two-storied hostel which can accommodate twenty-four participants. The professional staff comprises seventeen persons including a Director General, Three Directors (Training, Research and MIS), two Joint Directors (Training and Research), three Deputy Directors (Training, Research and MIS), a Documentation Officer, a System Analyst, a Programmer, and five Research Officers. An additional eight positions have been created, anticipated to be filled in 1990.

To the present AEPAM has been engaged mainly in the tasks of training educational planners and administrators; conducting research on problems and issues related to various aspects of educational development; and assisting in the establishment of an education management information system in the country.

Up to 1988, AEPAM had conducted fifty-two programmes for educational programmers and administrators. These programmes have varied from the long-term training course in educational planning and management (9–10 weeks), to short seminars (1–5 days). The participants in these programmes have included Provincial Education Secretaries, Directors of Education, District Education Officers, University Deans, and College Principals. Limited resources have inhibited the provision of training for lower echelon personnel, including Headteachers of Schools.

The Academy has also been engaged in research and evaluation studies related to education planning and management. The research activities undertaken and the list of publications are impressive, given the limited resources available. It is recognized, however, that the current overall capacity of AEPAM is inadequate for the tasks before it.

Plans for the immediate future which will enhance the functioning of AEPAM include additional training for the professional staff in training methods, policy analysis, and action-oriented research in education. The Academy will therefore be less dependent upon external faculty. However, external faculty always play an important role in the life of a training institution, bringing fresh ideas, new perspectives and practical relevance to the training provided. Being non-collegiate staff they also represent a cost effective way of securing expertise when needed.

usually considered. As Brian Caldwell commented to us: 'We must look for new modes of delivery of training and professional development for principals. For example, in Tasmania, we are doing some work at the beginning of each workday. We have twelve Thursday breakfast seminars conducted from 7.30–9.30 am commencing 14 September on the theme Creating an Excellent School based on the book. A total of ninety-two people will be participating, with about twenty-five doing the seminars as part of course requirements. We have clearly hit on a time slot which meets the needs of a lot of people.'

Mulford (1986) provides another timely reminder to those who engage in training/teaching educational administrators that 'most adults when entering a new learning experience begin with dependent-type behaviours' and, if the programme is good, '... move to independent behaviour and then to interdependent behaviour during the course of the learning activities' (p. 34). The progression can be facilitated by a readiness to provide 'some structure at the beginning of the learning activities; to move then to encouraging individual activities; and finally to provide opportunities for interdependent activities within the group'. Mulford concludes that 'adult learning behaviours tend to change as a result of increasing familiarity with the learning programme, content, or setting. Simultaneously, teaching modes need to change in response'.

The skilful teacher of adults knows that, within a sequence of teaching styles, there is a place for the didactic approach to teaching, and that the classroom methods of one-way communication — lectures, films, slide-talks, panel presentations, do have value and are necessary in certain circumstances. But he or she also knows that training must come alive for participants and this is achieved by having the adult learner fully and actively involved in the learning process. The diversity of approach which is required is well exemplified in the UK Open University's distance education programme (case study 6).

It is increasingly recognised that those who train educational administrators should themselves be trained to enable them to be fully involved in all of the processes necessary to build a good training programme, from needs analysis through syllabus and content development to presentation and evaluation/feedback. This involvement should apply equally to those whose training work takes place in either the formal sector, i.e. tertiary level award-bearing courses, or the non-formal sector, i.e. short courses, induction programmes, in-service programmes.

A training strategy incorporating the above has been developed and refined through successive implementations by Bernard *et al.* (1989). It comprises the following eight interrelated steps each building upon the output of the previous step:

(i) Training needs assessment and topic identification.
(ii) Preparation of training syllabuses.
(iii) Drafting of training materials.
(iv) Revision of materials and training of trainers.
(v) Implementation of training.

CASE STUDY 6
Open University/Distance Education Perspective
UNITED KINGDOM

The far flung nature of the teaching service in most countries makes it imperative that one means of providing preparatory or in-service programmes of either the short term or formal award variety be through the medium of external studies. Glatter (1988) summarizes much of what is entailed in distance education, and describes an Advanced Diploma in Educational Management introduced in 1985 at the Open University, UK.

For distance education learning materials are produced in a context separate from that in which the learner works. The pedagogy of distance education provides scope for the participant to combine study with work in ways which provide unique personal learning experiences.

Courses available usually comprise 'specially written teaching texts, recommended text books and audio-visual material (maybe special TV), face-to-face tuition at local study centres, and possibly residential schools'.

Important considerations in the development of these courses include a close collaboration with educational authorities in the design and implementation of phases. Such cooperation often leads to cohorts of teachers undertaking courses thus facilitating regular group meetings and provision of locally based materials, speakers and exercises etc. 'Group study methods enhance motivation, interpersonal contact and local relevance'. Study centres are an important formalizing aspect of distance education programmes.

An innovative Advanced Diploma in Educational Management requiring 800 study hours offered by the Centre for Educational Policy and Management in the UK's Open University, commenced in 1985. It has two distinct halves, the one having 'a relatively strong emphasis on exposition of theories, concepts, research and relevant contextual developments and issues … softened by substantial use of original case studies … to try to show the concrete significance of theories and concepts, in-text activities, exercises and assignments … , (and) local tutorial sessions … with wide relevant experience'; and the other being 'an experience-based course to provide students with an extended opportunity to apply their learning to particular working situations'. The logic which drives the programme introduces students to theory and research, gradually guiding them into the world of practice. The second half of the programme (nine months) requires 'the students to undertake and report on three small scale investigations of management issues in a school or college, though not necessarily the institution in which they are currently working.' The three projects are selected from a list of fourteen and are 'specified in broad terms, for example:

> *Identify the in-service education and training needs of teaching staff in an institution, department, or group, and make recommendations for a staff development policy and/or a programme of in-service activities. Consider the resource implications of any suggestions. ...*
>
> *... Substantial guidance in the conduct of small scale investigations is provided ... through specially provided materials ... appropriate methods require the students to engage in a high degree of structured (and often sensitive) interaction with colleagues, and, for some projects, with others such as parents, students, senior administrative staff and local employers.*
>
> *Early reactions to the course derived from surveys indicate that 'the course had broadened (the graduates') professional and managerial perspective as individuals, and had enhanced their capacity for fruitful personal reflection'.*
>
> *To the organizers the programme is satisfying but they realize it 'has limitations: there is provision for tutorial sessions, but not yet for residential schools; because of resource restrictions, the level of tutorial support to students is inadequate: and the scale of the operation makes briefing and follow-up very difficult to organize'.*

(vi) Follow-on reinforcement exercises.
(vii) Evaluation and review (of exercises and programme).
(viii) Preparation of guidebooks.

In the provision of training for educational administrators the planners and trainers should take account of the following themes developed by Pitner, (1987:)

- — provide opportunities for administrators to be away from the workplace;
- — allow administrators to personalize their training;
- — include opportunities for administrators to reflect on their actions;
- — build on the experiential base of administrators to foster cumulative learning;
- — incorporate modelling, and skill demonstrations in workshops and provide opportunities for participants to practise them;
- — include a component for training of trainers;
- — provide staff development for both personal and organizational growth and development;
- — design training that is cumulative;
- — allow administrators to recognize and act upon their problems;

— evaluate the outcomes of all staff development activities; and
— recognize that training can serve a variety of legitimate purposes. (pp. 36–9)

Women in Administration

The concerns that have been raised in this chapter concerning the selection, preparation, and professional development of educational administrators become even more evident when one turns to the position of women. Sanga, in case study 2, noted that there are no women principals in the Solomons. In response to the few women holding administrative positions, the Victorian State Board paper quoted earlier stressed the need for specific strategies to ensure that women gain administrative experience. Other countries express the same concerns.

As Usha Nayar (1986) noted:

> Women in educational administration and other professional leadership roles are noticeable by their scarcity both in the third world and the industrialized countries. In the former, their low participation is often resultant from the underdevelopment of women's education and hence low availability. In the latter, despite full education and high availability, very few women are to be found in educational and other leadership positions. In fact, in many third world societies the incidence of female 'seclusion' has thrown up more women educational administrators considering the low proportion of women who receive higher education in these societies. (p. 153)

Further in her paper (p. 165) she refers to research in India which has led to findings similar to those found in studies in the developed world — 'no significant differences are noticed in the leadership behaviour of male and female heads of schools along twelve dimensions'. The one dimension which did indicate gender differences, integration, suggests that 'female heads are better than males at working together as a team; settling conflicts when they occur in the group; coordinating the work; helping group members in solving their differences; and maintaining a closely knit group'. In summary, 'The perceived effectiveness of women principals was found to be as high as that of their male counterparts, if not higher ...'.

A recent study on factors affecting women's career decisions in Victorian secondary schools (Taylor, 1988), found that in a promotion system where the individual applies for and is interviewed for administrative positions 'such an application depends on the confidence of the prospective applicants that they can carry out the work and that they have some hope of gaining appointments' (*ibid*, p. 216). There is, however, a third factor that was found to be equally important — the application would be made only if it did not conflict with values that took precedence over career progress. These values may be related to personal life such as family responsibilities but they could also apply to the nature of the promotion positions being offered. Statements from the sixty-three women interviewed in the study suggest that role descriptions could benefit from a re-examination of the expectations they embody, not just to make them more compatible for women but also to provide schools with a more varied range of administrative styles' (*ibid*, 217).

If these findings which are consistently appearing, are correct, then those concerned with achieving the best administrative personnel for schools must note and act on them to ensure that women are enabled to achieve their full potential and be involved in roles that obviously match their abilities. All involved in education would gain from such moves.

Conclusion

Throughout the Commonwealth there is a continual ferment in the thinking of those charged with the responsibility of making system-wide changes in the administration of education. These changes are essentially in response to calls for greater efficiency in system administration, and to demands that the quality of education be improved. Thus a system's infrastructure must ultimately be geared and changed to support the teaching/learning activities of classrooms.

Teacher education and training, while still inadequate in many countries has hitherto received the bulk of attention. Currently the preparation and training of educational administrators has come increasingly into focus as the push for decentralization as a means to improve system efficiency and to make schools more responsive to quality improvement needs has gathered momentum. With this push comes: the concomitant redefinition of roles and responsibilities for systems' and schools' administrators; calls for school-based management and community participation; and the requirement that changes must occur in the organizational structure.

Further, the centrality and extraordinary complexity of the head of school's role as the facilitator and mediator of appropriate managerial responses to the changing administrative climate and environment has finally been recognized.

Still to be determined in almost all countries, is how best to select personnel for redefined administrative positions, and to provide training programmes in administration which are relevant to their positions and career stages.

This chapter has attempted to provide an overview of the progress made and the dilemmas faced in the selection and training of educational administrators. It has drawn upon the experiences of the workers, the scholarly literature, and the activities of contemporary practitioners. Numerous initiatives which are far reaching in philosophy, scope and potential, and are worthy of description have not been included. Examples of these would include the National Institute of Educational Management in Malaysia which provides residential training programmes for all involved in the administration of schools from office staff to senior systems personnel; similar institutions in India, Kenya, Mauritius, Sri Lanka and Tanzania; the Institute of Education in Singapore which is implementing the Government's policy that all principals of schools should receive one year of formal certificated training before taking up a position; and the Institute of Educational Administration in Victoria, Australia, which develops and presents short- and long-term residential programmes in educational leadership and management for a clientele ranging from senior secondary school students through parents to senior systems personnel.

It would be easy for those involved in advancing education through the professional development of educators to be overwhelmed by the magnitude of the task and by comparison to give the professional development of educational administrators a low priority. However, the quality of schools depends to a large extent on the quality of the administrators who need to be well prepared for this task for, in the words of Beare, Caldwell and Millikan (1989) 'school administration now takes place in an increasingly turbulent, politically charged environment; bluntly, running schools has become a tough job which involves very much more knowledge and skill than it did even a decade ago' (p. xiii).

It is therefore encouraging to see, across the Commonwealth, continued efforts to ensure that educational administrators will be well prepared to carry out their increasingly complex task for the benefit of those for whom schools are established — the students — and, ultimately, for the community at large.

Notes

1 The Institute of Educational Administration is a Statutory body established in 1977 under the Directorship of Dr. C.R. Moyle to provide administrative training programmes, to undertake research to ascertain methods by which the quality of educational administration may be improved, and to advise and assist educational institutions in matters relating to the administration of those institutions. Situated in Geelong, Victoria, its building comprises modern administrative, educational, residential, recreational and dining facilities. Over the years a range of long and short term programmes has been presented to persons ranging across the spectrum of those involved in school and system administration from student leaders to the Ministry's most senior personnel. Within the limits of its resources research and development activities including learning packages, have also been developed and implemented.

2 Local Administrative Committees consist of teachers elected to work with the Principal on administrative matters within the school.

References

Beare, H., Caldwell, B.J. and Millikan, R. (1989) *Creating an Excellent School: Some New Management Techniques*, London, Routledge.

Bernard, D., Moyle, C.R. and Pongtuluran, A. (1989) *Toward Decentralization in Education: Experiences of a Staff Training Program in Indonesia*, Paris, UNESCO.

Blank, D.M. (1987) 'School administration and reform in Botswana', *International Journal of Educational Development*, **7**, 2.

Cooper, B.S. and Boyd, W.L. (1987) 'The evolution of training of school administrators' in Murphy, J. and Hallinger, P. (Eds) *Approaches to Administrative Training in Education*, Albany, State University of New York Press.

Daresh, J. (1988) 'Learning at Nellie's elbow: Will it truly improve the preparation of educational administrators?' *Planning and Changing*, Fall, **19**, 3.

Farrugia, C. (1987) *Diploma Course in Educational Administration and Management*, Msida, University of Malta.

Glatter, R. (1988) 'University preparation for educational administration in the United Kingdom, with particular reference to distance learning', a paper presented to the University Council for Educational Administration Convention, Cincinatti, Ohio.

Judge, H. (1989) 'Is there a crisis in British secondary schools?', *Kappan*, June, **70**, 10.

Miklos, E. (1983) 'Evolution in administrator preparation programs', *Educational Administration Quarterly*, **19**, 3.

Mulford, W. (1986) 'Assessing the effectiveness in the field of professional preparation programs in educational administration' in Marshall, D.G. and Newton, E.H. (Eds) *The Professional Preparation and Development of Educational Administrators in Developing Areas: The Caribbean*, Ontario, Nipissing College.

Murphy, J. and Hallinger, P. (Eds) (1987) *Approaches to Administrative Training in Education*, Albany, State University of New York Press.

Nayar, U. (1986) 'Women in educational administration in the third world — The Indian case', in Marshall, D.G. and Newton, E.H. (Eds) *The Professional Preparation and Development of Educational Administrators in Developing Areas: The Caribbean*, Ontario, Nipissing College.

Olembo, J. (1986) 'Graduate programs in educational administration in developing countries', in Marshall, D.G. and Newton, E.H. (Eds) *The Professional Preparation and Development of Educational Administrators in Developing Areas: The Caribbean*, Ontario, Nipissing College.

Pitner, M.J. (1987) 'Principles of quality staff development: Lessons in administrator training' in Murphy, J. and Hallinger, P. (Eds) *Approaches to Administrative Training in Education*, Albany, State University of New York Press.

Rodwell, S. and Hurst, P. (1986) 'Learning resources in the training of third world educational administrators', in Marshall, D.G. and Newton, E.H. (Eds) *The Professional Preparation and Development of Educational Administrators in Developing Areas: The Caribbean*, Ontario, Nipissing College.

Sapra, C. (1984) *Report on the Study Group on Supervision and Inspection*, New Delhi, National Council of Educational Research and Training.

Scott, B. (1989) *Schools Renewal: A Strategy to Revitalise Schools Within the New South Wales State Education System*, Sydney, Management Review, NSW Education Portfolio.

Taylor, B. (1988) 'Exceptional women: Applicants for promotion in the Victorian teaching service, 1987, unpublished PhD doctoral dissertation, University of New England.

WEEKS, J. (1988) 'Current issues in professional development in developing countries: A personal view', *Journal of Educational Administration*, **26**, 3.

17 Theory and Research as Catalysts for Change

Meredydd Hughes and Tony Bush

Theory and Practice

The relationship between theory and practice has been a recurring theme during the twenty years since CCEA was established. Throughout this period various concepts and perspectives have been advanced and discussed in many Commonwealth countries. As is normal in an applied discipline, the acid test of the efficacy of theory has been its applicability in the 'real' world of schools and colleges.

Theories are sometimes normative in that they expound how educational institutions *ought* to be managed. They may seek to prescribe the 'right' way to organize schools and colleges. Arguably, however, theories are at their most useful when they *describe* events and situations. When they mirror practice they cannot be dismissed as irrelevant to the needs of teachers and managers.

Former CCEA President William Walker stressed the importance of theory in the very first issue of the Council's *Studies in Educational Administration*. He argues that theory is a most practical phenomenon:

> The commonly accepted dichotomy between theory and practice, so beloved of the 'down to earth' man, the product of the 'school of hard knocks' is a chimera, or, more likely, an excuse to avoid hard thinking. It is theory that guides what we do, explains what we have done and predicts what we will do next. There is no escaping it, for it is impossible for us to take actions independently of our motives. (Walker, 1973, p. 4)

In 1981 Douglas Thom made a similar case for the relevance of theory to practice. Focusing on bureaucracy, he too asserts that theory is useful for the educational practitioner:

> Bureaucratic theory provides the practitioner with a tool for the understanding of his or her environment. He is able to dissect situations and to become aware of where he fits in the hierarchy ... it provides the practitioner with ideas to sharpen his skills ... The theory helps the practitioner to formulate questions to be answered about his/her organization. (p. 5)

Goldwin Emerson takes up this theme in 1985. In advocating a range of theories borrowed from other disciplines, he urges a search for better theory and commends its use to practitioners and scholars. He endorses the view of Hoy and Miskel (1978, p. 435) that 'increasingly, performance will depend on the ability to use concepts, ideas and theories rather than skills acquired through experience' (Emerson, 1985, pp. 4–5).

The arguments in support of the systematic acquisition of theory by practitioners have been rehearsed by both the present authors (Bush, 1986 and 1989; Hughes, 1974 and 1984) and were also discussed in the paper by Walker cited earlier. These factors can be summarized as follows:

(i) Reliance on facts as the sole guide to action is unsatisfactory because all evidence requires *interpretation*. Practitioners cannot make decisions simply on an event by event basis if decision-making is to be consistent and not simply arbitrary and disconnected. Frames of reference are needed to provide the insight for decision-making.

(ii) Dependence on experience alone in interpreting facts is narrow because it discards the accumulated experience and ideas of others. Practitioners can be more effective if they deploy a range of experience and understanding in resolving problems. 'It is only fools who learn by experience. Wise men do not have to learn of the existence of every brick wall by banging their nose into it' (Jennings, 1977, p. vii).

(iii) Disastrous errors of judgment can occur while experience is being gained. Mistakes are costly in both material and human terms. Money is scarce but the needs of pupils and students are even more important. As one of the authors put it in an article reprinted in the CCEA journal, 'in education we just cannot throw away the flawed product as waste and start again' (Hughes, 1984, p. 5).

(iv) Experience in one situation is not necessarily applicable in another. Organizational variables may mean that practice in one setting has little relevance in the new context. To interpret behaviour and events in the fresh situation a broader awareness of possible approaches is necessary.

Despite these justifications for the applicability of theory, Duignan (1982) draws attention to the ubiquity of the *theory-practice gap*. Practitioners remain sceptical of the relevance of theory to their day-to-day work especially when it is propounded by academics who may have no experience of 'what life is *really* like on the firing line' (*ibid*, p. 4). As Dearden (1984) points out 'teachers commonly regard theory with ... suspicion because its bearings are unclear on the detailed decision as to what to do next Monday morning' (p. 4).

Theories are most useful for influencing practice when they suggest new ways in which events and situations can be perceived. Fresh insight may be provided by focusing attention on possible interrelationships that the practitioner has failed to notice, and which can be further explored and tested through empirical research. If the result is a better understanding of practice, the theory-practice gap is significantly reduced for those concerned. Theory cannot then be dismissed as irrelevant to the needs of those teachers and administrators.

We will begin by considering the organizational model, the bureaucratic perspective, which has been dominant in traditional administrative theory. We then examine alternative perspectives which have become influential during the past two decades, this leading us to the notion of multiple perspectives and diverse methodologies. In the following section we consider the application of the perspectives in research and in practice, the examples chosen from a vast field being inevitably somewhat arbitrarily selected. Finally we return to the issue of the relevance of theory and research for educational advance. Are they truly catalysts for change?

The Bureaucratic Perspective on Educational Administration

When the CCEA was established in 1970 the theory of educational administration was located primarily within the bureaucratic perspective. Walker (1973), for example, refers to the 'mechanistic' views of Taylor and Fayol as well as to the work of Weber, who defined the essentials of bureaucracy.

Thom (1981) also stresses the seminal influence of Weber on the development of bureaucratic theory and gives the following definition derived from Gerth and Mills (1946):

> The following organizing principles maximize rational decision-making and administrative efficiency; the use of a division of labour and specific allocations of responsibility; a well-defined hierarchy of authority; administrative thought and action based on written policies, rules and regulations; an impersonal, universalistic application of the bureaucratic environment to all inhabitants; and promotion and selection based on technical competence. (p. 2)

Bates (1980) has argued that administrative control is 'essentially bureaucratic in form' and that educational administration should be regarded as a *technology* of control (our emphasis):

> While it may be argued that mass education is *implicitly* a form of social control based upon the articulation of hidden interests or hegemonised relations, educational administration is quite *explicitly* a technology of control ... The solutions to management and control problems are sought through systems such as: planning, programming and budgeting systems (PPBS); programme evaluation and review technique (PERT); management information systems (MIS); management by objectives (MBO); operations research; productivity research; systems research and simulations studies ... The language used is a clear indication of a preoccupation with control. (p. 3)

As Walker (1973) emphasizes, techniques such as PPBS and MBO are strongly based in theory. Their proponents predicted that they would enhance administrator effectiveness. However, there is little evidence to support the efficacy of these techniques and they have been largely discredited as universal panaceas, the United Kingdom experience being one example.

Despite the comparative failure of these tools of bureaucracy the concept itself remains a pervasive element within the theory of educational administration. A recent issue of the BEMAS journal features an article extolling the virtues of bureaucracy.

> The last decade has seen fundamental changes in the way in which education is provided ... many of these changes can only be understood and accommodated in the context of a bureaucratic theory of educational organisation ... If schools are to make the best of the new demands that have, to a great extent, been imposed upon them, they have no choice but to make the best of bureaucracy. (Packwood, 1989, p. 9)

Thom (1981) joins with Packwood in regarding bureaucracy as inevitable yet, during the past fifteen years, there has been a growing chorus of voices pointing to the weaknesses of this approach and extolling the virtues of alternative theories of educational administration. The main limitations attributed to the bureaucratic perspective are as follows:

(i) Bureaucratic theories characterize organizations as *goal-seeking* entities but in practice it may be difficult to ascertain the goals of educational establishments. Many schools have formal written statements of their objectives but these may have little operational relevance as Perrow indicates:

> Official goals are purposely vague and general and do not indicate two major factors which influence organizational behaviour: the host of divisions that must be made among alternative ways of achieving official goals and the priority

> of multiple goals, and the many unofficial goals pursued by groups within the organization. (Perrow, 1961, p. 855)

(ii) Bureaucratic theories portray decision-making as a *rational* process. Managerial action is said to follow a careful evaluation of alternatives and a considered choice of the most appropriate option. In practice, however, much of human behaviour is irrational and this inevitably influences the nature of decision-making in education.

> People in organizations, including educational organizations, find themselves hard pressed either to find actual instances of those rational practices or to find rationalized practices whose outcomes have been as beneficient as predicted, or to feel that those rational occasions explain much of what goes on within the organization. (Weick, 1976, p. 1)

(iii) Bureaucratic models focus on the organization as an entity and ignore or underestimate the contribution of *individuals* within organizations. They assume that people occupy preordained positions in the structure and that their behaviour reflects their organizational positions rather than their individual qualities and experience. Such views have been challenged to varying degrees by human relations theorists who may still be regarded as essentially working within the bureaucratic perspective. The stance has been more radically attacked by Greenfield:

> Most theories of organization grossly simplify the nature of the reality with which they deal. The drive to see the organization as a single kind of entity with a life of its own apart from the perceptions and beliefs of those involved in it blinds us to its complexity and the variety of organizations people create around themselves. (Greenfield, 1973, p. 571)

(iv) Bureaucratic theories assume that power resides at the apex of the pyramid. Heads and principals have authority by virtue of their position as the appointed leaders of the institution. This focus on official authority leads to a view of educational administration which is essentially *top-down*. Such hierarchical approaches are most relevant for organizations which depend on tight discipline for their effectiveness. Soldiers, for example, are expected to carry out their orders without any questioning or elaboration. In education the perceived legitimacy of hierarchical authority is more ambiguous. Organizations such as schools and colleges with large numbers of professional staff tend to exhibit signs of tension between the conflicting demands of professionalism and the hierarchy. Professionals claim an authority of expertise which may come into conflict with the positional authority of the principal. The following passage from Hoyle (1981, p. 16) illustrates the dilemma and demonstrates the ambiguous nature of hierarchical authority in education.

> *Head*: I'm a little concerned Mr Dingle, that your English lessons pay little attention to inculcating good standards in written English.
>
> *Dingle*: I'm sorry to hear that, but I would like to know how you have come to your views on what goes on in my classes and, as a physicist, what knowledge you have in the teaching of English?
>
> *Head*: Mr Dingle, I regard those two questions as impertinent. I know what goes on in your classroom because I hear from other members of staff and from disgruntled parents who have been to complain. And although I am a physicist, I have been in this game long enough to know something about the teaching of English. In any case, as head of this school I am responsible for what goes on in it, and I don't like what I hear of your approach to the subject.
>
> *Dingle*: I'm sorry to hear that, headmaster, but as a professional I must insist on teaching English in the best way in which I know how.

(v) Bureaucratic approaches are most appropriate in *stable* conditions but are much less valid in periods of rapid change. In changing, dynamic, unstable organizations there may be little time or opportunity to engage in a rational process of choice. Bureaucratic perspectives require a measure of predictability to be useful as portraits of organizational behaviour. Yet, as March and Olsen (1976) point out, 'individuals find themselves in a more complex, less stable and less understood world than that described by standard theories of organizational choice'.

These weaknesses suggest that bureaucratic theories offer only a partial explanation of events and situations in educational establishments. We now turn to examine the other perspectives which have gained ground in the 1970s and 1980s.

Alternative Perspectives on Educational Administration

Political Perspectives

Baldridge expounded a new approach, the political model, in the early 1970s. Drawing on conflict theory, community power studies and interest group studies he articulated an alternative analysis of educational administration based on empirical work in universities in the USA.

> When we look at the complex and dynamic processes that explode on the modern campus today, we see neither the rigid, formal aspects of bureaucracy nor the calm, consensus-directed elements of an academic collegium. On the contrary ... (interest groups) emerge from the complex fragmented social structure of the university and its 'publics', drawing on the divergent concerns and life-styles of hundreds of miniature sub-cultures. These groups articulate their interests in many different ways, bringing pressure on the decision-making process from any number of angles ... Power and influence, once articulated, go through a complex process until policies are shaped, reshaped and forged out of the competing claims of multiple groups. (Baldridge, 1971, pp. 19–20)

Baldridge identified five stages of the policy process:

(i) *Social structure*. This is a configuration of social groups with different life styles and political interests. These differences often lead to conflict, for what is in the interest of one group may damage another;

(ii) *Interest articulation*. Groups with conflicting values and goals must translate them into effective influence. They try to exert pressure, make promises or threats and seek to translate their desires into political capital;

(iii) *The legislative stage*. Legislative bodies such as committees respond to pressures, transforming the conflict into politically feasible policy. In the process, many claims are played off against one another, negotiations are undertaken, compromises are forged, and rewards are divided;

(iv) *The formulation of policy*. The legislators determine policy which is the official climax to the conflict and represents an authoritative, binding decision to commit the organization to one set of goals and values;

(v) *The execution of policy*. The conflict comes to a climax and the resulting policy is turned over to the bureaucrats for routine execution. However, this may not be the end of the matter because the losers may engage in a new round of interest articulation and

> the execution of policy may cause a feedback cycle leading to a new round of political conflict.

Political perspectives have received considerable attention. In the United Kingdom, for instance, the British Educational Management and Administration Society (BEMAS) devoted its 1981 conference to 'the politics of educational improvement' (Pratt, 1982). A keynote speaker at the conference was Eric Hoyle who subsequently elaborated his ideas, arguing that schools are particularly prone to political activity for two reasons:

> One is their loosely coupled characteristics which yield the 'spaces' in which such activity can flourish. The second is the competing forms of legitimacy in decision-making which arise because the formal legitimacy of the head is challenged by alternative professional and democratic forms. (Hoyle, 1986, p. 148)

Political perspectives afford valuable insights into the operation of educational institutions. The focus on interests and the conflict between groups offers a persuasive interpretation of the decision-making process in schools. 'The political frame says that power and politics are central to organizations and cannot be swept under the rug. The perspective represents an important antidote to the antiseptic rationality sometimes present in structural analysis' (Bolman and Deal, 1984, p. 144).

A political perspective which, from a very different viewpoint, offers a radical critique of traditional organizational theory, has been developed by Richard Bates and colleagues at Deakin University, Australia. Drawing support from critical social theory as developed by Habermas (1976 and 1979), Bates focuses attention on

> the exercise of administrative authority during the negotiation of what is to count as culture in the school. A critical practice of educational administration would, necessarily, be reflective concerning such negotiations, placing them within the context of a critique of domination and a commitment to struggle in the interest of a better world. (Bates, 1982, p. 12)

Similarly Watkins (1986), in arguing for a critical theory of administration, affirms that 'the organization of teachers, students and parents to the various possibilities available is a central *political* activity of the educational administrator' (p. 97) [our emphasis], but adds that 'to facilitate the dialogue between the members of the organization administrators have to ensure the adequacy, legitimacy and openness of the way they communicate' (p. 97).

The critical theory version of the political model has had a mixed reception. It is criticized as 'not as reflective as its proponents claim' by Lane (1983, p. 1), while its method, according to Willower (1988) 'is not reflexive or self-critical' (p. 74). Lakomski (1987) argues that critical theory 'remains as far removed from "praxis" as the scientism it castigates' (p. 96). There have also been rebuttals of such criticism, for example, Bates (1984). The debate continues.

Subjective Perspectives

The Canadian writer, Thom Greenfield, is one of the most trenchant critics of bureaucratic perspectives. In a presentation at the International Intervisitation Programme in the UK in 1974, and in a series of papers (Greenfield, 1973, 1975, 1979b, 1980 and 1985), he strongly attacked conventional (primarily bureaucratic) organization theory. His main criticisms are as follows:

(i) He dismisses the concept of *organizational goals*, arguing that it is individuals who have purposes rather than organizations. 'What is an organization that it can have such a thing as a goal?' (Greenfield, 1973, p. 552). He argues that so called organizational goals tend to be the objectives of dominant individuals or groups within the organization. In this view principals or governing bodies are able to advance their own preferences as the goals of the school.

(ii) He treats *structure* as a product of human interaction rather than something which is fixed or predetermined. Organization charts are regarded as fictions because they cannot predict the behaviour of individuals. Greenfield criticizes the tendency of leaders to respond to difficulties by changing the structure rather than tackling the underlying attitudes of the people concerned:

> Shifting the external trappings of organization, which we may call organization structure if we wish, turns out to be easier than altering the deeper meanings and purposes which people express through organization ... we cannot solve organizational problems by either abolishing or improving structure alone; we must also look at their human foundations. (Greenfield, 1973, p. 565)

(iii) He focuses on the individual *meanings* of participants rather than the events and situations themselves. 'Organizations are to be understood in terms of people's beliefs about their behaviour within them' (Greenfield, 1975, p. 83). It is assumed that individuals may have different interpretations of the same event. Hoyle (1981, p. 45) suggests that in schools there may be competing realities. 'The head and the teachers see the world differently with each perspective having its own legitimacy'.

(iv) The interpretations of the researchers also come under scrutiny. If it is argued that 'the interpretation of human experience is the bedrock on which human life is built and upon which organizational theory should stand' (Greenfield, 1979a, p. 97), this must apply to meanings ascribed by researchers as much as to those of participants. The quest for knowledge thus inexorably involves a fundamental issue of methodology, as Everhart (1988) argues:

> Critical in this process is the recognition that the researcher carries certain interpretations of organizational life into researching. These conceptions are translated into basic research acts such as how problems are defined, what constitute data, and what data mean. (p. 709)

Subjective perspectives can be regarded as 'anti-theories' in that they emerged as a reaction to the perceived weaknesses of bureaucratic models. Greenfield sets out to destroy the central principles of conventional theory but consistently rejects the idea of proposing a precisely formulated alternative. The focus on individual meanings brings an additional dimension to our study of educational administration but it may be argued that subjective approaches alone do not provide a full understanding of the nature of educational organizations. Proponents would claim that this applies equally to other approaches.

Ambiguity Perspectives

In 1974 Cohen and March also challenged the bureaucratic perspectives in their standard work on *organized anarchies*. They claim that ambiguity is a prevalent feature of educational institutions which tend to exhibit the following characteristics:

> (i) *Problematic goals*. The organization appears to operate on a variety of inconsistent and ill-defined preferences. It can be described better as a loose collection of changing ideas than as a consistent structure.
> (ii) *Unclear technology*. The organization does not understand its own processes. It operates on the basis of a simple set of trial-and-error procedures, the residue of learning from the accidents of past experiences, imitation and the inventions born of necessity.
> (iii) *Fluid participation*. The participants in the organization vary among themselves in the amount of time and effort they devote to the organization; individual participants vary from one time to another. As a result standard theories of power and choice seem to be inadequate. (p. 3)

The authors suggest that the decision process can be likened to a 'garbage can' into which various problems and solutions are dumped by participants.

Decisions are the products of the interaction of four independent streams — problems, solutions, participants and choice opportunities. The outcomes of such decision processes are claimed to be unpredictable, a view challenged by political theorists. As Pfeffer (1981) has wittily observed, 'in organizational decision-making, some actors seem usually to get the garbage, while others manage to get the can' (p. 30).

The major contribution of the garbage can model is that it uncouples problems and choices. The notion of loose coupling is also at the heart of an alternative conceptualization of organizational ambiguity developed by Karl Weick (1976). Loose coupling means that events or organizational sub-units are coupled but each event also preserves its own identity and some elements of separateness.

In education the concept of loose coupling might apply to the relationship between faculties and senior management or to the links between governing bodies and individual teachers. Sub-units in particular may wish to retain a measure of autonomy from the central administration, for example to enhance their own reputation.

Ambiguity perspectives introduce some important dimensions into our study of educational administration. In particular they damage the bureaucratic notion that problems can necessarily be solved by a rational process. In conditions of turbulence and unpredictability decision-making is a much more uncertain business. However, ambiguity models tend to exaggerate the degree of uncertainty in educational institutions, which retain many predictable features. As Cohen and March (1974) themselves admit, 'no real system can be fully characterized in this way' (p. 91).

Collegial Perspectives

Unlike the other perspectives the development of collegial models cannot be tied to a specific date or a particular group of academics. These approaches have been an enduring feature in higher education but they also gained ground in primary schools during the 1980s.

Collegial approaches developed within the colleges of Oxford and Cambridge universities. According to Becher and Kogan (1980), 'collegium designates a structure or structures in which members have equal authority to participate in decisions which are binding on each of them' (p. 67). The authority of expertise is widespread in higher education and Williams and Blackstone (1983) claim that 'any organization which depends on high-level professional skills operates most efficiently if there is a substantial measure of collegiality in its management procedures' (p. 94).

In primary education also, the collegial perspective is widely advocated as 'best practice':

> The contemporary image of good practice has been promoted by the Inspectorate since 1978 ... It is of the 'collegial' primary school predicated on the two values of *teacher collaboration* and *subject expertise* ... It shows small working groups of teachers reporting back recommendations for school-wide change to the collectivity of the whole staff meeting for decision taking. These groups are led and organized by the curriculum postholders. (Campbell, 1985, p. 152)

The main features of collegial perspectives are as follows:

(i) They assume an *authority of expertise* in contrast to the positional authority associated with the bureaucratic models. Professional authority occurs when decisions are made on an individual basis rather than being standardized.

(ii) They stress a *common set of values* shared by members of the organization. These are thought to emanate from the socialization which occurs during training and the early years of professional practice. These common values are expected to lead to shared organizational objectives.

(iii) They assume that decisions are reached by a process of discussion leading to *consensus*. The belief that there are common values and shared objectives leads on to the view that it is both desirable and possible to resolve issues by agreement. The decision-making process may be elongated by the search for compromise but this is regarded as an acceptable price to pay to maintain the aura of shared values and beliefs.

Collegial perspectives may be regarded as highly normative and idealistic. They are attractive approaches because they encourage the participation of professional staff in decision-making. Moreover, the involvement of teachers in curricular and organizational change should lead to a sense of ownership of the new policies and enhance the prospect of successful innovation.

However, these models also have limitations. First, as Baldridge *et al.* (1978) suggest, 'the collegial literature often confuses *descriptive* and *normative* enterprises. Are the writers saying that the university *is* a collegium or that it ought to be a collegium?' (p. 33). The same criticism could be applied to collegial perspectives in schools. Secondly, the assumption of decision-making by consensus is flawed because schools and colleges have sectional interests. 'The collegial model ... fails to deal adequately with the problem of conflict ... (it) neglects the prolonged battles that precede consensus and the fact that the consensus actually represents the prevalence of one group over another' (*ibid*, pp. 33–4). Thirdly, collegial approaches may be difficult to sustain in view of the accountability of principals to external stake-holders. The requirements of accountability limit the extent to which heads are prepared or are able to share their power with their professional colleagues.

Multiple Perspectives and Diverse Methodologies

Considerable polarization of ideas and some acrimony were the immediate result as new perspectives were proposed. Commenting on the reception given to the Greenfield contribution to the 1974 IIP, the Proceedings Editor expressed unease: 'It would be regrettable if the academics of educational administration formed themselves into rival doctrinal factions of one-eyed true believers, whether of an "old" or a "new" ideology' (Hughes, 1975, p. 6). The writer proceeded to suggest that 'our understanding of complex issues will be enriched if we retain the ability and the will to appreciate that there are likely to be substantial merits as well as demerits in alternative perspectives'.

Similarly Baldridge *et al.* (1978) were stressing the partial nature of any one approach: 'the search for an all-encompassing model is simplistic, for no one model can delineate the intricacies of decision processes in complex organizations such as universities and colleges' (p. 28). In his earlier seminal work developing a political model and applying it to North American universities, Baldridge (1971) had been critical of both the bureaucratic and the collegial model, pointing to their limitations. In the later work, Baldridge *et al.* (1978) saw the political and bureaucratic perspectives as complementary: 'our original political model probably underestimated the impact of routine bureaucratic processes. Many decisions are made not in the heat of political controversy but because standard operating procedures dominate in most organizations' (pp. 42–3).

Some change of emphasis may also be detected in a UCEA seminar paper delivered by Greenfield in 1977. He called for tolerance of the existence of other possible perspectives and 'for research that attempts to look at social reality from a variety of perspectives ...' (Greenfield, 1979b, p. 179). In a concluding section he considered the implications for research:

> The attempt to reach an encompassing and consistent set of theories that explain social reality and order all its so-called facts is a mistaken path ... From this dilemma we should conclude that we should permit and encourage alternative and even conflicting theories. From these premises, it follows that methodologies must also be open and eclectic. (p. 187)

An interesting attempt to work out the implications of multiple perspectives and eclectic methodologies in a South American context was presented by Benno Sander at the 1982 IIP in Nigeria. He argued a need to conceive of 'multi-dimensional options' for the study and practice of educational administration, and provided a model of four interactive categories or dimensions: anthropological, political, pedagogical and economic (Sander, 1986, pp. 300–6). Relevance in coordinating activities is a basic criterion in the anthropological dimension; responsiveness to society is a primary concern in the political dimension; attaining educational objectives is the main consideration in the pedagogical dimension; while the economic dimension focuses on maximizing utilization of resources and materials. Crucial to the model, but not explained in detail, is the 'analysis of the confluences and contradictions between the different dimensions of the paradigm' (p. 306), taking account of differences of perspective and evaluative criteria.

The utility of multiple perspectives for improving practice is also a dominant theme for the American authors, Bolman and Deal (1984). They advance the idea of 'conceptual pluralism' as a means of developing a broader range of options for managerial action:

> Understanding organizations is nearly impossible when the manager is unconsciously wed to a single, narrow perspective ... Managers in all organizations — large or small, public or private — can increase their effectiveness and their freedom through the use of multiple vantage points. To be locked into a single path is likely to produce error and self-imprisonment. (p. 4)

Four 'relatively coherent' perspectives or 'frames' are identified, described respectively as natural systems, human resource, political and symbolical, each frame providing a different way of interpreting events and a different approach to effective management (pp. 241–2). Corresponding to Sander's 'analysis of the confluences and contradictions', 'reframing' is advocated, this involving 'switching across frames to generate new insights and options for managerial action' (p. 240). It is this which enables practitioners to 'diagnose the multiple realities of the people with whom we interact daily' (p. 255).

The notion of multiple perspectives has been supported by many other writers (Bush, 1986 and 1989; Cuthbert, 1984; Davies and Morgan, 1983; Ellstrom, 1983; Enderud, 1980; Griffiths, 1986; Sergiovanni, 1984). Ellstrom discusses four organizational models and integrates them into an overarching framework according to their degree of clarity and consensus concerning organizational goals and preferences and the level of ambiguity concerning technology and organizational processes.

Enderud (1980) extends this line of theory by presenting four organizational models as sequential phases of the decision process. He argues that there is an initial phase of ambiguity followed by a period of negotiation and bargaining. A possible solution emerges which is tested in collegial settings. The agreed outcome is then passed to the bureaucracy for implementation. Because there are four phases, 'participants often ... interpret the same decision as largely anarchic, political, collegial or bureaucratic, according to the phase which is most visible to them, because of their own participation or for other reasons' (Enderud, 1980, p. 241).

Davies and Morgan (1983) follow the Enderud approach in linking the same four models into sequential phases. They argue that the ambiguity of the decision process is heightened during periods of contraction and uncertainty. Policy is generated effectively only if adequate time and attention are given at each of the four phases. 'To miss any phase, or to allow insufficient time for it, is to invite problems subsequently ... Jumping over one phase may well create the necessity of a loopback (to an earlier phase)' (Davies and Morgan, 1983, pp. 172–3).

Although the Enderud and Davies and Morgan formulations are plausible it is certainly possible to consider alternative links between the perspectives. For example an apparently collegial process may lead to conflict and become political or anarchic. The optimum sequencing of the models cannot be predicted with confidence.

As we complete our review of bureaucratic and alternative perspectives on educational administration, it seems reasonable to conclude that the notion of a multiplicity of perspectives, accompanied by a readiness to use a diversity of methodologies, is likely to enable both academics and practitioners to achieve a fuller and deeper understanding of events and situations. Correspondingly they will be better placed to respond effectively and creatively to those events and situations.

Applying the Perspectives

Mainstream Studies Within the Bureaucratic Perspective

Until comparatively recently it would be true to say that the majority of research studies and discussion documents in educational administration can be located within the traditional organizational model which, for the purposes of this chapter, we have called a bureaucratic perspective. Three examples, from Australia, Canada and Britain, may be cited from the period when the creation of the CCEA was being mooted about twenty years ago.

In Australia Ross Thomas (1968 and 1969) carried out a study of innovation in a bureaucratic setting, namely the Queensland education system. A significant finding from a study of 164 innovations was that innovation tends to occur least in the central education system.

In Canada a succession of studies adopted a dimensional approach to bureaucracy, which led to the identification of a conceptually distinct professional element within Weber's characterization of bureaucracy (Punch, 1969). Punch found in a later study that the most important single determinant of school bureaucratization, as perceived by staff, is the principal's leader behaviour style (Punch, 1970).

In Britain Cohen (1970) used the Organizational Climate Description Questionnaire of Halpin and Croft (1963) to study role conceptions of secondary school heads, and found a bureaucratic role conception on the part of the head to be only partly related to the size of school. Heads of large schools laid greater emphasis on rules and formal procedures, but showed no less concern than the heads of smaller schools for the individual child, teacher and parental requests.

Over the last twenty years the salience of structural issues within the bureaucracy has been explored on a number of occasions. Thus Ben Ukeje, at the IIP 1974 in Britain, examined the variable roles of central, regional and local authorities in educational decision-making, drawing mainly on Nigerian experience, and warned of the problems created in most developing countries by 'the rapid multiplication of new administrative units which have to be coordinated with each other and with the existing departments' (Ukeje, 1975, p. 104). Ukeje returned to the same theme in an address at IIP 1982 in Nigeria, noting the state of 'structural fluidity' which tends to result from rapid socioeconomic and sociopolitical change:

> Hence there is always the urge or indeed the need to effect structural change in the system. But the parameters for the right choice at any given time and under a certain set of circumstances are generally not readily available or easily discernible. (Ukeje, 1986, p. 165)

Similar issues were discussed by Mukut Mathur (1983) in a study of multilevel educational planning and administration in India. Mathur favoured decentralization, but recommended more effective coordination within various sectors and agencies of education, and stronger linkages between the education sector and other sectors of development.

The issue of centralization versus decentralization in educational systems also emerged as a major theme at a 1976 Australian–New Zealand joint symposium on policies for participation (Watson, 1977), which was arranged by the newly formed New Zealand Educational Administration Society. As earlier chapters have shown, it is a topic which has recurred in Australian and New Zealand contexts, particularly in relation to institutional self-government, on a number of occasions: Mulford *et al.* (1977), Chapman (1988), Watt (1989) and Macpherson (1989).

The leadership role within a bureaucracy of the headteacher or school principal, already noted in the Canadian and British context, is also a key issue which has attracted considerable attention. It was taken as the theme of the 1980 CCEA Regional Conference in Cyprus (Cyprus Educational Administration Society, 1980). In his opening address, Andreas Anastassiades, the Cyprus Inspector General of Primary Education, quoted a UNESCO field study which highlighted an alleged lack of leadership by Cypriot headmasters. The report appeared however to exonerate the central bureaucracy of any blame, noting that 'though the role of the headmaster as leader and innovator is recognized by the administrators, it is not widely practised' (Wedell, 1971). Anastassiades, though himself a senior administrator, took the opportunity to reallocate the blame:

> In a centralized system of education all decision making on matters of importance and direction come from the top. For the headmasters the problem is not ability to show initative and leadership to solve the problems of his school but rather a lack of the administrative framework and structure in which he will be able to function properly and fully. (Anastassiades, 1980, p. 35)

While improving the bureaucratic structure within which the school and its head have to operate is eminently desirable as a first step, as Anastassiades recommended, it provides no guarantee that leadership and innovation will flourish. The adequacy of the bureaucratic perspective itself comes under challenge. Interestingly there were papers at the Cyprus Regional Conference— notably Farquhar's (1980) review of the management of change literature and Watson's (1980) advocacy of managerial discretion as a key concept for the principal in a centralized bureaucracy — which could be construed as providing support for the notion that alternative perspectives, new ways of perceiving and interpreting, are required to achieve a better understanding of leadership roles in educational organizations.

Some New Approaches: Dual and Alternative Perspectives

An early example of a dual approach was provided by Hughes (1976), who incorporated both a bureaucratic and a collegial perspective in the research design of a study of the secondary school head, conceptualized as a Janus-like professional-as-administrator role. Areas were identified in which the two perspectives were mutually supportive, in conflict or simply unrelated. Hughes proposed, and later elaborated, a dual (leading professional — chief executive) role model, the two sub-roles deeply interpenetrating each other in three areas of professional leadership: task achievement, group maintenance and development and the external domain (Hughes, 1985). It appeared that by facilitating authentic staff involvement and participation the professional-as-administrator could perform an effective integrative and coordinating role (Hughes, 1978).

The clash of bureaucratic and collegial perspectives is a recurrent concern in Ukeje's (1980) study of Nigerian university administration, and is the explicit focus of Lungu's (1988) case study of hierarchical authority in collegial structures at the University of Zambia. Lungu concludes that 'administrators may not entirely avoid clashes with collegial structures and processes' (p. 22), but considers that 'it is important to establish an equilibrium between hierarchical authority and collegiality' (p. 21).

The same duality is presented as a confrontation of alternatives in Ball's (1987) study of school headship in England and Wales. Using a political perspective, Ball identifies 'the twin problems of domination and integration' (p. 164) as analytical ambiguities of headship, a point elaborated as follows:

> Heads and their followers are trapped in this sealed political dialectic of colleagueship and hierarchy, professional and employee ...
>
> The management-line relationship is at heart disciplinary and punitive. On the other hand, heads find themselves confronted by pressures for high-speed organizational and curricular change, which demands high levels of creativity and personal initiative, and it is highly questionable whether traditional hierarchical management relationships are best suited to respond to such pressures. (pp. 164–5)

Ball takes the view, however, that — because of external pressures — it is the punitive bureaucratic approach which prevails in the UK context: 'In this situation the headteacher's role as leading professional is superseded by that as manager' (p. 260). Whether or not such a view is justified as a general conclusion, the unqualified use of the term 'manager' as an antonym for 'leading professional' can certainly be questioned. It appears to imply that 'managing' or 'administering' necessarily involves the adoption of a tight bureaucratic perspective, a proposition which attracts little support from Ball's own case studies.

Whether to work simultaneously using the methodologies of two disparate perspectives was a major issue for Best and his colleagues at an early stage of a research project, beginning in 1976, which resulted in a series of studies of pastoral care (student welfare) in English secondary schools. Originally conceived as basically a questionnaire study fitting neatly into our bureaucratic perspective, the project's rationale and methodology were soon being reassessed to take account of Greenfield's (1975) critique of conventional administrative theory. An interim paper (Best *et al.*, 1979) reported 'appreciable change in the theoretical and methodological orientation of the research' (p. 48), the researchers becoming convinced of the potential of an interpretive or subjective perspective for exploring the meanings given by individuals to pastoral care activities. Forgoing the 'comforting purity' of a single framework they argued that 'there may be much to be gained from drawing on both perspectives' (p. 51), and consequently adopted a dual approach. Interestingly however, they were already finding that their ethnographic study in a particular school, involving observations and interviews, was assuming 'a relatively more important place in comparison with the questionnaire study than we had originally envisaged' (p. 57). This became a significant trend, and the dual approach received little attention in their later research reports. Thus a qualitative study (Best *et al.*, 1983) of pastoral care at 'Rivendell' gave attention primarily to the views of teachers, fifty-nine of the eighty-two staff being interviewed. The researchers focused on eliciting the interpretations of these staff, rather than giving their own assessment of events'. 'We accept the force of the argument that to explain any social phenomenon it is necessary to establish the subjective meanings which relevant actors attach to the phenomenon' (Best *et al.*, 1983, p. 58).

A further example of a bureaucratic perspective and an alternative perspective in juxtaposition appeared in 1977 in the BEAS journal, *Educational Administration*. In two contrasting articles the school was conceived as a hierarchy (Packwood, 1977) and an anarchy (Turner, 1977), and each author then had an opportunity to comment on the other's position. The exchange highlighted a divergence of approach to issues such as professional autonomy and accountability, but revealed some commonalities. The relevance of the anarchy model has been tested empirically at a newly amalgamated comprehensive school in the English Midlands (Bell, 1989). The researchers found ambiguous goals, unclear technology and fluid membership; all features of the ambiguity perspective developed by Cohen and March (1974). Bell concluded that in conditions of organizational ambiguity 'the traditional notion of the school as an hierachical decision-making structure with a horizontal division into departments and a vertical division into authority levels needs to be abandoned' (p. 146).

A Diversity of Approaches and Methodologies

With the exception of two African references, all the examples in the previous section happen to be drawn from the United Kingdom. It must be stressed, however, that a similar widening of perspectives has been evident in many other parts of the Commonwealth, as we hope to demonstrate in this and the following section.

A notable example is provided by a University of New England volume, *Ways and Meanings of Research in Educational Administration* (Macpherson, 1987a), which brings together a collection of papers, mainly from Australia, and vividly demonstrates that research in the field 'has diversified in the last decade to straddle a range of philosophical, strategic, cultural and political questions in education' (Macpherson, p. ii). Macpherson's own study of regional directors of education adopted an interpretive approach derived from Greenfield's work (Macpherson, 1987b). A study by Augus (1987) of continuity and change in a Catholic school used a critical theory perspective, while Gronn's (1987) chapter on leader watching also placed emphasis on critical observation. A New Zealand contribution based on an action-research school development project (Prebble, 1987), drew eclectically on new perspectives 'to help (organizational members) to understand their own situation better and to help them design, implement and then evaluate action strategies that will improve the situation' (p. 246).

It is also of interest that a series of official studies of staffing and resource allocation in government schools in Australia and New Zealand was followed by further study of their adoption of different organizational perspectives (Sturman, 1986). Case studies of innovative schools enabled identification of examples which could respectively be described as bureaucratic, familial (corresponding broadly to the collegial perspective), loosely coupled and political, while many schools were more complex in their organizational patterns and relationships.

A general point that can be made is that unquestioned recourse in educational administration research to quantitative methods in the heyday of bureaucratic administrative theory is less evident as the merits of alternative perspectives have gained appreciation. Using qualitative or ethnographic methods, the actor's point of view is crucial and descriptive validity becomes the researcher's prime concern, as Duignan (1982, p. 4) argued in his study of behaviourally anchored measures of administrative effectiveness. Rather than interpreting events and behaviour within the framework of established theory, the researcher is able to consider the actors' accounts of events, theoretical understanding emerging as a result of that assessment. Such a process is akin to the 'grounded theory' advocated by Glaser and Strauss (1967), and is likely to be more appropriate for education and more acceptable to practising administrators than theory devoid of any input from practitioners.

Universal Versus Contextual Approaches

At the first IIP in 1966 Fred Enns (1969) warned that comparative research would require common categories of adequate description: 'Unless the researchers use the same concepts of system boundary and role, for instance, the studies will only lead to confusion' (p. 317). Given such universal agreement on perspective and methodology, the educational systems of the world could be regarded, as Reller and Morphet (1962) had enthusiastically proclaimed as 'a tremendous though relatively unused laboratory for the study of educational administration' (p. 425). The assumption, which underlay the traditional approach of the dominant bureaucratic perspective, is that structures and principles are universally applicable without regard to national or cultural differences.

It has to be admitted that transporting perspectives and procedures across the globe without regard to the circumstances and qualities of particular communities was a process which had some success. The most notable large scale example is the bureaucratic perspective itself, as witness the tight bureaucratic structures, with their strengths and weaknesses, which new nations have inherited from their colonial past.

Focusing on studies at the school level, structured observational research based on Mintzberg's (1973) leadership studies in the USA, has been conducted in Australia (Willis, 1980), in Britain (Webb and Lyons, 1982), in Canada (Duignan, 1980) as well as in the United States (Martin and Willower, 1981). Though the results proved to be broadly similar, Glatter (1983) pointed to a significant cultural difference: the 'inside focus' of the principals in the American study contrasted markedly with the external management emphasis identified in UK research on heads' tasks undertaken at the Open University (Morgan, Hall and Mackay, 1983). Similarly Gray (1983) has suggested that there are two broad schools of organization development in education, the American and the European, while Fullan (1976) has argued more generally that 'O D techniques are not culture-free and are not necessarily universally valid' (p. 47).

In an assessment of current professional development issues in developing countries, John Weeks (1988) notes that 'Sometimes models urged upon the Third World educational administrators do not fit comfortably into the alien environment' (p. 384). A vivid example of this was provided by Premadasa Udagama (1986) in a contribution to CCEA Studies concerning educational administration in small island states. In the social and political milieu which he described, bureaucratic impersonality as discussed by Weber would be a complete impossibility:

> In small societies administrative matters may be discussed openly as everybody virtually knows everybody else ... The governments too are closer to the people in small societies and informal communication is perhaps more important than the formal. Politics and administration are a perennial problem in developing countries, but in small countries the relationship is made more difficult by personal contacts ... Administrators face many problems. (p. 3)

Udagama is scathing of perspectives on administration 'with no politics, no economics and no culture. The theories have ignored, like the early missionaries, the politics of education' (p. 5).

Another CCEA Studies paper (Ocho, 1982) shows how political skills (using the term 'political' broadly as in our discussion of political perspectives) are a prime necessity for Nigerian school heads in dealing with party-political individuals and groups. The term 'political' is thus used in two different senses in Ocho's comparison of the headship skills required in Nigeria with the more technical North American requirements, which had been described in an earlier paper by Farquhar (1978):

> On the other hand the Nigerian school head may require more political skills to be able to manoeuvre through the contradictory demands of various political parties, members of which interpret administrative behaviour on partisan lines. He needs more skill and patience to work with ill informed, half literate and fanatical political appointees. Above all, the Nigerian school head needs more understanding of the need for internalization of acceptable values through education. Nigeria and other developing nations appear to be in a values dilemma arising from the sudden impact on our culture of contradictory foreign values and ideas that allowed little time for evolutionary acculturation, stabilization and synthesis. (Ocho, 1982, p. 6)

A case study of educational reform in Zambia (Lungu, 1986) again reports a high degree of politicization in the educational bureaucracy, but without the flexibility and openness to change characteristic of a more open bureaucratic structure. Lungu considers that, in developing countries such as Zambia, a reform programme, however well planned in system terms, fails to take off 'if objectives are not linked to the culture, norms, structures and resources of the target group' (p. 6). He dramatically concludes that 'To be an advocate of reform is to be a voice in the wilderness, or, more appropriately, a poorly armed African hunter confronting an infuriated wild elephant!' (p. 5).

The literature of official international organizations from about 1970 shows some awareness of the need for an international approach to educational administration to be sensitive to cultural and political factors. The report of an International Institute of Educational Planning Seminar (Kravertz, 1970) warned that there could be no universal panacea or package to be applied in all cases and referred to 'the doubtful effectiveness of even the most logical management procedures in the face of requirements for decisions coming from the conflicts which may arise among popular demand, political expediency, and economic resource feasibility' (p. 13).

Similarly Per Dalin (1973) at the end of a research project for the Organization for Economic Cooperation and Development on strategies for educational innovation in Europe and North America, appeared to regret having relied on a conceptual framework derived from the conventional literature on the management of change in which the comparative dimension is conspicuously absent. Recognizing that 'a structure for innovation would always have to have links with the administration of the existing educational system' (p. 263), he finally concluded:

> There is no *one* way to organize the process. A particular combination of factors in one country may call for a solution different from that required by the organizational pattern in another country, even if many basic factors (e.g. type of innovations, degree of centralization) are the same. (p. 263)

A third example is a UNESCO study of techniques for the improvement of school management (Van Gendt, 1976), which strongly opposed 'a tendency to transfer in an automatic manner the application of a management tool from one system to another and especially from developed to developing countries' (p. 93).

The indiscriminating transfer across cultures of managerial skills and concepts associated with the bureaucratic perspective has continued to be a cause of unease. At the same time there has been increasing recognition that alternative perspectives and methodologies are available which have much to offer in an international context. Such an occasion occurred at the 1982 IIP in Nigeria when Ben Ukeje (1986, p. 164) developed the concept of 'a culture-loaded theory of organizations', which he illustrated by reference to Greenfield's view of organizations 'not as structures subject to universal laws but as cultural artefacts dependent upon the specific meaning and intention of people within them' (Greenfield, 1975, p. 74). Similarly in Barbados, at the 1985 CCEA symposium on the professional development of educational administrators in developing areas, Earle Newton invoked Greenfield's critique in rejecting traditional models from the developed world for the training of Third World administrators (Newton, 1985). He drew also on other perspectives, including loose coupling and critical theory, and on Marshall and Newton's (1983) study of transferability across cultures in three distinct areas of skills and knowledge: the conceptual, the human relations and the technical areas.

It may also be noted that, even when the reference to new perspectives is not explicit, many *CCEA Studies* over the years have in fact placed emphasis on a sensitive appreciation of the perceptions and interpretations of those involved as participants in educational processes and those affected by them. An excellent example is a study of the views of Cattle Fulani nomadic families in Northern Nigeria concerning the education of their children (Ezeomah, 1978 and 1981), where the 'culture-loading' of the research design, to use Ukeje's phrase, was very high. The study depended crucially on obtaining the understanding and cooperation of the Fulani tribal chiefs and community leaders, and patiently working over a period of time to overcome suspicion concerning the purpose of the study. The research itself, as it developed, relied mainly on observation and oral interviews with family members in the Fulani language, using open-ended questions, and was essentially an ethnographic study.

Other *CCEA Studies*, some in more conventional contexts, can similarly be cited: a study of the social background of members of a group of Papua New Guinea students (Thomas, 1979); a case study of administrative team development in Queensland (Hampstead *et al.*, 1980); school self-evaluation in the English Midlands (Hewlett, 1982); the comprehensive school in Guyana, South America (Olembo, 1983); Australian primary principals observed (Phillips, 1986); school effectiveness in a Pacific small island (Thaman, 1987); scenarios being tested as research tools (Small and Briggs, 1987), with a Commonwealth perspective added by John Weeks.

Scenarios and case studies may be used for in-service training as well as for research. In exploring the international dimension it is therefore relevant to note finally the thought provoking case studies from across the Commonwealth brought together by Harry Harris, former CCEA Executive Director, firstly in *The Penang Case Book* (Harris, 1975), and more extensively, with a careful analysis of theoretical and methodological issues, in the *Commonwealth Case Book for School Administrators* (Harris, 1982). A similar volume for administrators in post-secondary education (McCaig, 1985) was also produced, both being published by the Commonwealth Secretariat. As noted in the Preface to the 1982 volume, 'It is the great advantage of the case study approach that as a flexible instrument ... its use for training purposes recognizes local circumstance as well as general principle' (p. 1).

Catalysts for Educational Change?

The concerns and priorities of academics, even as they develop new perspectives and research methodologies, may still appear remote and unreal to hardpressed and inadequately resourced practitioners in many parts of the world faced with new developments and unexpected challenges. We therefore briefly return to the crucial issue of the relevance of theory and research which we posed at the beginning of the chapter.

We have considered a number of contrasting perspectives on educational organizations. Drawing mainly on Commonwealth sources, we have noted examples of their application, and of the adoption of a multiple perspectives approach, in research and practice over the last two decades. It might well have been even easier to cite a host of educational developments *not* contaminated by any conscious recourse to theory and research!

Catalysis is a strong metaphor, and its applicability to educational administration theory and research since 1970 is by no means obvious. In the very practical world of chemical engineering effective catalysts are highly prized. They are substances which facilitate and accelerate chemical change, thereby enhancing productivity, sometimes dramatically. In the practical world of administering education it is difficult to cite clear cut examples of new perspectives and methodologies having a similarly spectacular catalytic effect in advancing administrative practice.

And yet, new ways of perceiving organizations and their members are beginning to have an effect. It is as uncontested assumptions are exposed as never before to the challenge of alternative ways of seeing that practitioners and theorists alike find themselves liberated from being imprisoned by a single and closed set of metaphors. As William Taylor (1984) has pointed out in an educational context, metaphors should not be dismissed as mere stylistic embellishments. They are powerful means of shaping thought. In similar vein Gareth Morgan (1986) has teased out the implications of a number of different images of organization: organization as machine, as living organism, as a political system, as a culture, and so on. Potentially it would appear that theory and research can have a dramatic and profound effect on the actual administering of education. This will occur as practitioners generally become critically aware of the metaphors they are constantly using, including their strengths and limitations, and of the range of metaphors that are also relevant, each with its own strengths and limitations.

It may be illuminating to compare two metaphors which have been proposed for the role of theory. The first comes from the early days of the American 'Theory Movement' when a spatial metaphor was used to justify theory in educational administration. According to Getzels (1960), administrative theory is a mapping of the territory within which the administrator has to operate. Just as a good map gives an accurate representation of the complexities of the landscape, so that the traveller may choose and vary a route in accordance with prevailing circumstances, administration theory, it is claimed, uncovers the pattern of relationships and structures of which the wise practitioner will take note, as he/she takes decisions on administrative matters. By implication theory and practice are very distinct and easily separable activities. It is the practitioner who goes out and does the travelling, coping with traffic congestion and changing the route as necessary because of road works or adverse weather. The theorist firmly stays at base, and is essentially a cartographer producing ever more accurate maps of 'the world out there' and receiving research reports from time to time concerning the accuracy of the maps produced.

The second, and more recent, metaphor, also providing a spatial image, implies a closer and more interactive relationship between theory and practice. The practitioner and the theorist/researcher are together in a helicopter, jointly investigating and skilfully manoeuvering their craft to explore the territory of operation from different angles and perspectives, landing at various places to appreciate the situation on the ground and lifting off again as appropriate. The metaphor is commended to educational administrators by Everard (1984, pp. 17–18), who claims that 'helicopter quality' is a major determinant of managerial success, quoting supporting evidence for management research undertaken for Shell. Helicopter quality, Everard explains, is 'the statesmanlike attribute that enabled a manager easily to shift his position between the particular and the general and abstract, so that he could relate seemingly unrelated experiences in his day-to-day work and make a coherent pattern of them (seeing both the wood and the trees and how they relate)' (pp. 17–18). The consequent 'broadening of mental horizons' for practitioners which Everard advocates sharply contrasts with his view of earth-bound administration: 'narrow-minded, nose-to-the-grindstone parochialism and compartmentalization, which can be rife and counterproductive unless active steps are taken to avoid it' (p. 17).

In the mapping metaphor the roles of the traveller and the cartographer are quite distinct. Characteristically, however, in the more contemporary model it is not easy to distinguish between the roles of practitioner and theorist/researcher in the helicopter, and any precise division would be arbitrary and somewhat artificial. As we have seen in this chapter, 'helicopter quality', to use Everard's phrase — including an appreciation of multiple perspectives and an ability to 'switch frames', as described by Bolman and Deal (1984) — is as desirable for the theorist and researcher as it is for the practitioner.

The standpoint suggested is in close accord with Schön's (1983) concept of the *reflective* practitioner and his advocacy of professional education which enhances the practitioner's ability for reflection-in-action. It is also in tune with the increasingly active involvement of practitioners across the Commonwealth as seminar group members and as individual researchers within in-service courses for professional development, as noted in the previous chapter. Edited volumes in Australia (Macpherson, 1987) and in the United Kingdom (Hughes *et al.*, 1985) are the outcome of such involvement.

As a part of their in-service training, teachers in schools and colleges are increasingly encouraged to conduct small-scale investigations in their own institutions, and there is encouraging evidence that such research leads to modifications of practice in these institutions. An example is the participant feedback from an Open University project-based distance learning programme (c.f. Case Study 6 in chapter 16) which indicated both an effect on participants' own management approach, thinking and practice, and an effect on actual and proposed changes in institutional policy and practice (Glatter *et al.*, 1989, p. 257). Such 'in-house' research may be expected to help in developing more reflective practitioners who will draw on academic expertise and relevant theory in tackling practical problems.

Looking to the future it may be surmised that reflective practice, grounded in theory that draws on multiple perspectives and diverse research methodologies, will contribute substantially to narrowing the theory-practice gap. Indeed the metaphor of a 'gap' may itself become outmoded and we will prefer to envisage a 'tension' between theory and practice, which is creative and which, we may hope, will always persist as a challenge to new thinking and better practice.

We were hesitant about claiming that theory and research in educational administration have been catalysts for educational change over the past two decades. There has, however, been so much change and development and new thinking, only a fraction of which has been briefly sketched in this chapter, that we may surely speculate that during the second twenty year span of CCEA's existence, theory and research in educational administration will truly become catalysts of worldwide educational change and development.

References

ANASTASSIADES, A. (1980) 'Background to school management in Cyprus' in CYPRUS EDUCATIONAL ADMINISTRATION SOCIETY, *Managing the School of the Future: Focus on Principals*, Nicosia, Cyprus, CEAS.

ANGUS, L.B. (1987) 'A critical ethnography of continuity and change in a catholic school' in MACPHERSON, R.J.S. (Ed) *Ways and Meanings of Research in Educational Administration*, Armidale, Australia, University of New England.

BALDRIDGE, J.V. (1971) *Power and Conflict in the University*, New York, John Wiley.

BALDRIDGE, J.V., CURTIS, D.V., ECKER, G. and RILEY, G.L. (1978) *Policy Making and Effective Leadership*, San Francisco, CA, Jossey-Bass.

BALL, S.J. (1987) *The Micro-Politics of the School: Towards a Theory of School Organization*, London, Methuen.

BATES, R.J. (1980) *The Function of Educational Administration in the Processes of Cultural Transmission*, Paris, International Sociological Association.

BATES, R.J. (1982) 'Towards a critical practice of educational administration', *CCEA Studies in Educational Administration*, **27**, pp. 1–15.

BATES, R.J. (1984) 'How critical is critical theory?: a short statement on Lane's critique', *CCEA Newsletter*, **6**, 4, p. 12.

BECHER, T. and KOGAN, M. (1980) *Process and Structure in Higher Education*, Aldershot, Gower.

BELL, L. (1989) 'Ambiguity models and secondary schools: A case study' in BUSH, T. (Ed) *Managing Education: Theory and Practice*, Milton Keynes, Open University Press.

BEST, R.E., JARVIS, C.B. and RIBBINS, P.M. (1979) 'Researching pastoral care' in HUGHES, M.G. and RIBBINS, P.M. (Eds) *Research in Educational Administration*, **8**, 1, pp. 48–74.

BEST, R., RIBBINS, P., JARVIS, C. and ODDY, D. (1983) *Education and Care*, London, Heinemann.

BOLMAN, L.G. and DEAL, T.E. (1984) *Modern Approaches to Understanding and Managing Organizations*, San Francisco, CA, Jossey-Bass.

BUSH, T. (1986) *Theories of Educational Management*, London, Harper and Row (reprint 1988 published by Paul Chapman).

BUSH, T. (1989) 'The nature of theory in educational management' in BUSH, T. (Ed) *Managing Education: Theory and Practice*, Milton Keynes, Open University Press.

CAMPBELL, R.J. (1985) *Developing the Primary School Curriculum*, London, Holt, Rinehart and Winston.

CHAPMAN, J.D. (1988) 'Decentralization, devolution and the teacher: participation by teachers in the decision making of schools', *Journal of Educational Administration*, **26**, 1, pp. 39–72.

COHEN, L. (1970) 'School size and headteachers' bureaucratic role conceptions', *Educational Review*, **23**, pp. 50–8.

COHEN, M.D. and MARCH, J.G. (1974) *Leadership and Ambiguity: The American College President*, New York, McGraw-Hill (reprint 1986 by the Harvard Business School Press, Boston).

CUTHBERT, R. (1984) 'The management process', *E324 Management in Post-Compulsory Education*, Block 3, Part 2, Milton Keynes, Open University.

CYPRUS EDUCATIONAL ADMINISTRATION SOCIETY (1980) *Managing the Schools of the Future: Focus on Principals*, Nicosia, Cyprus, CEAS.

DALIN, P. (1973) *Strategies for Innovation in Education, Case Studies of Educational Innovation, Volume 4*, Paris, OECD Centre for Educational Research and Innovation.

DAVIES, J.L. and MORGAN, A.W. (1983) 'Management of higher education in a period of contraction and uncertainty' in BOYD-BARRETT, O., BUSH, T., GOODEY, J., MCNAY, I. and PREEDY, M. (Eds) *Approaches to Post-School Management*, London, Harper and Row.

DEARDEN, R.F. (1984) *Theory and Practice in Education*, London, Routledge and Kegan Paul.

DUIGNAN, P.A. (1980) 'Administrative behaviour of school superintendents: A descriptive study', *Journal of Educational Administration*, **18**, 1, pp. 5–26.

Duignan, P.A. (1982) 'Developing behaviourally anchored measures of administrative effectiveness: some problems and possibilities', *CCEA Studies in Educational Administration*, **25**, pp. 1–10.

Ellstrom, P.E. (1983) 'Four faces of educational organizations', *Higher Education*, **12**, pp. 231–41.

Emerson, G. (1985) 'Will it ever fly?', *CCEA Studies in Educational Administration*, **39**, pp. 2–5.

Enderud, H. (1980) 'Administrative leadership in organized anarchies', *International Journal of Institutional Management in Higher Education*, **4**, 3, pp. 235–53.

Enns, F. (1969) 'The promise of international co-operation in the preparation of educational administrators' in Baron, G., Cooper, D. and Walker, W.G. (Eds) *Educational Administration: International Perspectives*, Chicago, IL, Rand McNally.

Everard, K.B. (1984) *Management in Comprehensive Schools — What Can Be Learned from Industry*? (2nd. edn.) York, Centre for the Study of Comprehensive Schools, University of York.

Everhart, R.B. (1988) 'Fieldwork methodology in educational administration' in Boyan, N.J. (Ed) *Handbook of Research on Educational Administration*, New York, Longman.

Ezeomah, C. (1978) 'Educating the nomads: The attitudes of the Cattle Fulani towards education', *CCEA Studies in Educational Administration*, **12**, pp. 1–10.

Ezeomah, C. (1981) 'Strategies for training nomadic teachers', *CCEA Studies in Educational Administration*, **23**, pp. 1–8.

Farquhar, R.H. (1978) 'Recent developments in the professional preparation of principals', *CCEA Studies in Educational Administration*, **11**, pp. 1–19.

Farquhar, R.H. (1980) 'New wine in old bottles: Managing change?' in Cyprus Educational Administration Society, *Managing the Schools of the Future: Focus on Principals*, Nicosia, Cyprus, CEAS.

Fullan, M. (1976) 'OD in schools: An overview and critique' in Open University, *Organization Development: The Case of Sheldon High School*, Milton Keynes, Open University Press.

Gerth, H.H. and Mills, C.W. (Eds) (1946) *From Max Weber: Essays in Sociology*, New York, Oxford University Press.

Getzels, J.W. (1960) 'Theory and practice in educational administration: An old question revisited' in Campbell, R.F. and Lipham, J.M. (Eds) *Administrative Theory as a Guide to Action*, Chicago, IL, Midwest Administration Center, University of Chicago.

Glaser, B.G. and Strauss, A.L. (1967) *The Discovery of Grounded Theory*, London, Weidenfeld and Nicolson.

Glatter, R. (1983) 'Implications of research for policy on school management training' in Hegarty, S. (Ed) *Training for Management in Schools*, Windsor, NFER-Nelson for the Council of Europe.

Glatter, R., Bush, T. and Preedy, M. (1989) 'Applied studies in educational management: A project-based distance learning programme' in Blum, R.E. and Butler, J.A. (Eds) *School Leader Development for School Improvement*, Leuven, Belgium, ACCO.

Gray, H.L. (1983) 'Organization development (OD) in education', *School Organization and Management Abstracts*, **2**, 1, pp. 7–19.

Greenfield, T.B. (1973) 'Organizations as social inventions: Rethinking assumptions about change', *Journal of Applied Behavioural Science*, **9**, 5, pp. 551–74.

GREENFIELD, T.B. (1975) 'Theory about organizations: A new perspective and its implications for schools' in HUGHES, M.G. (Ed) *Administering Education: International Challenge*, London, Athlone Press.

GREENFIELD, T.B. (1979a) 'Organization theory as ideology', *Curriculum Enquiry*, **9**, 2, pp. 97–112.

GREENFIELD. T.B. (1979b) 'Ideas versus data: How can the data speak for themselves?' in IMMEGART, G.L. and BOYD, W.L. (Eds) *Problem-Finding in Educational Administration*, Lexingtion, MA: Lexington Books.

GREENFIELD, T.B. (1980) 'The man who comes back through the door in the wall: Discovering truth, discovering self, discovering organizations', *Educational Administration Quarterly*, **16**, 2, pp. 26–59.

GREENFIELD, T.B. (1985) 'Theories of educational organization: A critical perspective' in HUSEN, T. and POSTLETHWAITE, T.N. (Eds) *The International Encyclopedia of Education*, Oxford, Pergamon Press.

GRIFFITHS, D. (1986) 'Theories in educational administration: Past, present and future' in UKEJE, B.O., OCHO, L.O. and FAGBAMIYE, E.O. (Eds) *Issues and Concerns in Educational Administration*, Lagos, Macmillan Nigeria.

GRONN, P.C. (1987) 'Notes on leader watching?' in MACPHERSON, R.J.S. (Ed) *Ways and Meanings of Research in Educational Administration*, Armidale, Australia, University of New England.

HABERMAS, J. (1976) *Legitimation Crisis*, London, Heinemann.

HABERMAS, J. (1979) *Communication and the Evolution of Society*, Boston, MA, Beacon Press.

HALPIN, A.W. and CROFT, D.B. (1963) *The Organizational Climate of Schools*, Chicago, IL, University of Chicago.

HAMPSTEAD, T.F., FORD, J.E. and HIRD, W.N. (1980) 'An administrative team development programme', *CCEA Studies in Educational Administration*, **18**, pp. 1–10.

HARRIS, H. (1975) 'The Penang Case Book', *CCEA Studies in Educational Administration*, **5**, pp. 1–8.

HARRIS, H. (1982) *The Commonwealth Case Book for School Administrators*, London, Commonwealth Secretariat.

HEWLETT, M. (1982) 'Adjusting the focus: Practical pre-conditions for successfully implementing evaluation procedures', *CCEA Studies in Educational Administration*, **28**, pp. 1–10.

HOY, W. and MISKEL, C. (1978) *Educational Administration: Theory, Research and Practice*, New York, Random House.

HOYLE, E. (1981) 'The process of management', *E323 Management and the School*, Block 3, Part 1, Milton Keynes, Open University.

HOYLE, E. (1986) *The Politics of School Management*, Sevenoaks, Hodder and Stoughton.

HUGHES, M.G. (Ed) (1974) *Secondary School Administration: A Management Approach*, 2nd edn, Oxford, Pergamon.

HUGHES, M.G. (Ed) (1975) *Administering Education: International Challenge*, London, Athlone Press.

HUGHES, M.G. (1976) 'The professional-as-administrator: the case of the secondary school head' in PETERS, R.S. (Ed) *The Role of the Head*, London, Routledge and Kegan Paul.

HUGHES, M.G. (1978) 'Reconciling professional and administrative concerns', *CCEA Studies in Educational Administration*, **13**, pp. 1–10. Also in BUSH, T., GLATTER, R.,

GOODEY, J. and RICHES, C. (Eds) (1980) *Approaches to School Management*, London, Harper and Row.

HUGHES, M.G. (1984) 'Educational administration: pure or applied', *CCEA Studies in Educational Administration*, **35**, pp. 1–11.

HUGHES, M., RIBBINS, P. and THOMAS, H. (Eds) (1985) *Managing Education: The System and the Institution*, London, Holt, Rinehart and Winston (Reprint 1987 published by Cassell.)

JENNINGS, A. (1977) 'Introduction' in JENNINGS, A. (Ed) *Management and Headship in the Secondary School*, London, Ward Lock Educational.

KRAVETZ, N. (Ed) (1970) *Management and Decision-making in Educational Planning: An IIEP Seminar*, Paris, UNESCO International Institute of Educational Planning.

LAKOMSKI, G. (1987) 'Critical theory and educational administration', *Journal of Educational Administration*, **25**, 1, pp. 85–100.

LANE, T.J. (1983) 'How critical is critical theory?', *CCEA Studies in Educational Administration*, **32**, pp. 1–7.

LUNGU, G.F. (1986) 'Attacking the elephant: Reforming educational administration in Zambia', *CCEA Studies in Educational Administration*, **40**, pp. 1–12.

LUNGU, G.F. (1988) 'Hierarchical authority vs collegial structures in an African university: Lessons from the University of Zambia', *CCEA Studies in Educational Administration*, **47**, pp. 1–24.

MCCAIG, R. (1985) *The Commonwealth Casebook for Administrators in Post-Secondary Education*, London, Commonwealth Secretariat.

MACPHERSON, R.J.S. (Ed) (1987a) *Ways and Meanings of Research in Educational Administration*, Armidale, Australia, University of New England.

MACPHERSON, R.J.S. (1987b) 'System and structural man, politician and philosopher: being a Regional Director of Education' in MACPHERSON, R.J.S. (Ed) *Ways and Meanings of Research in Educational Administration*, Armidale, Australia, University of New England.

MACPHERSON, R.J.S. (1989) 'Radical administrative reforms in New Zealand education: The implications of the Picot Report for institutional managers', *Journal of Educational Administration*, **27**, 1, pp. 29–44.

MARCH, J.G. and OLSEN, J.P. (1976) 'Organizational choice under ambiguity' in MARCH, J.G. and OLSEN, J.P. (Eds) *Ambiguity and Choice in Organizations*, Bergan, Universitetsforlaget.

MARSHALL, D. and NEWTON, E. (1983) 'The professional preparation of school administrators in developing countries: Some critical issues for decision-making', *Department of Educational Foundations Centre for International Education and Development, Occasional Paper Series No. 3.* Edmonton, Alberta, University of Alberta.

MARTIN, W.J. and WILLOWER, D.J. (1981) 'The managerial behavior of high school principals', *Educational Administration Quarterly*, **17**, 1, pp. 69–90.

MATHUR, M.V. (1983) 'Multi-level educational planning and administration in India' in MALPICA, C. and RASSEKH, S. (Eds) *Educational Administration and Multi-level Plan Implementation: Experiences from Developing Countries*, Paris, UNESCO International Institute for Educational Planning.

MINTZBERG, H. (1973) *The Nature of Managerial Work*, New York, Harper and Row.

MORGAN, C., HALL, V. and MACKAY, H. (1983) *The Selection of Secondary School Headteachers*, Milton Keynes, Open University Press.

MORGAN, G. (1986) *Images of Organization*, Beverley Hills, CA, Sage Publications.

MULFORD, W.R., CONABERE, A.B. and KELLER, J.A. (1977) 'Organization development in schools: Early data on the Australian experience', *Journal of Educational Administration*, **15**, 2, pp. 210–37.

NEWTON, E.H. (1985) 'Critical issues in the professional preparation and development of educational administrators in developing areas' in MARSHALL, D.G. and NEWTON, E.H. (Eds) *The Professional Preparation and Development of Educational Administrators in Developing Areas: The Caribbean*, North Bay, Ontario, Canada, Nipissing University College, on behalf of CCEA.

OCHO, L.O. (1982) 'Achieving educational objectives in Nigeria', *CCEA Studies in Educational Administration*, **26**, pp. 1–11.

OLEMBO, J. (1983) 'The unilateral (comprehensive) secondary schools of Guyana, South America', *CCEA Studies in Educational Administration*, **30**, pp. 1–6.

PACKWOOD, T. (1977) 'The school as a hierarchy', *Educational Administration*, **5**, 2, pp. 1–6.

PACKWOOD, T. (1989) 'Return to the hierarchy!', *Educational Management and Administration*, **17**, 1, pp. 9–15.

PERROW, C. (1961) 'The analysis of goals in complex organizations', *American Sociological Review*, **26**, pp. 854–6.

PFEFFER, J. (1981) *Power in Organizations*, Marshfields, MA, Pitman.

PHILLIPS, D. (1986) 'But soft, he is observed: Primary principal "on an even keel"', *CCEA Studies in Educational Administration*, **43**, pp. 1–16.

PRATT, S. (Ed) (1982) 'The micropolitics of educational improvement', *Educational Management and Administration*, **10**, 2.

PREBBLE, T. (1987) 'School research: Action research for the whole school' in MACPHERSON, R.J.S. (Ed) *Ways and Meanings of Research in Educational Administration*, Armidale, Australia, University of New England.

PUNCH, K.F. (1969) 'Bureaucratic structure in schools: Towards redefinition and measurement', *Educational Administration Quarterly*, **2**, pp. 43–57.

PUNCH, K.F. (1970) 'Interschool variation in bureaucratization', *Journal of Educational Administration*, **8**, 2, pp. 124–34.

RELLER, T.L. and MORPHET, E.L. (1962) *Comparative Educational Administration*, Englewood Cliffs, NJ, Prentice Hall.

SANDER, B. (1986) 'Educational administration: Challenges, prospects and options' in UKEJE, B.O., OCHO, L.O. and FAGBAMIYE, E.O. (Eds) *Issues and Concerns in Educational Administration: The Nigerian Case in International Perspective*, Lagos, Nigeria, Macmillan Nigeria.

SCHÖN, D.A. (1983) *The Reflective Practitioner*, San Francisco, CA, Jossey-Bass.

SERGIOVANNI, T.J. (1984) 'Cultural and competing perspectives in administrative theory and practice' in SERGIOVANNI, T.J. and CORBALLY, J.E. (Eds) *Leadership and Organisational Culture*, Chicago, IL, University of Illinois Press.

SMALL, M.B. and BRIGGS, D.K. (1987) 'Scenarios as research tools for investigating social issues', *CCEA Studies in Educational Administration*, **45**, pp. 1–15.

STURMAN, A. (1986) 'The application of organizational models to the study of schools', *Journal of Educational Administration*, **24**, 2, pp. 187–212.

TAYLOR, W. (1984) 'Metaphors of educational discourse' in TAYLOR, W. (Ed) *Metaphors of Education*, London, Heinemann.

THAMAN, K. (1987) 'Good schools (and bad): Some issues in assessing school effectiveness in Pacific Island contexts', *CCEA Studies in Educational Administration*, **44**, pp. 1–12.

THOM, D.J. (1981) 'Questioning bureaucracy', *CCEA Studies in Educational Administration*, **22**, pp. 1–10.

THOMAS, A.R. (1968 and 1969) 'Innovation within a bureaucratic system', *Journal of Educational Administration*, **6**, 2, pp. 116–31 and **7**, 1, pp. 20–36.

THOMAS, E.B. (1979) 'A Papua New Guinea elite: A study of the background of twenty-eight students of the Diploma of Educational Administration Programme at the University of Papua New Guinea, 1972–74', *CCEA Studies in Educational Administration*, **14**, pp. 1–15.

TURNER, C. (1977) 'Organizing educational institutions as anarchies', *Educational Administration*, **5**, 2, pp. 6–12.

UDAGAMA, P. (1986) 'Educational administration in small island states: Success or failure?', *CCEA Studies in Educational Administration*, **42**, pp. 1–8.

UKEJE, B.O. (1975) 'Structure and educational decision-making: The roles of central, regional and local authorities' in HUGHES, M.G. (Ed) *Administering Education: International Challenge*, London, Athlone Press.

UKEJE, B.O. (1980) 'University administration: The case of Nigeria', *CCEA Studies in Educational Administration*, **20**, pp. 1–21.

UKEJE, B.O. (1986) 'Educational administration and planning at the crossroads: A general overview' in UKEJE, B.O. *et al.* (Eds) *Issues and Concerns in Educational Administration*, Lagos, Macmillan Nigeria.

UKEJE, B.O., OCHO, L.O. and FAGBAMIYE, E.O. (Eds) (1986) *Issues and Concerns in Educational Administration: The Nigerian Case in International Perspective*, Lagos, Macmillan Nigeria.

VAN GENDT, R. (1976) *Tools for the Improvement of School Management: A Study in Two Phases*, Reports and Studies No. S18, Paris, UNESCO Division of Educational Policy and Planning.

WALKER, W.G. (1973) 'Theory and practice in educational administration', *CCEA Studies in Educational Administration*, **1**, pp. 1–19.

WATKINS, P. (1986) 'From managerialism to communicative competence: Control and consequences in educational administration', *Journal of Educational Administration,* **24**, 1, pp. 86–106.

WATSON, J.E. (Ed) (1977) *Policies for Participation: Trends in Educational Administration in Australia and New Zealand*, Wellington, New Zealand, New Zealand Educational Administration Society.

WATSON, L.E. (1980) 'Managerial discretion: A key concept for the principal', in CYPRUS EDUCATIONAL ADMINISTRATION SOCIETY, *Managing the Schools of the Future: Focus on Principals*, Nicosia, Cyprus, CEAS (also in *CCEA Studies in Educational Administration*, **24**, pp. 1–9).

WATT, J. (1989) 'Devolution of power: The ideological meaning', *Journal of Educational Administration*, **27**, 1, pp. 19–28.

WEBB, P.C. and LYONS, G. (1982) 'The nature of managerial activities in education' in GRAY, H.L. (Ed) *The Management of Educational Institutions*, London, Falmer Press.

WEDELL, E.G. (1971) *Teachers and Educational Development*, Paris, UNESCO.

WEEKS, J. (1988) 'Current issues in professional development in developing countries: A personal view', *Journal of Educational Administration*, **25**, 3, pp. 382–92.

WEICK, K.E. (1976) 'Educational organizations as loosely coupled systems', *Administrative Science Quarterly*, **21**, 1, pp. 1–19.

Williams, G. and Blackstone, T. (1983) *Response to Adversity*, Guildford, Society for Research into Higher Education.

Wills, Q. (1980) 'The work activity of school principals: An observational study', *Journal of Educational Administration*, **18**, 1, pp. 27–54.

Willower, D.J. (1988) 'Synthesis and projection' in Boyan, N.J. (Ed) *Handbook of Research on Educational Administration*, New York, Longman.

18 CCEA and the Commonwealth: Living Organizations for Development

John Weeks

The two earlier chapters in this section, have referred extensively to CCEA-related activities and publications across the world. Indeed, the worldwide perspective and broad understanding across national and cultural boundaries shown by all contributors to this volume may be regarded as a reflection of their common membership of the CCEA network. In this final chapter it is therefore appropriate to return to the theme of the Commonwealth and its institutions, introduced by Professor Walker in the first chapter, and to consider, in particular, the role of the Commonwealth Council for Educational Administration as a powerful and dynamic resource for educational advance.

The Commonwealth

Sir Kenneth Wheare, a former Vice-Chancellor of the University of Oxford, once said: 'If the Commonwealth did not exist it would be impossible to invent it'. 'But the Commonwealth does exist', says Peter Lyon, Editor of *The Round Table*, and Secretary of the Institute of Commonwealth Studies at the University of London, 'and is a continuing, innovatory, activist association. There is good reason not only to study it but also to promote it ... in humanity's interest'. He adds that it is among the best known and least understood of international associations. We need to help people to understand its role and appreciate its worth.

The London Declaration in 1949, issued by the then eight Commonwealth leaders, set the seal on the modern Commonwealth and showed it to be an association that was flexible, adaptable, innovative and ready to meet the challenges and realities of the changing times. Lester Pearson (1973), at that time Prime Minister of Canada, wrote in his memoirs: 'So began the new Commonwealth of Nations: British Empire to British Commonwealth to Commonwealth: Emperor to King to Head. This was one of the most important landmarks in the history of the Commonwealth. It was a critical moment in her post-war development'.

The Commonwealth, then, is concerned with and for people: concerned to help people help themselves, to strive to strengthen those global links and to make full use of the great potential which is inherent in those more than one billion people in fifty countries.

In its diversity of peoples, religions, languages and governments there is a unity of purpose, of fundamental beliefs — a collegiality — a family feeling. I wrote, after attending the Tenth Commonwealth Conference of Education Ministers in Nairobi in August 1987

> There is absolutely no doubt, when a meeting like the 10CCEM takes place, that there *is* such a quality as the *Commonwealth spirit*. It is a unique atmosphere in which — despite often quite strongly held, diverse opinions, expressed in heated argument — the freedom to be outspoken and a willingness to compromise and modify combine with a commonality of will to produce unity and consensus.

It's difficult to capture the essence of a 'spirit' in words. This indefinable spirit has to be felt, to be experienced, for one to appreciate its full significance.

So we see a Commonwealth as 'a partnership for progress based on the human values necessary for mutual support ... [and] ... interdependency' (*Commonwealth Today*, 1989). Or, as Davidson Nichol of Sierra Leone put it, 'A multi-faceted crystal has emerged in the form of a Commonwealth'.

The Commonwealth Secretariat

The light from that 'multi-faceted crystal' is reflected, refracted through the global network by the Commonwealth Secretariat which helps to turn ideas, schemes, resolutions into reality through its various agencies. It is the purveyor of the Commonwealth's collective wisdom, creating, to use a cliché, light and heat wherever they are needed. As Julius Nyerere aptly put it in 1977

> ... the Commonwealth is people meeting together, consulting, learning from each other, trying to persuade each other and sometimes cooperating with each other, regardless of economics or geography or ideology or religion or race.

The Secretariat, that 'main agency for joint endeavours' was established in 1965, as described by Professor Walker in chapter 1. It coordinates the work and continuing development of associations with a limited but extraordinarily effective staff. Eighteen divisions and programmes, each with its director, and staff from all member countries: an 'agency for action' as it is well called, the nucleus of the network. It makes use of the rich diversity in the Commonwealth to assist development, share expertise and experience to help countries and people to build confidence and to achieve goals.

Figure 18.1 provides an indication of the Secretariat structure in a nutshell. It shows boxes but within those boxes lies its strength — the people committed to its values.

The Secretariat coordinates and organizes intergovernmental consultations, services Commonwealth meetings and committees, conducts programmes of cooperation, implements projects and is a clearing-house for information. It also maintains links with professional associations like the Commonwealth Council for Educational Administration (CCEA) and the developing group of such non-Government organizations (NGOs).

Let us consider more closely two of the important programmes of the Human Resource Development Group (HRDG): Education and Fellowships and Training, both of which are closely associated with CCEA.

The Education Programme is the oldest area of Commonwealth cooperation. The present Education Programme is one of the six programmes brought together in the Human Resource Development Group to concentrate on consolidating the Secretariat's work in helping governments strengthen their manpower resources and provide guidance and opportunities for personal professional development.

CCEA has, over the years, enjoyed the support and encouragement of the Programme in the area of educational administration and currently continues this close association in a variety of projects, for example:

* selection, training and support of personnel in isolated situations in small states;
* the role of the multi-faceted administrator;
* organization and administration of ministries and departments in small island states.

The Programme makes considerable use of professional associations in its work in higher education, science, teacher education, non-formal education and, of course, educational administration.

Providing the resources for many of the projects developed by the Education Programme in association with Commonwealth governments is the **Commonwealth Fund for Technical Cooperation**. The CFTC's Fellowships and Training Programme makes available awards for training projects and supports the various seminars and workshops which form an important part of the Education Programme's activities. The Education programme helps countries and people to fulfil those great expectations which depend on the human face of education development.

All these projects rely not only on links between governments but also on links between professionals across the Commonwealth. This potential resource for national and Commonwealth development was a scattered, diverse group

Figure 18.1 Administrative Structure of the Commonwealth Secretariat

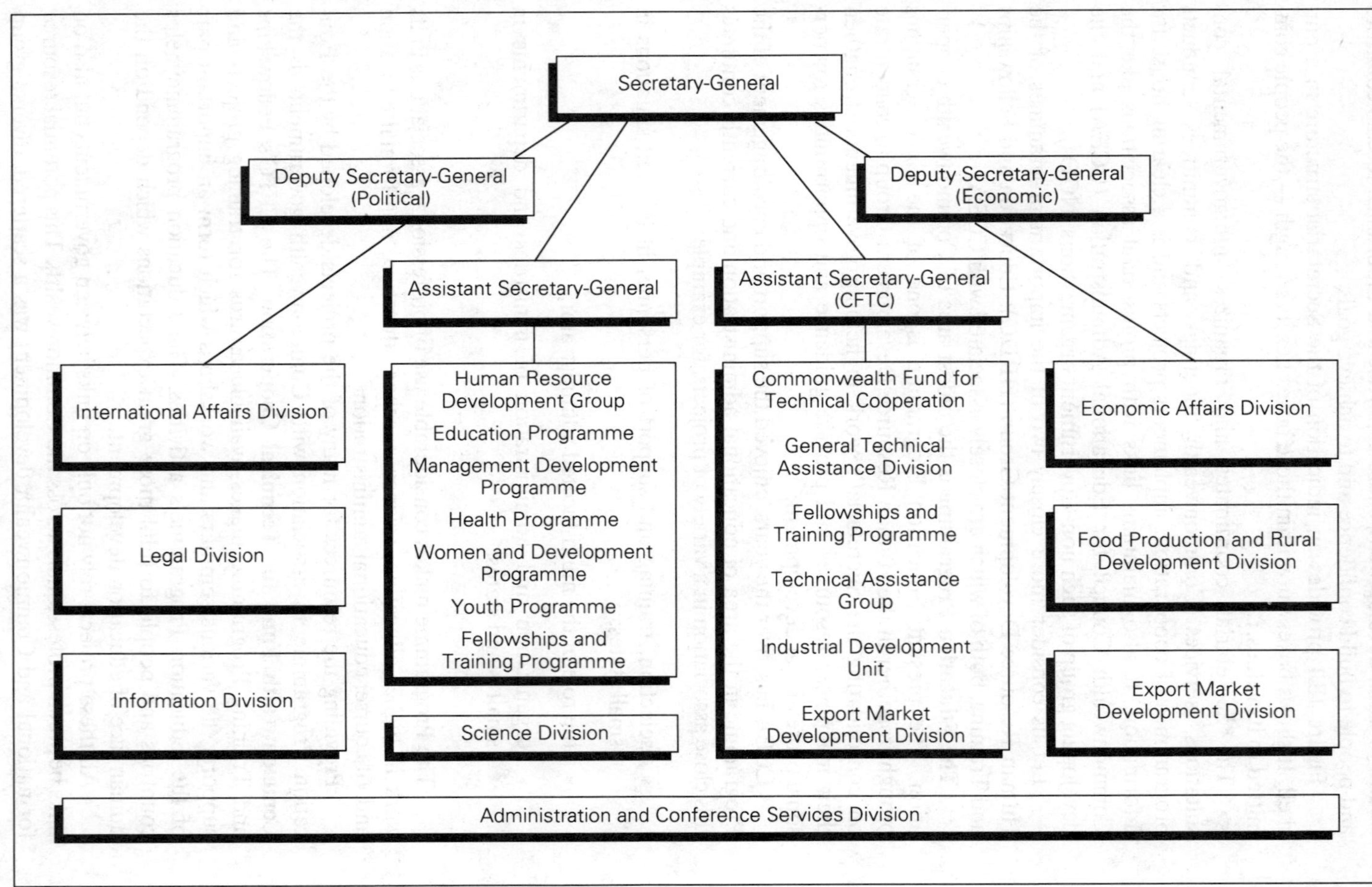

in professional, often non-Government, associations which needed a focus, a coordinating, supportive agency to make full use of the vast reservoir of talent available. The Commonwealth Foundation was the Heads of Governments' inspired answer to the need.

The Commonwealth Foundation

The Foundation, the agency which, as Professor Walker points out, was to show enough faith in *the concept* of CCEA to turn it into *a reality*, was established in 1966 as an autonomous body after the 1965 meeting of Commonwealth Heads of Government in London. Its role was to promote closer professional cooperation within the Commonwealth and its mandate was extended in 1979 to include non-Government and voluntary organizations. Continuing its development, the Foundation was reconstituted as an international organization. All this was a daunting task for an agency with a Director and a small staff but it was a task so well carried out that its budget was increased regularly as the work expanded.

The Foundation now cooperates in the activities of thirty-three Commonwealth Professional Associations (CCEA is one of the CPAs) and has supported the setting-up and conduct of eighteen interdisciplinary Professional Centres and Associations. These are just two examples from the Foundation's comprehensive list of activities — all innovative and providing the practical encouragement and support which, it is hoped, will lead to self-reliance and independence. The Foundation provides the enabling resources for enterprises to be launched and supported until they develop sufficient strength to carry on alone. It truly provides a *foundation* on which successful ventures are built.

The threads drawing together its diverse activities are the Foundation's aims for the promotion of Commonwealth cooperation among people and associations and the professional development of all those involved. Recent endorsement at the highest level was provided in the CHOGM Communique issued after the 1989 meeting in Malaysia:

> 23 Heads of Government ... commended the work of the Foundation in promoting stronger links with the large, diverse family of non-Governmental organizations through the establishment of Commonwealth Liaison Units and acknowledged the increased potential this created for sharing their Commonwealth relationships. They noted the increased efforts of professional cadres to promote wider intra-professional cooperation and consultations.
>
> 24 Heads of Government particularly welcomed the proposed establishment of a regular Commonwealth Forum of non-Governmental organizations to provide focus for the many forms

of consultations that continue at all levels of Commonwealth contact ....

25 In recognition of the growing importance of the varied programmes developed to promote better Commonwealth understanding, Heads of Government approved an increase in the Foundation's target income over current levels by an aggregated 10 per cent over the next two year period 1990/91–1991/92.

The varied programmes to which the Heads of Government refer include the following CCEA projects which have been supported by the Foundation in recent years:

* **New Zealand** – N.Z. Educational Administration Society's annual conferences/workshops. South Pacific participants funded by CF through CCEA.
* **Kenya** – Sixth CCEA Regional Educational Administration conference/workshop. Strong financial support from CF for regional participants and encouragement given to the Kenya Educational Administration Association responsible for its organization.
* **Women in Educational Leadership** – a project to investigate the role of women in education in Malaysia, Sri Lanka and India.
* **Professional Development of Educational Administrators in Grenada** – a special Foundation support programme implemented by CCEA's Caribbean and Canadian affiliated associations.
* **South Pacific Young Administrators Exchange Programme** – a pilot project to encourage cooperation among educators, countries and systems.
* **Regional Fellowships for Young Administrators** – a project designed to broaden administration horizons and strengthen association links. It stems from the South Pacific pilot project and is open to all CCEA regions.
* **Publishing** – provision of funds by CF for CCEA's two main publications, *Newsletter* and *Studies in Educational Administration*, and also for upgrading publishing facilities. Since publications are CCEA's main lines of communication in the network and communication is our lifeline, this is a vital project.
* **Small Scale Projects for Small States** – a fund to assist the associations in small states to carry out limited operations in order to strengthen isolated associations not able to get together with other associations in the region. It has been welcomed by such associations, Mauritius being the first to try out the concept.

* **Network Interaction Programme** — modest but significant projects to link people and associations. An early project involves New Zealand and Tonga. Others will follow as practical, supportive programmes are planned.
* **Network Interchange Fund** — many fledgling affiliated associations have problems in the initial stages and need some collegial support to see them safely launched. This support fund provides that much-needed boost and encouragement. The fund will facilitate association interchange between well-established groups working with newly-formed societies.
* **Foundation Fellowships** — CCEA's nominees from Singapore, Western Samoa, Brunei and Tonga have received awards for the past four years.

The wide range of activities carried out by CCEA's worldwide network, largely financed and encouraged by the Foundation, makes a very positive contribution to the Foundation's aims and objectives — to strengthen Commonwealth links across frontiers and to support development programmes. These projects were and are Commonwealth-wide and are excellent examples of Commonwealth cooperation.

The Commonwealth Council for Educational Administration

As described by Professor Walker in chapter 1, CCEA came into existence at the University of New England, Armidale, Australia, in 1970. Its first *Newsletter*, published in 1971, announced that the Council's membership was to be

> ... open to all those involved or interested in the administration of education. This prescription thus enables educationists from all levels — pre-school to tertiary — to participate in Council activities. Similarly it permits membership for practising administrators, for scholars and professors involved in the study and teaching of educational administration, for teachers aspiring to administrative status, for politicians and civil servants.

Newsletter No. 1 also made it clear that the primary concern of the new body would be to improve administrative practice within education in Commonwealth countries:

> *The Case for a Council*
>
> In most countries of the Commonwealth expenditure upon education accounts for a very large proportion of national resources. Yet the people chosen to administer these expensive educational enterprises

> have often been ill-prepared and in the professional sense of practice in the field of administration, ill-supported by the necessary human contacts with colleagues of similar interests, by the supply of journals in the area or by opportunities to discuss matters of mutual concern in conferences, meetings and the like.
>
> There is ample evidence of the problems referred to above. In no Commonwealth country, with the possible exception of Canada, is there a nation-wide association of educational administrators. Certainly, until recently, there was no Commonwealth-wide association of this type. There are pitifully few journals or magazines devoted to the practice of educational administration. There are surprisingly few universities and other tertiary institutions which are interested in training educational administrators for senior or even relatively junior positions. The extent of research in the field is, of course, very limited.
>
> Clearly, assistance in the preparation of educational administrators is required urgently in virtually all Commonwealth countries. (p. 1)

Since that time the Council has stimulated and helped more and more individuals, institutions, ministries and departments of education to be involved in thinking about and planning for the development of educational administration. As George Baron, an early pioneer in the field of educational administration at the University of London, wrote in 1973:

> Perhaps the most significant of all the trends of the present time is the growing consciousness of administration as a field of study to which *practitioners* can make significant contributions.

Growth

From modest beginnings CCEA has grown into an international association of more than twenty-five active associations with almost 6000 members in forty countries: the only organization of its kind in the world. That is no small achievement and while this is not the place to recite all the links in the network, a random selection does reveal CCEA's wide horizons — the rich store of resources availabe in people, ideas and philosophies, experiences and systems — to be shared by all. These growing inter-association links are typified by:

* the Queensland Institute's provision of its *Practising Administrator* journal (now published by the Australian Council for Educational Administration) and professional books to fledgling overseas groups;
* the British Educational Management and Administration Society's links with the Bombay association;

* New Zealand's joint professional development programme with Tonga;
* the African interactive grouping – Kenya, Uganda, Nigeria, Ghana, The Gambia, Tanzania and Zambia.

There is also a growing interest from non-Commonwealth countries through associate membership: Thailand, the Philippines, China, Burma, Japan and other countries. In addition to close association with the Commonwealth Secretariat and the Commonwealth Foundation, strong links have been forged with UNESCO (Paris, Bangkok and the Pacific), the US University Council for Educational Administration, the Inter-American Society for Educational Administration (ISEA), the European Forum, universities, libraries and foundations. The list grows each year.

The network concept is strengthened through CCEA's links within the family of the Organization of Commonwealth Associations associated with the Commonwealth Foundation. Many of the OCA groups' activities are relevant to CCEA – the work of the Commonwealth Association for the Education and Training of Adults being a good example. Similarly some CCEA projects are of interest to other Commonwealth professional associations across the world. This is a widening contact which adds materially to the professional resources of the Council.

In all its work it is salutary for CCEA to keep its role firmly in mind as explained by Harry Harris (1980), Executive Director 1975–1983:

> The role of CCEA is not to be the focal point of *all* activity. Rather its function is that of diffusing, encouraging, multiplying through *collective* effort .... We need to encourage: improvization, imagination, divergent ways of thinking, how to be positive, to say 'How can it be done?' to strengthen leadership qualities in everyone.

During its period of growing and maturing, CCEA has worked to achieve such a cooperative approach, as described by Mark Hewlett in *Studies* No. 28. He argued:

> ... for harnessing together the efforts of academics, administrators and teachers in order to bring about practical improvements in schools. It seems particularly appropriate to place this argument in the arena of CCEA, one of whose essential and distinctive functions is to bring together people from different spheres of the educational world.

As Hewlett notes, this harnessing of effort, this harmonization of resources is indeed CCEA's role, just as the Commonwealth is a force for concerted action in facing problems. The Hong Kong Council for Educational Administration, lively and active, exemplifies this coordinating role, this bridging of credibility gaps in a number of its activities linking HKCEA, university, schools and the Department of Education. These items from a recent annual report show that HKCEA, a CCEA affiliated association, is responsible for organizing professional development courses for the Department of Education which are accredited by the University.

* The Hong Kong University Extra-mural course on the Management of Educational Institutions is in its fourth year and still in heavy demand. My thanks to all HKCEA members involved in organizing and conducting the course.
* This year the Council's other HKU Extra-mural courses under the umbrella of the In-Service Teacher Education Programme (INSTEP) includes a Management Course for Secondary School Department Heads.
* The Council was continuously invited by the Training Unit of the Education Department to develop and conduct courses for the new secondary school heads and deputy heads.

There are many other similar examples of bridge-building from Kenya, Singapore, Nigeria, India and beyond. This building of bridges was demonstrated as the Chairman of the New Zealand Educational Administration Society explained at a NZEAS Annual General Meeting in 1990:

> We came together rather like a large family — 100 in number. The family ranged from a West Australian principal who has spent the last year in Auckland to a school committee member from Dunedin and others from so many places and positions in between as well as Vanuatu and Tonga. Our family covered the broadest of spectrums across New Zealand educational enterprise and the extended family which NZEAS is part of — the Commonwealth Council for Educational Administration.

A further illustration of CCEA's role in 'encouraging through collective effort' is the case of Uganda's newly-formed Uganda Council for Educational Administration. Nearly 400 members from all branches of education, full of enthusiasm after years of stress and lack of resources have come together in great need of support. The Secretary of UCEA writes:

> Dear Mr John Weeks,
> It is a long time since I wrote you a letter. May be you have been wondering as to what might have befallen on UCEA. There have been ups and downs. But the urge to press on forward has been strong enough and we have at least established enough tentacles nation wide. We have secured the support of the secondary school Headteachers'

> Association, the Principals' Associations and individual teachers from primary schools, teacher training colleges and secondary schools. We are trying to publicize the association using our meagre resources.
>
> The members are very grateful to the QIEA [*Queensland Institute of Educational Administration, Australia. Ed.*] for the continued supply of literature and desk kits. Recently a lecturer from Makerere University, Faculty of Education glanced at one of the magazines which had been sent to our Deputy Principal, and expressed the desire to circulate some of the articles to a wider range of the teaching and administrative population. I have requested the President of QIEA, that if it were possible UCEA would be allowed to extract some articles from the *Practising Administrator* and be published in one of our home papers here in Uganda. [*No problem here.*]
>
> We intend to organize a national seminar, the first of its kind here in Kampala in December this year. The *registered* membership has reached 300, but 180 have so far paid both their membership and annual subscription ...
>
> There is so much which is lying before us and it demands trained personnel. This stage requires every participant to sacrifice as much as can possibly be. We therefore extend our hopeful request to CCEA for more parental closer links with us. We need proper setting and organizing as already the teachers and administrators have indicated much expectation from the association.

Other associations have responded quickly to Uganda's needs and CCEA, through its recently established Network Interchange Fund financed by the Commonwealth Foundation, will provide 'pump-priming' funds to boost the UCEA's own efforts.

Other means by which the network communication is strengthened are national, regional and international workshops, conferences and seminars, inter-association exchanges and publications. The 1986–90 President, Emeritus Professor Meredydd Hughes, noted in his last report 'With our scattered Board and equally far-flung association secretaries — twenty-one Board members in ten countries, twenty-seven Association secretaries in twenty-four countries — we try every means possible, short of using carrier-pigeons, to maintain strong collegial links.' One means of maintaining the network and supporting the associations, especially those newly-formed like that of Uganda, is through CCEA's own *Newsletter* and *Studies in Educational Administration*, substantial publications which appear twice a year. Both are vital communication channels not only between those 'far-flung' Board members and secretaries but our much-further-flung 6000 members. The preparation, printing, packing and despatching is quite an enterprise for the small CCEA staff consisting of two half-timers — the Executive Director and his Secretary, plus a couple of casual helpers.

Conferences, workshops and seminars are spread round the network in an endeavour to maintain the sense of wider identity and fellowship (perhaps the Australian term 'mateship' catches the essence) within the Commonwealth and have been held, so far, in Australia, Bangladesh, Barbados, Canada, Cyprus, Fiji, Grenada, India, Kenya, Malaysia, New Zealand, Nigeria, Singapore, Tonga and the United Kingdom.

'Educational administration', as Harry Harris put it, 'in the context of Commonwealth sentiment and diversity has a richness and variety transcending the local scene. By giving expression to that diversity while providing a focus for the many things that unite the Commonwealth, CCEA has established itself as a worthwhile and a vigorous professional organization.'

The Future

We have seen what CCEA has become over the years — but that is only the beginning. We have also seen that CCEA has not arrived but is still on its way. The story continues and CCEA has a vision, of what it must continue to strive for. As Patrick Duignan (1982), a CCEA member now at the University in Brunei, has affirmed:

> I firmly believe that any organization, in order to survive and achieve success, must have a sound set of beliefs in which it premises all its policies and actions.

CCEA does have a sound set of beliefs, a vision for its being: administration is the means not the end; administration means people helping people; administration means bringing people together from different spheres of the educational world as members of a team; administration is helping people to become confident and competent to act positively, to turn words into deeds. For CCEA, people are women and men and children 'enabled to achieve their aspirations and be involved in roles that match their abilities' in fact, to reach full development. Julius Nyerere (1988) had this vision of development:

> ... development has a purpose: that purpose is the liberation of man. It is true in the Third World that we talk a lot about economic development — about expanding the number of goods and services, and the capacity to produce them. But the goods are needed to serve men; services are required to make the lives of men more easeful as well as more fruitful. Political, social and economic organization is needed to enlarge the freedom and dignity of men. Always we come back to man — to liberated man — as the purpose of activity, the purpose of development. But man can only liberate himself or develop himself. He cannot be liberated or developed by another. For man makes himself. It is his ability to act deliberately, for a self-determined purpose,

> which distinguishes him from the other animals. The expansion of his own consciousness, and therefore of his power over himself, his environment and his society, must therefore ultimately be what we mean by development.

An implication of such thinking is that things happen through people and administrators need to accept that understanding people is the beginning of salvation; that plans are achieved through all those people working in the system.

CCEA's role is to provide the means to this end, to help people to help themselves so that those in every area of education are able to arrive at the 'developed' stage. To use words from the 1989 conference of the New Zealand Educational Administration Society, we have 'a significant role ... of networking across the crowded educational administration scene ... to reduce the trauma and the noise and to focus on the essentials!'

Finally I would emphasize the need for us to grasp the reality of Commonwealth, to realize that it does exist, that it works, that we are all part of it, something unique to be prized. With that realization will come the feeling of belonging to a living organism, of being part of the whole and not isolated, the feeling that visions can be realized through one another — as long as we have faith and are prepared to work for success.

Within that wider system CCEA is a worldwide organization trying to cater for the professional needs of educational administrators. In its philosophy, in its practical activities and in the way it endeavours constantly to adapt to the changing needs of its members, CCEA itself vividly exemplifies a thought recently expressed in *CCEA Studies in Educational Administration*:

> We in educational administration are concerned with living systems, *not* non-living systems ... Living systems are not just self-renewing. They are self-organizing. (Sungaila, 1990)

References

Baron, G. (1973) 'Trends in educational administration in Britain', *CCEA Studies in Educational Administration*, 3.

CCEA *Newsletter*, **1,** 1 (1971).

Chadwick, J. (1982) *The Unofficial Commonwealth: The Story of the Commonwealth Foundation 1965–80*, London, Allen & Unwin.

Commonwealth Secretariat (1989) *Commonwealth Today*, London.

Doxey, M. (1989) *The Commonwealth Secretariat and the Contemporary Commonwealth*, London, Macmillan.

Duignan, P. (1982) 'Near enough is not good enough: Developing a culture of high expectations in schools', *CCEA Studies in Educational Administration*, **37**.

Harris, H.T.B. (1980) 'Some aspects of educational administration in the Commonwealth,' paper presented at the National Institute of Educational Planning and Administration, New Delhi.

HEWLETT, M. (1982) 'Adjusting the focus: Practical preconditions for successfully implementing evaluation procedures', *CCEA Studies in Educational Administration*, **28**.

LYON, P. (1989) 'Empires of the mind', *Times Educational Supplement*, 10 February.

NYERERE, J. (1977) Speech at the Third Commonwealth Regional Conference, Dacca.

NYERERE, J. (1988) 'Adult Education and Development No. 30'.

PEARSON, L.B. (1973) *Memoirs: Through Diplomacy to Politics*, London, Gollancz.

SUNGAILA, H. (1990) 'Organizations alive! Have we at last found the key to a science of educational administration?', *CCEA Studies in Educational Administration*, **52**.

WEEKS, J. (1987) *CCEA Newsletter*, **8**, 2.

Notes on Contributors

M. Kazim Bacchus is Professor, Sociology of Education, and Director of the Centre for International Education and Development, Faculty of Education, University of Alberta, Canada. He has taught in Guyana and England, was Assistant Director of Education in Guyana, and has carried out educational projects in Papua New Guinea, Tanzania, Uganda, Nepal and the West Indies. He was Professor of Education in Developing Countries at the Institute of Education, University of London 1985–86, and has also lectured at other universities, including the University of Guyana, the University of the West Indies, and the University of Chicago Comparative Education Centre.

Hedley Beare has been Professor of Education at the University of Melbourne since 1981, where he specializes in educational administration and policy. He has degrees from the Universities of Adelaide, Melbourne and Harvard University. He has been a Harkness Fellow, a Fulbright Senior Scholar, and a Visiting Scholar at the University of Oregon, Stanford and Bristol. During the 1970s he was in succession the foundation Chief Executive of Australia's two most recently established public school systems, those of the Northern Territory and the Australian Capital Territory. He is a Fellow of the Australian Council for Educational Administration, the Australian College of Education and the Australian Institute of Management.

Ray Bolam is Director of Further Professional Studies and Director of the National Development Centre for Educational Management and Policy in the School of Education, University of Bristol, England. He has carried out numerous research and consultancy projects for national governments, for the OECD, and for the European Commission. Dr. Bolam has published widely on teacher induction, in-service teacher education, the management of educational change, headteacher training, and teacher appraisal, and has been editor of *Educational Management and Administration*, the journal of the British Educational Management and Administration Society.

Tony Bush is Senior Lecturer in Educational Policy and Management at the Open University, Milton Keynes, England. He was formerly a teacher in secondary schools and a professional officer with a local education authority. His principal publications are *Theories of Educational Management* (1986), *Managing Education: Theory and Practice* (1989) and *Directors of Education: Facing Reform* (1989) (with Maurice Kogan and Tony Lenney). He has recently been appointed to a new Chair in Educational Management at the University of Leicester.

Judith Chapman is Director of the School Decision Making and Management Centre, Faculty of Education, Monash University, Australia. She is a member of the Board of the Commonwealth Council for Educational Administration and a Fellow of the Australian Council of Educational Administration. Dr. Chapman has worked extensively in the field of educational administration and has undertaken projects on behalf of OECD, UNESCO, and the Australian Commonwealth Government.

Wayne L. Edwards is Senior Lecturer in Education at New Zealand's Massey University. His graduate study was in anthropology and educational administration and he holds a PhD from the University of New England, Australia. He has taught and undertaken research in the USA, Canada, Australia and Britain, his research interests including the principalship, professional development and ethnography. Dr. Edwards was President, 1984–90, of the New Zealand Educational Administration Society, and has been a member of the CCEA Board since 1986.

Robin H. Farquhar is President and Vice-Chancellor of Carleton University in Ottawa, Canada, where he is also Professor of Public Administration. He has previously served as President and Vice-Chancellor of the University of Winnipeg, Dean of Education at the University of Saskatchewan, Assistant Director of the Ontario Institute for Studies in Education in Toronto, and Deputy Director of the University Council for Educational Administration in the United States. Dr. Farquhar has been President of the Canadian Society for the Study of Education, and Director of the Canadian Education Association, the Inter-American Society for Educational Administration, and the US National Academy of School Executives. He is a Fellow of the Commonwealth Council for Educational Administration and was CCEA President 1982–86. He has published widely in the fields of comparative and higher education administration, the professional preparation of educational leaders, and the novels of Ernest Hemingway.

Claudia Harvey is the Director of Curriculum in the Ministry of Education, Trinidad and Tobago, West Indies. Previously she has been a secondary school teacher, a curriculum officer, and Head of the Training Unit in the Ministry of Education. She also lectures part-time in methods of social research, educational administration, and adult education. Her main research focus has been in the area of educational practice. Dr. Harvey is Chairperson of the Caribbean Regional Council for Adult Education.

Meredydd G. Hughes is an Emeritus Professor of Education of the University of Birmingham, UK, having been Head of the Department of Educational Studies and Dean of the Faculty of Education, and previously Senior Lecturer at University College, Cardiff. He was founding editor of *Educational Administration*, journal of CCEA's newly established UK affiliate association, BEAS. Professor Hughes was National Chair 1978–82, when the association's title became 'The British Educational Management and Administration Society'. More recently he has been substantially involved in international assignments for UNESCO and CCEA, and was CCEA President and Standing Committee Chairman for the International Intervisitation Programmes, 1986–90. At the 1982 IIP in Nigeria he was awarded the Fellowship of CCEA.

Tunku Ismail Jewa is Dean of the School of Educational Studies and Professor of Educational Administration at the Universiti Sains Malaysia in Penang, Malaysia. Having undertaken teacher training at the University of Birmingham, England, he became a school principal before joining the university's academic staff. He obtained his MEd in Pennsylvania State University under a Fulbright award, obtained his PhD at the University of Malaya, and proceeded to Harvard University for post-doctoral study. Professor Jewa is Chairman of the Penang Educational Administration Society and a CCEA Board Member. He is a member of the Malaysian Ministry of Education Advisory Board on Teacher Education and Educational Research.

Samuel S. Maneno is currently Principal of Lenana School, Kenya. His previous wide administrative experience has included headship of the highly regarded Alliance High School and four other secondary schools. He was appointed Deputy Director of Education to coordinate the implementation of a new structure for secondary education in Kenya. Other responsibilities have included the Chairmanship of the Kenya Secondary School Headteachers Association and the Kenya Secondary Schools Sports Association. He has also been a member of the National Examinations Council, the Institute of Education Academic Board, and the Presidential Working Party on Education and Manpower Training for the Next Decade and Beyond.

Colin Moyle is currently Expert in Educational Administration and Management with Unesco. Dr. Moyle former career has been with the Ministry of Education of Victoria, Australia. He was the founding Director of the Institute of Educational Administration. He has also been a primary school teacher and head, a secondary school teacher, a Teachers' College Lecturer in English, an Inspector of Schools and a Regional Director of Education.

Nicholas Nwagwu is Provost of Alvan Ikoku College of Education, Owerri, Nigeria. Following his BA degree at the University of Nigeria, he obtained an MEd at Leicester University, UK, and an MA and EdD at Columbia University. For several years he was a high school principal, and subsequently became Professor and Dean of Education at the University of Benin. He is a Fellow of CCEA and of the Institute of Administrative Management of Nigeria, and is the current President of the Nigerian Association for Educational Administration and Planning. A UNESCO consultant on the training of education managers in Africa, he has published several books and journal articles and has travelled widely.

Jotham Ombisi Olembo is Associate Professor of Educational Administration at Kenyatta University. After obtaining his EdD at Ball State University, Indiana, USA, he was a Lecturer, and then Senior Lecturer, at Kenyatta University, being appointed Chairman of the newly created Department of Educational Administration, Planning and Curriculum Development. He has published two books and several research articles. He is a Fellow of CCEA and currently a member of the CCEA Board; he is also the founder and present chairman of the Kenya Educational Administration Association. Professor Olembo has presented conference papers in Cyprus, India, Barbados, Guyana, Britain, the USA, and Mauritius.

Kenneth A. Rae is a Senior Policy Analyst in the Managerial/Organization Policy Section of the Ministry of Education in Wellington, New Zealand. He was previously a secondary school teacher, and in schools in the Auckland province held positions of Head of English Department and Deputy Principal. He served in both head and regional offices of the former Department of Education and from 1 October 1989 for five months was a foundation consultant in the Development Unit of the Education Review Office. He has been since 1984 National Secretary of the New Zealand Educational Administration Society, assisted in the management of IIP86, and gave a paper on Rural Education to the CCEA Regional Conference in Kenya in 1988.

Larry Sackney received his PhD from the University of Alberta. He is currently a professor in the Department of Educational Administration, University of Saskatchewan and the Director of the Saskatchewan Educational Leadership Unit. He has been President of the Canadian Association for the Study of Educational Administration and a member of the CCEA Board. He is presently the Vice-President of the International Congress for School Effectiveness. His research interests include school effectiveness, rural education, leadership improvement and supervision.

Chaman L. Sapra is the former Professor and Head of the School and Nonformal Education Department of the National Institute of Educational Planning and Administration, New Delhi. He worked in the Planning Commission of the Government of India, and the National Council of Educational Research and Training, and was associated with the Indian Education Commission and the Indian Teachers Commission. Dr. Sapra is a Fellow of CCEA and currently a CCEA Vice-President, and has been a Distinguished Visiting Professor at the University of Alberta, Canada. Singly or in collaboration, he has authored or edited seventeen books, and he has published numerous research papers and articles on various aspects of educational planning and management in professional journals in India and abroad.

Andrew Sturman was educated at London University. He worked for seven years at the Home Office criminological research unit during which time his research and publications focused on the study of vandalism and community development. Dr. Sturman settled in Australia in 1978 and until 1989 was employed at the Australian Council for Educational Research where his interests and publications have been in the areas of school organization, transition from school to work, multiculturalism and curriculum decision-making. In July 1989 he took up a position at the Victorian State Boar of Education as a Policy Analyst.

Bernadette Taylor is Principal of Malvern Girls' High School, Victoria, Australia. She has recently served as Acting Deputy Director at the Institute of Educational Administration in Geelong, Victoria. Her role there included developing and running professional development programmes for educational administrators and potential educational administrators. Dr. Taylor's PhD was obtained for a study of women in administrative posts.

Emeritus Professor W.G. Walker, A.M. was the founding President of the Commonwealth Council for Educational Administration and in 1986 became its 'Honorary President'. He retired in late 1989 as Chief Executive and Principal of the Australian Management College Mt Eliza, having previously been Professor of Educational Administration and for a long time Acting Vice-Chancellor of the University of New England. He was a Professorial Fellow in the Graduate School of Management of Monash University and a Director of the Melbourne office of TASA Executive Search, specializing in the field of higher education. In 1990 he was awarded the Gold Medal of the Australian Council for Educational Administration. Professor Walker died in July 1991.

John Weeks has had wide experience in the service of education in the Commonwealth and for Commonwealth and international agencies over a period of thirty-five years. He is now Executive Director of the Commonwealth Council for Educational Administration, and has been elected a Fellow of CCEA. He is also an Honorary Fellow of the University of New England, Australia, where the headquarters of CCEA are situated. John describes himself as an administrator who has a firm belief in people.

Gwendoline Williams is a Lecturer in Management Studies and in Women Studies at the University of the West Indies, St. Augustine, Trinidad and Tobago. Earlier in her career she was involved in teacher education at the Valsayn Teachers' College, and has been a staff development facilitator throughout the school system in Trinidad and Tobago. Mrs Williams is currently a member of the National Advisory Committee on Education and the National Planning Committee, and is Deputy Chairperson of the Management Development Centre. Her main foci of research are institutional development and social change and educational management.

Kevin Wilson's career began in Tasmania where he served as a teacher, an administrator, and a Teachers' College Lecturer with the Department of Education. He completed his MEd and PhD in educational administration at the University of Alberta in 1970 and joined the Department of Educational Administration at the University of Saskatchewan in 1971. He is currently Professor and Head of this Department. Other positions he has held in the University include Director of the University Studies Group, Director of the Field Services Bureau and Associate Dean of Education. He has been a Visiting Professor at the University of Uppsala, Sweden; the University of New England, Australia; and the University Council on Educational Administration at Arizona State University. His conference presentations include sessions in England, Denmark, Sweden, New Zealand, Australia and throughout Canada. Dr. Wilson's research interests include the preparation of administrators and organizational effectiveness.

Index